FROM RACHEL
CHRISTMAS 20

REBELLION

REBELLION

THE INSIDE STORY OF FOOTBALL'S PROTEST MOVEMENT

EDITED BY
DOUGIE BRIMSON

JOHN BLAKE

Published by John Blake Publishing Ltd,
3 Bramber Court, 2 Bramber Road,
London W14 9PB, England

www.blake.co.uk

This edition first published in hardback in 2006

ISBN 1 84454 288 2
ISBN 978-1-84454-288-8

British Library Cataloguing-in-Publication Data:

A catalogue record for this book is available from the British Library.

Design by www.envydesign.co.uk

Printed and bound in Great Britain by William Clowes Ltd, Beccles, Suffolk

1 3 5 7 9 10 8 6 4 2

Images courtesy of Clevamedia, Action Images, Getty Images, Mick
Cunningham, John Barnes and Gary Firmager.

Every attempt has been made to contact the relevant copyright-holders,
but some were unobtainable. We would be grateful if the appropriate
people could contact us.

Papers used by John Blake Publishing are natural, recyclable
products made from wood grown in sustainable forests.
The manufacturing processes conform to the environmental
regulations of the country of origin.

This book would not have been possible without the help and support of supporters from clubs all over England.

It is dedicated to them and all those fans battling to keep their clubs alive.

And for Tina

CONTENTS

INTRODUCTION

EDMUND BURKE, THE famous British statesman and philosopher, once said, 'For evil to triumph, all it takes is for good men to do nothing.' Whilst the fact that he died in 1797 suggests it highly unlikely that he was talking about the great game, the simple fact of the matter is that if ever a statement applied to football and its fans, it is that one.

Make no mistake, it might be the beautiful game, but some of the things that have gone on in the name of English football over the years are nothing less than evil.

I'm not talking about horror tackles or even the worst excesses of hooliganism but something much more fundamental than that. I'm talking about the business end of the game. An area which for decades seems to have fallen outside the control of anybody and, as a consequence, has witnessed everything from clubs being run as quasi-dictatorships by corrupt chairmen through to players, grounds and even whole clubs being sold to line the pockets of agents, managers and all kinds of other dubious individuals.

Traditionally, and tragically, such actions usually went by unopposed. Government hasn't ever really been interested in the idea of dirtying its hands in the grubby world of football, whilst the FA, the body charged with administering the game, has always preferred to adopt a 'sit back and do nothing' approach to issues that impact on supporters.

As a result, it is the supporters who have suffered most over the years. Not simply because of the damage they've witnessed being done to their clubs, but because in most cases they've been the ones who have ended up picking up the pieces. A process which has often involved raising funds to refill coffers emptied by inept or corrupt staff, often with little more than a grudging thanks.

But no more. Now, at last, supporters have begun to cry 'enough'. Although, to be fair, the idea of football fans actually having the temerity to protest about a problem surrounding either the game or – more likely – their club, began in earnest before Malcolm Glazer set out to wrest control of Manchester United.

In fact, as we shall see, it is fair to say that whilst there have been major developments in recent years in the way supporters go about things, they have been complaining about football almost as long as the game has existed. That said, it is a sad indictment of our beloved sport that the fans – the people who ultimately fuel the game – still have no direct say in the way the majority of clubs are run.

Criminal though that is, the truth is that much of the reason for it can be put down to apathy. It's one thing handing over a few quid at a turnstile, it's quite another getting involved in something which will take every second of your spare time, if not your life. Especially when it'll be done for no financial reward and usually, little gratitude.

INTRODUCTION

Anyone who does that has my utmost respect because I'm not sure I would or could do it.

And that, in effect, is what this book is about. Those individuals who have got off their arses and made good things happen. Or at least tried to!

I am, however, well aware that there is a degree of irony in the fact that it is my name on the front cover. After all, I've spent the bulk of my writing career constructing books about the darker and unpalatable side of football. Hooliganism all but destroyed football in the '70s and '80s and its impact on the game continues to this day. One only has to witness the police presence at the average local derby or watch the frenzy surrounding an England away trip to see that.

In part, I am responsible for that. Whilst I was never a hard-core hooligan, I was one of those who skirted the edges of the scene back then and occasionally became involved in trouble. Yet it was actually that very thing which gave me the idea for this book. For whilst working on my last project, *Kicking Off*, I wrote:

The fact that it [hooliganism] causes so many problems for so many others isn't simply irrelevant, it actually adds to the experience. Those police, that CCTV, those ticket restrictions... they are because of you, they are your fault. Have you any idea how that feels when you're walking along a street in a strange town with a group of mates? That's the buzz.

That arrogance, self-confidence, bottle, call it what you like but the bottom line is that it's what these lads live for. Not because they are yobs or thick but because that's the way they follow football.

People who don't understand that are, in many

respects, missing an important point in that supporting a football club – as opposed to being a supporter of football – isn't simply about watching football. It's about belonging to something which will not only take you from the highest of highs to the lowest of lows emotionally, but which will almost certainly have an irrational and disproportionate impact on your life at some point or another.

As I read over that later on, I was struck by the ease with which I felt able to explain away the fact that the activities of violent criminals – for that is, in essence, what hooligans are – can be justified. And the more I thought about it, the more I realised that if hooligans are at one end of the supporting spectrum, then guys such as Mark Perryman, who runs the excellent Philosophy Football organisation and has been instrumental in changing the image of the national team's support, are at the other.

Here I was, providing even more exposure for the more negative aspects of the game, whilst the other, more positive side of supporting was being almost entirely ignored. So I decided to think about how I could redress that balance and, fairly quickly, came up with the idea of recording some of the more high profile protests to provide some kind of acknowledgement of the efforts put in by some of these amazing individuals. The title, *Rebellion*, was an obvious choice.

The important thing was to get the right mix of teams and protests which, to be fair, wasn't the toughest of assignments as they pretty much picked themselves.

Wimbledon, Charlton, Bournemouth, Brighton, West Ham and Manchester United were penned in immediately and were quickly supplemented by Manchester City, Norwich and Reading. I've also included something from my own club, Watford. Well what did you expect?

Together, this list provides a very good range of why and how protests come about as well as what has been done by the fans to achieve a variety of outcomes. Some protesters have been successful and can be classed as winners, others are clearly losers. There are also some who lost, but who ended up winning!

This is not, however, a definitive list. Indeed, I have been genuinely shocked not only by the nature but the number of problems and issues fans have had to deal with over the years. Many of which are still ongoing.

One of the more interesting was the highly vociferous campaign waged by a section of Birmingham City supporters to stop the club signing Lee Bowyer. A player with what can only be described as a colourful history!

What marks this protest out as significant was not that the fans eventually succeeded, but that both the board and the manager came out and verbally attacked the fans for what they had done. A clear indication that they had missed the entire point by a country mile. Fans aren't fools and they have standards they expect players to reach if they are to represent their club. In their eyes, rightly or wrongly, Bowyer fell below those standards and so they knew they would never be able to support him on the pitch. Therefore, as far as they were concerned he was potentially trouble. Why invite that when there was no need?

Ironically, we experienced much the same thing at Watford some years back when our then-manager, Glenn Roeder, signed former Luton and Chelsea striker Kerry

Dixon, despite assurance he would never bring a Luton player, ex or otherwise, to the club.

However, in this case, the outcome was entirely different as no one found out until it was too late and the signing split the fans down the middle. Some, myself included, refused to attend games while he was there whilst others claimed we should support the shirt, not the player. Sadly, so nasty did it all become that Watford fans ended up fighting amongst themselves at Roots Hall one Saturday. For the record, Dixon was a disaster for Watford – proof that we were right all along.

Of course, it isn't just at club level that fans have protested. Wider issues such as a return to safe terracing, the boycotting of advertisers using Carlton and Granada during the collapse of ITV Digital and even the whole Kick Racism movement, are all worthy causes.

But for me, it's the stuff going on at club level which holds the real interest, and so that's where I decided to focus my energy. From that point on, it was all about research, but it soon became apparent that the background to some of the protests was so complicated that for me to do them justice would take years.

To speed up the process, I began by contacting some of the principal figures involved, told them what I wanted to do and asked them if they'd like to give their side of the story. To a man, they agreed and the results, as you will see, make for astonishing reading.

In addition, I have provided a brief look at the history of our often fraught relationship with the game and finally, taken a look at how things could, maybe even should, develop in the future.

But ultimately, this is more than a book which relates a

series of events, no matter how important they might be. Instead, I hope *Rebellion* will prove to be an inspiration.

The guys involved in all of the protests featured here will be the first to tell you that they are nothing special. Rather, they are just average, normal fans who, for whatever reason, felt the need to get involved and do something to save their clubs.

But they are more than that, much more. They, like the many thousands of men and women up and down the country working tirelessly to keep their clubs alive, are the true soul of football and we should all be proud we have people like them fighting our corner.

This book is dedicated to all of them. And if it inspires just one person to get involved in something that is going on at their own club, then all the hard work, late nights and very early mornings will have been worth it.

Dougie Brimson

CHAPTER ONE

THE EARLY DAYS – FROM DOWNTRODDEN TO DETERMINED

BY DOUGIE BRIMSON

IT IS FAIR to say that until the 1980s the game's relationship with the fans was almost entirely one way. They took, we gave. It really was as brutal as that. This wasn't just at the turnstiles either. Supporters' clubs were originally established by clubs as nothing more than a way for getting more money from the pockets of the largely working class fans. Even the few who had any money weren't granted any influence within the club structure they were busily propping up. Indeed, the slightest inkling of militancy would usually see them simply shut down. Sometimes for a short while, often altogether.

Bizarrely, the body established to represent these clubs, The National Federation of Football Supporters Clubs (NFFSC), was instrumental in allowing this to go on. It might have boasted a membership of over 500,000 in 1953 but its motto 'To Help, not hinder' speaks volumes for its non-confrontational approach to the sport. In fact, its only real success came in 1956 when it helped convince parliament that the relaxation of the gaming laws – thus allowing supporters groups to run fund-raising lotteries – was a good idea. A 'success' which eventually backfired badly when, with support from the FA, the clubs were granted authority to run their own lotteries.

Although their power was minimal, the basic idea of the Federation was a sound one. Football was the nation's major pastime and those people who funding it by walking through turnstiles needed some kind of representation. It just needed one with a bit more bite. Incredibly, it wasn't until 1985 that it finally got it.

The catalyst was a horrific catalogue of events, all of which took place when football was already on its knees as a result of the continuing hooliganism problem.

The Bradford fire, the death of a young supporter during rioting at Birmingham City, the televised riot at Luton and worst of all, the Heysel disaster when 39 Italian fans died, all combined to drive football to the brink of collapse. Fans of the game, who had already been demonised to the extent that all were regarded by both the press and the police as potential hooligans, began to fear for the future.

Then, out of nowhere, a group of Liverpool fans cried 'enough'. Sick of being tarred with the hooligan brush and desperate to finally provide some kind of authentic link between the game and the people who funded it, they decided to establish the Football Supporters Association (FSA). It was an almost instant success.

The key difference between the NFFSC and the FSA was that whereas the Federation was established to umbrella the various supporters clubs, the FSA represented the fans as a whole.

More importantly, the FSA were extremely pro-active and

certainly not afraid to get their collective teeth into the political side of the game. They certainly fought tooth and nail to stop the ID card scheme Margaret Thatcher was so keen on and later on became heavily involved with the campaign to rid football of racism.

Although they were also active in lobbying for the provision of increased ticket allocations for fans at cup finals and for 10 per cent of all grounds to be allocated to visiting fans, in recent years, they have become most well known for organising the fans embassies at major international tournaments. Something which has proved to be an astonishing and worthy success.

However, the FSA always had one major problem – membership. At its peak, it hovered around the 5,000 mark. A tiny number when compared to the overall figures for people attending games on a regular basis. Looking back, it can be argued that this problem was largely of their own making. Football fans have always been apathetic to organisations linked with the game, particularly those not directly involved with their own clubs. However, many were quick to note the success the FSA enjoyed through its campaigning and this was instrumental in the formation of a number of club-based Independent Supporters Associations (ISAs). The bulk of these came about in an effort to make clubs more accountable to their own fans or in response to specific problems. For example, one of the early ISAs sprang up at QPR in response to plans to merge the club with Fulham. Another was formed at Tottenham in 1991 when the club faced financial ruin.

ISAs at West Ham, Brighton and Manchester United have also enjoyed massive successes in battles with their clubs as we shall see later on. Indeed, almost every professional club in the land now has or has had an ISA, the vast majority of which are extremely well organised and, most importantly, respected by the clubs they support.

With fans finally becoming more organised at club level, the role and influence of the FSA began to diminish and, in 2002, they merged with the NFFSC to form the Football Supporters Federation (FSF), which currently has a membership of well over 100,000. Still not great, but a significant number. However, the FSF is extremely well organised and enjoys a high media profile. It has also developed a very good working relationship with all sides, so who knows what it might achieve in the future. Hopes are certainly high.

Another supporter-driven initiative to come to the fore in recent years has been the Supporter Trusts (ST). These came about through the government funded 'Supporters Direct' initiative set up in 2001 as a result of recommendations made by former MP David Mellor's Football Task Force.

STs have provided a significant move towards democratising football, largely because they work by seeking to acquire a degree of ownership of the club. Something which not only leads to more direct involvement in the day-to-day running, but also provides a degree of influence within the decision-making process at board level.

The first ST was formed in 1992 at Northampton Town when the club, like so many before and since, was teetering on the edge of bankruptcy and it was an immediate success. By working in conjunction with the local council, not only did they save the club but they helped it build a new ground. It also earned the right to place two members on the board which was something of a first.

The success at Northampton inspired other groups to follow suit at clubs such as Exeter, Bournemouth, York,

Notts County and Chesterfield, as well as others almost ruined by the collapse of the ITV Digital deal in 2002.

But it wasn't just clubs in financial straits who saw them formed amongst their support. Shareholders United was formed at Old Trafford during the battle to stop Rupert Murdoch taking over Manchester United.

In total, there are now over 100 Supporters' Trusts across England, Wales and Scotland with 61 of those holding a stake within their football clubs. But just as significantly, there are now 39 football clubs with supporter representation on their boards with 4 league clubs and 8 non-league clubs being wholly owned by their respective ST. This is an amazing achievement by any stretch of the imagination.

Hopefully, the success of the STs will continue and, all being well, will lead to more significant supporter influence not just at club level, but at national level. This would certainly be of huge benefit to groups such as englandfans and campaigns such as 'Stand Up, Sit Down', which fights tirelessly for the return of safe terracing.

There have, however, always been plenty of supporters who, whilst they would never have dreamed of becoming involved in any kind of organised group, have plenty to gripe about. For them, an outlet came, not in the shape of organised protests, but in the form of small easily-read and often anarchic magazines known universally as Fanzines.

The term 'fanzine' actually dates back to the late '40s, when it was coined by the American publishers of magazines aimed at science fiction fans. Some 30 years later, the term had crossed the Atlantic and was adopted by unofficial and often self-published periodicals covering music, the Scooter scene and, most importantly, football.

The first football fanzine was *Foul,* which was published in 1972 and ran for four seasons. However, it was the mid-1980s when they really exploded on the scene. With titles such as *Talk of the Toon* (Newcastle), *When Skies are Grey* (Everton), *Through Wind and Rain* (Liverpool) and *The Almighty Brian* (Nottingham Forest), they provided an alternative look at the game mixing as they did informed comment with terrace banter.

Some of the fanzines were humour-based, while others focused on hooligan groups and the culture of Casual, the most famous being *The End*. One of the very first fanzines, this was very much a Scouse creation and covered everything from clothes and music through to early '80s youth politics.

There were, however, some who simply went too far. Southampton FCs *On the March* once placed a picture of the manager Ian Branfoot on its cover under the headline 'Hope you die soon'.

It is estimated that there have been in excess of 600 different titles produced over the years, but key to their success has been the fact that they were, and remain, wholly independent. It was this which has allowed them to provide a platform for the airing of grievances and often controversial comment in a way that was often as far away from being politically correct as it is possible to get. Anyone who has ever read a copy of Birmingham City's *The Zulu* will know that!

It is fair to say, however, that many fanzines have been extremely influential over the years. Certainly *Back to the Valley* was instrumental in Charlton's return to its spiritual home whilst Manchester United fanzines have been always been at the forefront of events at Old Trafford. It was inevitable that sooner or later a fanzine would emerge that would take things beyond the local scene and target a national readership, and in the spring of 1986, two arrived at once. The first was *Off The Ball,* which folded after 16 issues, and the other was *When Saturday Comes* (WSC).

WSC was an almost instant success and has grown into a highly-respected magazine featuring contributions from a wide range of both established writers and genuine football fans, something which allows it to provide informed and intelligently-written articles about anything and everything related to the great game. The fact that many of them retain that slightly anarchic feel which made the original fanzines so popular is a real and continuing attraction.

However, I have to say that I am no real fan of WSC. I find much of the writing borders on anal and many of the subjects obscure in the extreme. However, there is little doubt that it fulfils a valuable and important role. Not least by reminding everyone that football fans aren't the Neanderthal beasts that people used to think they were but are instead reasonably intelligent and, above all, normal individuals. Many of whom have a great deal to say and contribute.

But more importantly, WSC provides a national and credible forum for football fans to gather information about what is going on. At a time when so much of the game is bordering on the edge of disaster, that has never been more important.

Like the ISAs, the STs and the FSF, long may it continue.

CHAPTER TWO

CHARLTON FC – BACK TO THE VALLEY

BY JOHN BARNES

FOR A WHILE at least, it seemed that everything was going to be okay.

It was 3.30 pm on Thursday, 8 March 1984 and Charlton Athletic Football Club, having endured decades of chronic under-investment and a disastrous fiscal regime that at times had tended towards utter recklessness, emerged at last, intact, from the High Court.

Theirs had been a grave situation that had seemed irredeemable just eight days before when, on 27 February 1984, the club was officially wound up and the gates of The Valley, the club's home for the preceding 65 years, were locked by the Official Receiver. Hope was scarce then. But in an act of blind faith, the Football League did what little it could, agreeing to postpone Charlton's next fixture against Blackburn Rovers at Ewood Park (to the great annoyance of the Blackburn club, who'd already ordered the pies), offering them the most valuable commodity – time. For if, even at the eleventh hour, there was a chance

9

that someone would come forward to launch a last ditch rescue bid, every last moment counted.

Of course, with nothing new to report, each day that passed made Charlton's predicament increasingly desperate. But even as the fans prepared to pay their last respects, behind the scenes frantic negotiations were taking place until finally a deal was brokered and Charlton Athletic (1984) Limited was born.

Responsible for their timely redemption were Sunley Holdings, a large Surrey-based building and property company who were now the proud new owners of Charlton Athletic, with their Managing Director John Fryer, appointed as the Chairman of the new company. And although Mr Fryer claimed to be a genuine Charlton fan, it was nevertheless a mystery as to why any building and property company thought it might be nice to become involved in running a basket case of a football club, especially one that had no real estate attached.

In the circumstances, Charlton fans were nothing less than truly grateful, but most gave little regard as to who the new owners were. Indeed, amid the deep sense of relief and jubilation nobody really cared. For now the only thing that mattered was that after this most major of dramas, Charlton had survived, normality could resume and everything was going to be okay – or so they thought.

In footballing terms, normality at Charlton had, for decades, meant sustained mediocrity punctuated occasionally by brief moments of exhilarating inspiration. It was a familiar pattern that only served to make those inspirational moments all the more special, and in that respect, normality had its merits. But mostly, normality was comfortable, cosy and familiar. And perhaps because of the club's recent near-death experience, players and fans alike eagerly embraced normality once more; existence alone was cause for celebration. Not so in the boardroom where, for many long years, normality had been something of a rarity. Here, already, moves were being made, as the new regime busied itself recruiting three new directors. In came Derek Ufton, a former player and club captain, Bill Strong, a member of Greenwich Council and Jimmy Hill, the former Coventry City manager and one-time chairman of the Professional Footballers' Association (PFA), now a well-known TV pundit, and indeed it was he who would very soon find himself acting as chairman, whilst the ailing Mr Fryer recovered from surgery.

The remainder of the 1983/84 season and the one that followed would pass uneventfully and the cosy normality of pre and post winding-up seemed to merge together so seamlessly that it was impossible to see the join. Charlton fans, although small in number, were largely content, and after the long period of uncertainty, who could blame them? Now, as the 1985/86 season approached, there was even cause for cautious optimism as a series of seven new signings were made by manager Lennie Lawrence who, with the modest £300,000 budget he'd been granted, significantly improved the squad. Yes, it looked certain that everything was going to be okay.

Back in June 1982, former Chairman, Michael Gliksten had terminated his family's 50 years in control of Charlton Athletic when he sold the club to Mark Hulyer, the young, brash incoming Chairman. In selling the club, Gliksten secured ownership of The Valley through his company Adelong Limited, whilst Hulyer signed a 30-year lease on the stadium, as well as the club's training ground at New

Eltham, at a rate of £110,000 per annum. Gliksten loaned a further £300,000 in order to cover half the existing overdraft, which he had guaranteed, and the remainder of which he paid off. The shares in the club would change hands for the modest sum of £1,000. The terms provided for Hulyer to repay the outstanding amounts, plus interest on the loan, in quarterly instalments over four years and at a fixed rate of interest.

Sadly Hulyer's tenure would be short. And although his stated intention was to lead Charlton back to the first division, the cumulative costs of the ill-considered signing of former European player of the year, Allan Simonsen, and the financial burden of his takeover agreement with Gliksten, meant that instead of a bright new dawn, the only place Hulyer would lead Charlton was alarmingly close to oblivion.

At the time of the winding-up order, and even as Hulyer left, Sunley Holdings negotiated more favourable terms with Gliksten for a ten-year lease of the ground, at a rent of £70,000 per annum, and with a view to eventual purchase. However, as was later to prove significant, the new lease did not provide for the use of two acres of the site located behind the West stand, an area that was to remain available to Mr Gliksten. Precisely who had insisted that this piece of land should be excluded is not clear. Charlton would later claim Gliksten had insisted on it, and Gliksten would vigorously reject such a claim. According to Gliksten, at the meeting where the deal was agreed, Charlton director Richard Collins had produced a drawing showing the boundaries of the land the club required, and the two acres in question were outside of this. Collins, it was alleged, had suggested that Gliksten might like to develop this parcel of land in order to recover some of the losses he'd incurred in his dealings with Hulyer.

As the new season drew near, amid the optimism came some depressing news as the Greater London Council (GLC) successfully applied for a closure order on the Valley's East terrace on the grounds that it was no longer safe, effectively reducing the ground's capacity to 10,500; this in a stadium that had, only a few short years before, been able to boast the biggest capacity in the Football League.

In the wake of the terrible tragedies of Heysel and Bradford only the season before, safety in football stadia had become a hot political issue, and given the condition the terrace was in, the order should not have come as any great surprise. Of course Charlton disputed the decision, arguing that a terrace that had once accommodated 40,000 people or more could surely, even now, safely hold a reduced capacity of perhaps 3,000 regardless of its current condition. But the GLC stood firm and their position was fully supported by the courts, so the terrace was closed. Despite these tribulations, the new season commenced and on the pitch it seemed the earlier optimism of the fans was justified as Charlton made their best ever start to a league campaign, with the first four games producing three wins and a draw, which was a great start to the season. But, although the fans didn't know it at the time, normality would very soon be snatched from their grasp once more, and seemingly for good.

Charlton's fifth league fixture of the 1985/86 season was played at home to Crystal Palace on Saturday, 7 September. In the days leading up to the game a story surfaced in the *South London Press* and the *Kentish Times*. Both newspapers claimed that, without prior warning, former owner and Chairman Michael Gliksten had demanded that the football club vacate the two acres of land at the rear of the West stand, with effect from 30th September. In response, John Fryer expressed the club's complete and utter shock, claiming that the loss of the land and the twenty-three associated turnstiles, would make future segregation of fans impossible, a situation that would not be acceptable to the police.

With the benefit of hindsight, the timing of the news leaves little doubt that the story was fed to the press in a premeditated and cynical attempt to provide a ready-made scapegoat for what was to come next. Of course they already knew that Gliksten could request the use of this land at any time, so it was no real surprise. And anyway, on the face of it, the loss of the land seemed to offer an opportunity to make segregation easier rather than more difficult. The only genuine, but minor disruption, was that a new entrance and turnstiles would have to be constructed in order to give access to away fans.

Now, with Gliksten suitably discredited and Saturday fast approaching, the bombshell was primed and ready to be dropped.

The weather was fine and warm, and the streets and pubs around The Valley steadily filled with fans from both clubs, all attending to their various pre-match rituals. There was a good feeling about the day with Charlton fans looking forward to improving on their fantastic start to the season, and Palace fans, having seen their team knock Charlton out of the Milk Cup only days before, feeling confident of another good result. But as the afternoon wore on, some distressing rumours began to circulate. Only whispers at first, they became steadily louder and more persistent. Apparently Fryer intended to move Charlton to Selhurst

Park to ground-share with Palace. The initial reaction was that the rumours must be bogus. How on earth could they be true, since, without thoughtful planning, a ground share arrangement couldn't possibly work? It simply didn't make any sense. But then again, with the closure of the East terrace and Gliksten forcing the club to vacate the land behind the West stand, then... perhaps?

It wasn't long before the tentatively curious Charlton fans discovered the truth. As they entered the stadium, each was handed a single sheet of paper that bore the stark heading, 'MESSAGE TO OUR SUPPORTERS'. It began, 'It is with great regret that we must announce that we will be obliged to leave The Valley the home of Charlton Athletic Football Club for 66 years'. It went on to explain that, due to the situation with the East terrace and the loss of the land behind the West stand, from 5 October 1985 Charlton Athletic would play their home games at Selhurst Park, the ground of rivals Crystal Palace, and continued by giving some very helpful directions on how to get there.

The news was cruel enough in itself, but the fact that the club felt it appropriate to inform the fans of their ill-conceived intentions in such a vulgar and thoughtless way, only served to compound the sense of bemusement and injustice.

With the majority of the crowd in a state of shock, the atmosphere was very low-key. Yes, thankfully Charlton went on to win 3-1, but the celebrations were muted. On the final whistle, most simply turned and headed for home to contemplate the horrible implications of the day's news, while a few chose to linger, for reasons only they knew.

Throughout the ensuing weeks the local papers were inundated with letters of outrage and protest at the club's plans. Most of which, whilst scathingly critical of the board's decision, also expressed genuine heartfelt concerns for the future well-being of their club. Others, it seemed, just wanted to put on record the fact that they would refuse to watch Charlton at Selhurst Park. The football club, too, received large numbers of letters, although Mr Fryer said later in the match-day programme, that most supported the board, although at the same time, they felt sad at what was happening.

There were further words of protest from former Chairmen Gliksten and Hulyer. Now being painted the villain of the piece, Gliksten was anxious to clarify the situation regarding the two acres of land and the earlier negotiations. While Hulyer, his successor, simply echoed the feelings of many fans when he said, 'moving to Crystal Palace is not the answer; it makes every game an away game'. Despite these protests, the board was undeterred.

The final game at The Valley was scheduled for 21 September. As the day approached there was talk that some fans were planning to break into The Valley and damage the pitch in an effort to sabotage the game. Although this defiant but futile act was never realised, the night before the game others did get in to daub slogans attacking both Gliksten and Fryer. As with all of the protests at this time, and for some considerable time after, these actions were independent and uncoordinated, carried out by small groups and individuals. Indeed, although among the fans there was profound unhappiness at what was happening to their football club, without a united voice, each was left to articulate their feelings in whatever way they could; leaving the way clear for the board to proceed with their plans largely unopposed.

This was to be the final football match played at The Valley. After 66 years, the people who owned and managed the club would no longer consider it the home of Charlton Athletic. From now on, they told anyone prepared to listen, Selhurst Park will be home. But not so the fans, the vast majority of whom, would never, ever consider home to be anywhere other than London SE7.

The match that day was of little consequence, and although Stoke City were comfortably dispatched 2–0 , it was only the occasion that was of any real significance to the majority of Charlton fans. The earlier sense of bemusement had now given way to anger. And just being there, letting those feelings be known to anyone within earshot was the least they could do in order to release their pent up frustrations. Better still, if there was a chance to direct their bile in the direction of the director box.

Before the game there was a small but symbolic protest when a dozen or so fans got on to the pitch to lay wreaths in the centre circle. Shortly before kick-off a group of a few hundred invaded the closed East terrace, where they sat until persuaded to move by the police. Around the ground the chant of 'we hate Palace' was repeated over and over. Banners and placards were displayed, most telling Fryer precisely where he could stick his Selhurst Park; others were perhaps more subtle. There was one in particular that seemed rather poignant: 'Don't let the Sunley set on The Valley' was the simple plea.

At half-time hordes of young fans managed to get on to the pitch, delaying the restart by almost ten minutes. Although the rest of the crowd expressed their support for the demonstration, once a small group broke away and decided to try to snap one of the crossbars, they were roundly booed until they desisted.

As the match neared its conclusion, the mood of the crowd

grew uglier by the minute, prompting the directors to leave their seats early in order to take refuge under the West stand. And when the final whistle was blown, players and officials fled as if running for their lives, whilst thousands of angry fans poured onto the pitch hurling abuse towards the empty directors' box.

With the intended recipients of their venom nowhere to be seen the abuse soon turned into defiant chants of 'we're not going to Selhurst Park'. Now no one, it seemed, knew quite what to do next; that is until a group of fans made their way to the top of the East terrace to dismantle a large, signed hoarding, which read, 'Sunley welcomes you to Charlton Athletic'. One fan registered his protest by climbing one of the floodlight pylons as far below him people hacked up lumps of turf from the pitch and others secured larger and less portable souvenirs.

Almost an hour after the match had finished thousands still lingered, many with tears in their eyes. They didn't know how to say goodbye. This was the place where all of their most treasured footballing memories were. The Valley was Charlton Athletic and Charlton Athletic was The Valley, and now that seemingly unbreakable bond was being destroyed, and what is more, nobody really understood why. Yes, people recognised that to spend the money required to repair the East terrace, and to construct new access and turnstiles behind the West stand, was not an attractive proposition, especially since the club didn't own the stadium. But nevertheless, the alternative option now being pursued, looked certain to have greater financial implications in the long term, and many believed that ultimately it would jeopardise the club's very existence all over again.

As had been mooted in the sporting press for some years,

ground sharing did make financial sense on the face of it, but this simplistic belief ignored the very real emotional attachment most football fans have for their club's stadium. So why did the directors refuse to see what was so painfully obvious? Was Fryer really naive enough to believe the fans would follow the team across south London regardless, and that ground sharing would be an unqualified success? Was he simply seduced by Ron Noades, the Palace Chairman, who for years had been touting for a club to come and share Selhurst Park? Or perhaps it was all the work of Jimmy Hill who, having been largely responsible for the introduction of three points for a win, and the abolition of the player's maximum wage, saw himself as one of the game's great innovators. Did he want to be the first in the anticipated proliferation of successful ground sharing arrangements?

At about 6.00 pm on Saturday, 21 September 1985, the police, fearing an arson attack on the mainly wooden-floored West stand, finally cleared the stadium for the last time.

Leaving The Valley with indecent haste, Charlton became the new tenants at Selhurst Park. Curiously, Fryer announced that Palace and Charlton would become equal partners and joint owners of the stadium, although Palace Chairman Ron Noades denied this in the local press.

However, around this time a company named Selhurst Valley Limited was registered at Company House, which would appear to confirm the true intentions of the parties involved. In the event, and for reasons never revealed, such an arrangement didn't materialise. Instead Charlton negotiated an agreement whereby Palace would receive 10 per cent of their gate receipts, plus half towards the cost of any maintenance or safety work, thus giving themselves some protection at least should attendances prove to be poor. And indeed, they were poor. In their most successful season for 30 years, the team clinched promotion to division one by finishing runners-up to Norwich City. Despite this success, Charlton recorded their lowest ever attendance figure for a second division match when 3,059 turned up on November 30 for the visit of Carlisle United. And they could only average 5,916 for all of the 18 league matches played at Selhurst Park that season.

The dissent from the fans showed no signs of abating. 'We should have stayed at The Valley', became the new anthem, sung home and away. Banners could still be seen on the terraces demanding the club return to The Valley. At the same time, though, no one seemed ready to step forward and take the lead in opposing this nonsense, least of all the supporters' club, whose committee members meekly accepted the decisions of the football club's board regardless of their implications. It would appear that, as an organisation, they defined their functions only as those of fundraising and arranging travel to away games. They refused to accept that it would have been wholly appropriate for them to become involved in the politics of the football club at this time, and in this respect they let their members down badly.

As the season drew to a close, despite all the evidence to the contrary, there were still some fans who harboured a vain hope that the directors might yet realise their error of judgement and take the club home; but no. Even as supporters celebrated promotion, Fryer was quoted in the Croydon Advertiser saying, 'We shall never, never return there. It is not going to happen. It would cost £3 million to put things right at The Valley. Here at Selhurst Park we have the use of the best stadium in south London. Mr Noades has made considerable developments to the ground which we could never have done at The Valley. Our future is here and now that we are in the first division we shall try to make sure that we stay there.' No doubt Mr Fryer's assertion was based on the expectation that gates would improve dramatically with the team's promotion. It was an assertion that would very soon be put to the test.

Charlton were at home to Sheffield Wednesday in their first game back in English football's top flight. The game ended in a 1–1 draw, watched by a crowd of only 8,501, which was easily the lowest in the first division that day, and lower than seven attendances in the second. It would seem that Fryer was once again mistaken.

Thus, what should have been a glorious return was, in many ways, a major disappointment, prompting life-long Charlton fan and the *Mail on Sunday* sports writer, Patrick Collins, to express the feelings of many as, under the headline 'No grounds for celebration,' he wrote: 'Charlton Athletic returned to the first division after an absence of 29 years. Those of us who had waited, hoped and thrown in the odd desperate prayer for such an event, had imagined an occasion awash with joyful nostalgia. It would be one of The Valley's most memorable days. But The Valley is no more than a derelict monument, with vandalised stands, decaying terraces and a pitch ablaze with towering weeds. Charlton slipped away from Charlton 11 months ago and their traditions died with the move. Football has changed, Charlton have changed. And not, I fear, for the better.'

Since the move was first announced, Peter Cordwell, the sports editor of the *South East London & Kentish Mercury*, had set out on a lone crusade against Fryer and his directors. Although not a Charlton fan himself, he nevertheless saw the objectionable nature of what was unfolding and seemed almost to take it personally. His campaign began on 12 September 1985. At first he focused on what it all meant for the fans, how the younger ones felt devastated at the prospect of their club leaving The Valley, and how the older ones, who'd perhaps followed the team for many decades, could not face the thought of that awful journey to Selhurst Park. Later, he viciously slammed the directors for the way they had unceremoniously dismissed most of The Valley ground staff, many of whom had given the club sterling service over a long period. Next he was critical of Greenwich Council who, as part of the deal that rescued the club in 1984, were paying Charlton £50,000 per year in return for use of the stadium's facilities, plus some community work. Now with the club residing in Croydon, the deal looked pretty pointless. Needless to say Greenwich terminated the agreement immediately.

The attendances for the next few home games were even less impressive than on the opening day. Crowds of 6,531, 5,312 and 5,527 watched league fixtures against Wimbledon, Norwich City and Coventry City respectively. By the time a crowd of 2,319 had seen Charlton beat Lincoln City 3-1 in the Littlewoods Cup, Cordwell had decided that enough was enough. In his match report he wrote, 'Only an Emperor with a penchant for parading around starkers would fail to see that Charlton have no real future at Selhurst Park. It cannot go on like this.'

The following Thursday the *Mercury* gave over its entire back page to a petition form under the heading, 'Our home is The VALLEY'. Inside Cordwell continued: 'Stick your name down – and get others to sign too – if you believe that Charlton should return to The Valley from Crystal Palace's ground, Selhurst Park. It's your chance, if nothing else, to voice your frustrations at being stranded miles from home. Hardly a day goes by without *Mercury Sport* receiving a phone call or a letter pleading the case for a planned return to The Valley or a new site in Greenwich. Talk among fans at Selhurst Park always gets around to The Valley. A banner opposite the press box always carries the same poignant message. Chants of "Back to the Valley", echo eerily around Norwood Junction station.' Cordwell went on to make a plea for a massive response to the *Mercury* petition to impress Greenwich Council. 'We're talking sack loads,' he added.

Within two weeks, the response was an impressive 15,000 signatures. What was even more impressive was the fact that the *Mercury* was only distributed in the London boroughs of Greenwich and Lewisham, which between them were home to between 30 and 40 per cent of the club's fans. Had the paper's circulation reached into the club's traditional heartlands of northwest Kent, then who knows how many signatures the petition would have produced?

As luck would have it, the chance to hand over the petition presented itself almost immediately, with the advent of the supporters' club AGM, which would be attended by members of the board of directors. Charlton fan, Rick Everitt, who would later go on to publish the *Voice of The Valley* fanzine, tipped Cordwell off about this opportunity. Cordwell however, somehow managed to interpret Everitt's letter as an official invitation from a member of the supporters' club committee. His response came just four days before the meeting, with a back page headline that joyously proclaimed: 'We'll be there', together with a story urging everybody else to come along too.

By now the national press had heard about the petition,

the story was getting some exposure and the campaign was gaining momentum. On the day of the AGM the *Daily Express* even reported that club captain Mark Aizlewood backed the fan's campaign. 'Even the players who never played at The Valley want to go back,' he allegedly said. 'It's a joke, all the players are nursing hopes that the club will somehow be able to move back. We only go to Selhurst Park just before the kick offs. That's all we see of the ground. If the traffic was rerouted, I would get lost going to games.'

The Valley Club was a single storey building located on the corner of The Valley site, behind the Covered End, and it was the regular venue for supporters' club functions and meetings. At the time the football club moved, the lease had only recently been taken over by former Charlton team captain and manager, Mike Bailey, together with his business partner Ken Hunt, and over the next four years, the Valley Club provided the only regular activity at the old ground. The building itself could accommodate about 400 people, which, on most occasions, was more than adequate, but this AGM was nothing like most occasions.

It was 20 October 1986, and as the appointed time of the meeting approached, hundreds of fans started filing into the building. It wasn't long before the place was packed and the decision was taken to lock the doors in order to prevent a dangerous situation developing. Nevertheless, those already inside simply opened the fire exits for the benefit of those still desperate to witness the proceedings. By now there were probably more than 1,000 people inside and with more arriving by the minute, the police were called in order to disperse the gathering crowds.

Eventually the delegation from the football club arrived, including directors Derek Ufton and Mike Norris, recently appointed Chief Executive Tony Shaw, and the ever-popular Mark Aizlewood. In the packed hall Aizlewood was welcomed warmly, due mainly to his comments reported in the *Daily Express*. The directors however, were booed and heckled at every opportunity, which made it almost impossible to hear the questions put to them, or indeed the responses given. Eventually when some semblance of order was achieved and voices could just about be heard via the decrepit PA system, the directors revealed that they had no authority to answer questions regarding finance, couldn't say how long Charlton could survive on their current attendances and didn't know whether the club would be prepared to buy The Valley from Michael Gliksten, assuming he was willing to sell. And so, being unable to offer any pertinent information, the members of the delegation were ready to leave.

However, before they could push their way to the exits, Greenwich Council leader John Austin-Walker took the microphone and promised that as long as Charlton remained in exile, the council would refuse any planning applications that might be made for the redevelopment of The Valley. Then, pointing towards the directors he proclaimed, 'They owe that club to this borough.' Not surprisingly, Mr Austin-Walker was cheered to the rafters that night, but he hadn't finished just yet, going on to demand that the directors attend a fact-finding meeting with the council and fans, in order to discuss possible ways that the club might return. In the circumstances, Ufton and Norris were in no position to refuse. Finally, with the handing over of the *Mercury* petition, the meeting ended.

Peter Cordwell, in his role as sports editor of the *Mercury*, had started his one-man campaign just over a year before.

Now, at last, things were beginning to move apace. Thanks to his doggedness, for the first time in the 13 months since Charlton left The Valley, disgruntled fans were given the opportunity to confront some of the directors who'd been party to that decision. Not only that, but thankfully, the campaign was now attracting some national publicity, with the headline 'Rumpus at The Valley,' on the back page of the *Daily Express*, the following day.

The meeting between council, directors and fans took place on 6 November 1986, just two days after a ridiculously small Selhurst Park crowd of 821 had witnessed Charlton's 3-2 win over Birmingham City in the Full Members Cup. This time, Richard Collins joined Ufton and Norris, and they confirmed that they had full authority to speak on behalf of the board. There was also representation from the supporters' club. But since it was now recognised that their credibility had been severely compromised due to their extreme inertia, six 'ordinary' fans were also present, along with a number of councillors.

After two hours or so, John Austin-Walker emerged from council room five to deliver an agreed statement to the fans waiting patiently outside. 'The representatives of the board and Greenwich Council express their wish for Charlton Athletic to return to the borough at the earliest opportunity. Both sides accept that a return to The Valley does not appear to be a viable proposition. The council and the directors are anxious to explore the possibility of a new Valley stadium at a location in the borough. The council will do all in its power to assist the board in exploring that possibility and agree to reconvene tonight's meeting with representatives of the supporters on January 15 1987, to give a progress report.' In conclusion, Richard Collins, who had recently been appointed as club vice-chairman, took the opportunity to appeal to fans to end their boycott of games at Selhurst Park. But, as was later shown, this appeal was largely ignored, which was just as well, since it would seem certain the low attendances were the very thing now persuading the board to soften their position.

January 15 came and went without the promised meeting. Negotiations, it was claimed, had reached a very delicate stage and the meeting would be re-arranged to take place a few weeks later. But that never happened either. When questioned, the club referred all enquiries to the council, whilst from the council there was only silence.

Meanwhile, on the pitch, Charlton's first season back in the first division had been one long struggle. Threatened with relegation throughout, they finally won their battle to stay up in dramatic fashion in the newly introduced play-offs. Competing with Charlton for a place in the top flight were Oldham Athletic, Leeds United and Ipswich Town, who'd finished third, fourth and fifth respectively, in the second division.

In the semi-final Charlton made hard work of it, but managed to edge past Ipswich. Their reward was a final tie, over two legs, against Leeds, which would only produce a stalemate. So it went to a deciding match at neutral St Andrews, Birmingham. Locked at 0-0 at the end of ninety minutes, the game went into extra-time. With the prospect of a penalty shoot-out looming, the deadlock was finally broken when Leeds went ahead from a John Sheridan free-kick. With less than seven minutes remaining, Charlton were staring relegation squarely in the face; that is until Peter Shirtliff equalised from a Mark Stuart pass. Just to show that it was no fluke, he repeated the trick three minutes from time to secure Charlton's first division status for another season.

On the terraces, contrary to the hopes of the optimistic John Fryer, the crowds failed to respond to the attractions of top-flight football. A tiny crowd of 4,205 watched the home fixture against Oxford United, which was easily Charlton's lowest ever in the first division. And the average for all 21 regular league games played at Selhurst Park was a mere 9,012.

Shortly after the play-off victory, the ailing John Fryer stood down as chairman in favour of Richard Collins, and became joint president of the football club, along with his business partner John Sunley. Meanwhile, the board was further strengthened by the addition of Lloyd's broker, farmer and Charlton fan, Roger Alwen. Alwen's arrival was to herald significant changes, with the acquisition of a new training ground in New Eltham giving the club a base in the borough of Greenwich for the first time in nearly two years. At the same time, Sunley Holdings became the club's major shareholder, which to Charlton fans at least, sounded so much better than sole shareholders, as had previously been the case. Notable too was the fact that ownership of the training ground was with Alwen and Norris, rather than with the football club, who were granted the lease on very favourable terms.

Dashed hopes were raised once more when, at the end of October 1987, under the headline, 'Charlton look to The Valley again,' the *Daily Express* carried a story claiming that Alwen and Norris had entered into negotiations with Michael Gliksten with a view to acquiring The Valley. When questioned, Norris described the report as ridiculous, whilst Alwen explained that the money needed to return to The Valley was not available at present. Significantly, this was the first time since the club left that a Charlton director had spoken openly about a possible return there. This, in itself, was a promising development, despite the denials.

Steve Dixon was a dissident voice on the supporters' club's, rather conservative, committee. Passionate about his football club, he was one of only a few prepared to speak out, whilst most of his colleagues continued to avoid any criticism of the board. Like most Charlton fans he had become increasingly frustrated with the apparent lack of progress since the meeting with Greenwich councillors and Charlton directors, more than a year earlier. In consequence he had come to the conclusion that some proactivity was required in order to try to force the issue. Much to the dismay of some of his supporters' club colleagues, Dixon was advocating a mass boycott of a forthcoming home fixture, in an attempt to shake the board out of its apparent inertia.

Around the same time, Rick Everitt was finalising his preparations for the launch of *Voice of The Valley*, a new Charlton fanzine. On hearing of Dixon's idea, it immediately struck a chord, and so he decided to promote it by way of his new publication, whilst Peter Cordwell enthusiastically splashed the story all over the back page of the *Mercury*. The match earmarked was the fixture versus Oxford United, which was due to be played on 26 March 1988. It was decided that in order to try to gain maximum publicity, fans would congregate en masse in the streets around The Valley. Charlton's worst-ever first division crowd had watched the corresponding fixture the previous season, making it the obvious choice. The date was also far enough away to give the organisers sufficient time to promote the boycott, put all necessary measures in place, and turn up the heat on the Charlton board.

The idea really captured the imagination of the fans, and it was soon a major topic of conversation on the streets and in the pubs of southeast London. With such a positive reaction there was genuine hope for a massive turnout at The Valley, and wouldn't it be interesting to see what sort of crowd would actually attend the game? On hearing of the proposed boycott, and realising how embarrassing the situation might become, the Charlton board pleaded with fans not to go ahead. They appealed to their sense of loyalty, arguing that the team needed all the support they could get at this particular stage of the season, especially with relegation a real possibility. Nevertheless, the fans remained steadfast.

Despite all of the planning and publicity, the boycott was destined never to go ahead once the beginning of March heralded some incredible news. Apparently, two Charlton directors had purchased the freehold of The Valley, precisely as the article in the *Daily Express* had predicted three months before. However, as exciting as this new development was, the question remained – was there now any real intent to return to The Valley or not? Eventually Charlton issued a statement: 'Following amicable negotiations, Adelong Limited, a company controlled by the Gliksten family, has been acquired by Mr Michael Norris, vice-chairman of Charlton Athletic Football Club, in his personal capacity, with the financial assistance of Laing Homes. It is intended that any benefit from this transaction will be for Charlton Athletic, who will continue to play at Selhurst Park while an alternative and feasible solution to play in Greenwich is finalised.'

In view of this fantastic news, the situation was now the most promising it had been since before the move. But even though it was clear the wheels of change were very slowly beginning to turn, at this stage it would seem the club's preferred destination was not The Valley, but a new stadium to be built elsewhere in the borough of Greenwich. Even though such an option would not be ideal, as far as the fans were concerned, just about anywhere would be better than Selhurst Park. Nevertheless, it was a return to The Valley that they really yearned for, and so yet another petition was organised, this time urging Greenwich council to do everything possible to facilitate Charlton's return to The Valley. In the event, it would seem this particular petition was aimed at the wrong target.

On the pitch, 1987/88 was yet another season of struggle. After looking certainties for relegation for most of the year, it was only an uncharacteristically strong finish that enabled the team to retain their status, finishing in seventeenth position. As for attendances, even with an uncommonly large crowd of 28,095 for the visit of Liverpool in January, the average was down on the previous year at a dismal 8,681.

On the first day of June there was further good news when Michael Norris and Roger Alwen successfully acquired the club's controlling shares from Sunley Holdings, in a £3.25m deal. However, disappointingly, it appeared that Sunley continued to have some financial interest in the club (as indicated by John Sunley becoming a director), whilst Richard Collins remained as chairman.

Later that month, a supporters' delegation comprising of Everitt and three of the supporters' club committee members, were invited to meet with Norris and Ufton at the former's Knightsbridge office. Norris explained quite openly that his preferred choice was to build a new stadium on the Blackwall peninsular (somewhere close to where the

Millennium Dome now stands), which would be financed by the redevelopment of The Valley site by Laing Homes. In his efforts to promote his cause and preclude any campaign against a new stadium and in favour of The Valley, it was the *Voice of The Valley* that seemed to be his main concern. At first, he tried to persuade Everitt to abandon his fanzine completely. Failing that, he next urged him to consider allowing the fanzine to become an organ of the supporters' club. Everitt refused both requests until finally Norris asked that the name of the fanzine be changed; but all to no avail.

Having promised the fans improved future communication, on 7 September 1988, Norris, Ufton and team manager, Lennie Lawrence, attended a public meeting at the Greenwich borough hall. The new leader of the council, David Picton, was also in attendance, along with about 600 fans. In the face of a barrage of questions from the floor, Norris was not very forthcoming and refused to be drawn on whether a return to The Valley was a possibility. Picton meanwhile promised that: 'If Charlton get together a deal involving The Valley, the council would not stand in its way' – words that would later come back to haunt him. The meeting was concluded with a promise of more news before Christmas.

Over the ensuing months, there was growing speculation as to where in Greenwich Charlton might return. While the Blackwall peninsular was not yet completely discounted, it seemed that not a week passed without another site being discussed in the local press.

Christmas came and went with no further news, only continued rumours. At the turn of the year, the *Mail on Sunday* ran a story forecasting that within a few weeks there would be an announcement from the club regarding a move to a site within 'a stone's throw' from The Valley.

But yet again, time passed and no such announcement was forthcoming.

The fans were beginning to lose patience with what seemed to be yet another endless wait. Any enquiries made to the club were, once more, deflected in the direction of the council, and, as before, the council remained silent. It was mid February before Charlton made any comment at all. At the specific request of the supporters' club, the following notice appeared in the match day programme: 'The directors of Charlton Athletic Football Club would like the supporters to know that they are continuing with the discussions concerning the plans for the club to return to the London Borough of Greenwich. At the supporters' meeting at Greenwich borough hall last autumn, it was stated that an announcement would be made by Christmas last. Regretfully this was unable to take place because the proposed arrangements are taking longer to finalise than at first thought. Every effort is being made to conclude the terms and a meeting will be convened with the supporters as soon as we have something firm to report and discuss.'

It was early March when, completely out of the blue, Roger Alwen became the new chairman of Charlton Athletic Football Club. Increasingly frustrated at the time and effort being wasted in the search for an acceptable site in Greenwich (when it had already become obvious no such site was available), he'd reached the conclusion that the only realistic option was the one that had been staring them squarely in the face all along, and so he'd decided to put up the money to refurbish The Valley.

The plan was to announce this uplifting news at a public meeting, which was to be held at Greenwich borough hall on 23 March 1989. The meeting was arranged under the pretext of the launch of a new club fund-raising scheme. However, somehow, Peter Cordwell got wind of the story and, with the little information he had, he pieced together a reasonably accurate account of what was about to be revealed. The story was published on 16 March, and the *Mercury* managed to steal Mr Alwen's thunder, much to the dismay of the football club.

So now the news was out in the open. But naturally the fans wanted to hear it for themselves before they dared to believe. With limited space in the hall, admission to the meeting was by ticket only, and numbers were limited to 600 places with many more turning up on the night. Some were fortunate enough to get in even without tickets, allowed to stand on either side of the hall, and it was only when no more could be safely admitted that the doors were firmly locked. Outside in the drizzling rain hundreds more waited patiently, while many others took refuge in the pubs of Woolwich, all anxious to hear confirmation of the news.

In the hall, seven club directors and officials, as well as new council leader, Dave Picton, took their seats on the stage. Mr Alwen's time had arrived as, with quivering voice, he delivered these words: 'During the past two and a half years, and particularly since the recent acquisition of The Valley, we have had numerous meetings and lengthy conversations with various parties to enable Charlton Athletic to return to the London Borough of Greenwich and there has been much publicised speculation as to their outcome. We appreciate that many of you have felt left in the dark by the club. However, we hope that you understand that this has not been intentional and we have tried to keep you as well informed as possible. The club has had, of course, to respect the confidential nature of these conversations. We have had favourable indications from the council that a planning consent may shortly be given on part of The Valley and we are therefore very happy to put in hand a major refurbishment programme which will enable Charlton Athletic Football Club to once again play football at The Valley.'

The last few words were lost as the hall spontaneously erupted in unbridled celebration. After some minutes, the new chairman managed to quieten the happy gathering sufficiently for him to continue: 'The work involved will be substantial and costly, but we hope that it will begin in the next few weeks and be completed early in 1990, so that for part of next season, football can be played at The Valley. Following the purchase in 1987 of the training ground in New Eltham, we feel this is another step towards helping Charlton Athletic to once again be a major force in English football. For our move back to be successful and completed on time we need total support from every Charlton supporter and we will be looking at ways the many offers of help can be taken up. Our aim is to provide a modern stadium of which we can all be justly proud. Finally, we would like to thank Laing Homes Limited, for without their assistance this decision to move back to The Valley would not have been possible, and also the council and their leader, Dave Picton, for their support.' To add to the joyous mood inside, cheers from those standing in the rain could now clearly be heard, as the wonderful news seeped slowly onto the nearby streets. Curiously, almost as a footnote to the meeting, Picton urged fans to write to the council in support of the club's forthcoming planning application. In addition he said, 'Charlton have a great past and I think they now have a great future. And I'm sure that when the formal processes have been gone through, the future is going to be back at The Valley.'

At the suggestion of the football club, on the morning of Sunday, 2 April, a vast army of happy fans congregated in the rain amid the ruins of their long neglected temple, in order to clear the weeds and refuse that had accumulated during the years of exile. Their efforts would mark the first small steps towards preparing for the return. And in the place where wreaths had once been laid, the gathered debris was piled high and put to the flame. It was a scene that resembled a mournful funeral pyre, but no one grieved. Here, there was only euphoria as the flames danced higher and higher.

The club's new plans for The Valley included a 20,000-capacity stadium, which would include both seating and terracing. There was also to be a very modest housing development. In the circumstances the proposal was very much a case of the club cutting their cloth according to the means at their disposal at that time. And although many fans felt that such a limited capacity was far too conservative, in the circumstances everyone was happy to express their support. Tragically though, it would not be long before any debate over the adequacy of the proposed plans would become irrelevant. On 15 April 1989, ninety-six Liverpool fans were killed at Hillsborough, crushed to death against the perimeter fence of an overcrowded Leppings Lane terrace, at the start of their FA cup semi-final against Nottingham Forest.

In the aftermath of such shocking events an inquiry was launched. Led by Lord Justice Taylor, it not only concerned itself with the circumstances surrounding this particular incident, but looked also at the general situation regarding public safety in and around football stadia. The subsequent report made a range of recommendations, and significantly for Charlton, these included the phasing out of terracing for all first division clubs, with no standing areas remaining by the summer of 1994. In the light of the report, Charlton's plans for The Valley were already obsolete.

Of course, when compared to the horror and grief endured by the Hillsborough victims and their friends and families, this was nothing more than a minor inconvenience. Nevertheless, it was to be the first in an increasingly frustrating series of obstacles that Charlton had to overcome before they could return.

It was precisely three months since Mr Alwen's emotional announcement of the club's intended return, and the implied acceptance that Charlton's ground-share adventure had been total folly, when, with coincidental symmetry, the man who'd led the club into exile, lost his long battle against cancer. At the time it seemed to many that John Fryer's passing was also the herald of the club's rebirth.

In response to what he called 'deep concerns' felt by local residents, Norman Adams, the Greenwich council planning chair, distributed 2,000 letters to homes around The Valley detailing the pros and cons of Charlton's plans. 'It's our job to put people in the picture so that they won't feel alienated,' he told the *Mercury*. 'It's council policy to support the club's return to the borough but within certain guidelines. People must have the right to carry on their peaceful existence.' After the council leader, Dave Picton, had happily expressed support for a return to The Valley only two months earlier, it now seemed ominous that Adams talked only of the council supporting a return to the borough of Greenwich, and not specifically to The Valley. But Picton would very soon claim he'd only been voicing his own opinion on that particular occasion.

Although the proposed housing required planning permission, due to The Valley's status within the council's development plan as designated community open space, and its previous use as a football ground, Charlton did not require permission in order to simply return. They did however need to have the closure order on the East terrace removed, and obtain a safety certificate from Greenwich council. An application for permission to build 54 flats and 27 two- and three-bedroom houses behind the West stand, had been submitted in the summer of 1988, but had not been progressed whilst there was uncertainty over the plans for the football club. That application was later revised when permission was sought for a more modest 66 flats with 12 two- and three-bedroom houses.

With the publication of the interim Taylor Report in August 1989, and the subsequent all-seater requirement, a major rethink was necessary for the proposed standing areas behind both goals and on the East terrace. It was also realised that, since the West stand would be bigger than the one it would replace, planning permission would certainly be required for that. In the event, Charlton decided to apply for planning permission not only for the West stand, but also for development of the north and east sides of the ground. A model of how the new stadium might look was unveiled at the club's New Eltham training ground on 20 August 1989, and according to director Michael Norris, the redevelopment would be carried out in three stages, giving an initial capacity of 18,500, which might ultimately be increased to around 25,000. Stage one of the redevelopment was to be the construction of a new West stand, stage two would see the demolition of the old covered end and the Valley Club and the emergence of a new North stand incorporating offices and banqueting facilities, and stage three would see the elimination of all standing with the provision of a new East stand.

On 30 August 1989, Greenwich council received a detailed planning application for the West stand and an outline application for the North and East. A further application had already been submitted for the extension and conversion of a building previously used as club offices, to provide premises for a new club shop.

By now, Charlton were reluctantly admitting that there was no way the club could return during the 1989/90 season, and at a press briefing, Norris warned, 'now it is entirely up to the council to see that we are able to get back in time for next season.'

In response to the planning applications, the council sent out 1,500 leaflets to local residents giving details of the club's plans. On 17 October, six weeks after the applications had been submitted, Charlton attended their first meeting with the planning department to discuss the proposals. It seemed that the purpose of the meeting was to explain the scheme and to confirm that the commercial elements were essential to the club returning to The Valley. The council informed the club that the application for the West stand could not be considered in advance of the other applications, and that the committee would consider all the applications simultaneously.

There was also some bad news concerning the timescale for a decision, when it was confirmed the applications would not go before the committee until mid-January. In a press release, the new chair of the planning committee, Simon Oelman gave the following reasons for the delay: 'Not all residents of the borough, and particularly some of those living in the immediate vicinity of The Valley, share the fans' enthusiasm for the club's return. The applications are not solely concerned with rebuilding the stadium but include a sizeable area of housing, offices and a banqueting facility. Whether such activities are appropriate in the area is a major question. They also involve the erection of a far more substantial structure located closer to people's homes than were the original stands. In terms of timescale in dealing with the application, I feel sure no one would wish the plans to be approved until the safety of all the spectators and residents has been guaranteed in the design. The club has recently changed its mind on the stadium development and the proposed housing has also been altered. A revised planning application for these alterations has only very recently been submitted and the council is also awaiting a response concerning the problems of parking which would undoubtedly arise. We are dealing with a stadium for the 21 century. Times, requirements and standards have changed since the club first came to The Valley and the council would be failing in its duty if it ignored questions of safety and of wider environmental concerns.'

The council arranged for a series of public meetings regarding the club's proposed return, and insisted on consulting locally on whether or not the commercial proposals were appropriate, which was a total nonsense since the answers could readily be found in their own development plan.

As expected, there was some resentment locally and in November a leaflet emerged which ferociously attacked the scheme. 'Do you really know what's proposed at The Valley? As well as a new stadium the club want speculative offices. The stadium will be massive, 60–70 feet high. It will dominate, overlook and cut out light to nearby houses. The whole scheme is expensive and the club are bound to want to use it as much as possible to pay for it. There won't just be football every two weeks! Find out more! Object to these crazy ideas not fit for a residential area! Object now in writing to the council – they cannot ignore all of us.' The leaflet ended with the contact details of Ms Eve Oldham of the North Charlton Community Centre, who had previously been the chair of two of the public meetings held around the ground.

By December, the council had been aware of Charlton's proposals for more than three months, and had known about the housing application for twice as long, yet it took them that long to inform Charlton that their proposals were in conflict with the council's development plan. At a meeting, they confirmed that the plans were largely unacceptable and the outline scheme would be refused. However, the West stand would be approved subject to certain conditions: the club were to finance a survey and then partly fund a traffic management scheme aimed at preventing commuters from using a road adjacent to The Valley as a rush hour short-cut. They were also to provide parking for spectators' cars on match days and a compound for residents' cars. Finally, they were to give public access to the pitch and the gym.

Charlton considered these conditions to be utterly unacceptable and, in particular, they argued that since the club enjoyed existing use of The Valley as a football stadium, the parking issue should not be a planning consideration. In response they withdrew their detailed application for the West stand and instead sought outline approval for all four sides of the ground.

Two days later, Greenwich council issued a press release:

'Charlton Athletic have been asked to compromise on plans to redevelop their old ground at The Valley. At a meeting with Greenwich council on December 4th, Charlton were urged to drop their controversial plans to include speculative office space and a banqueting suite as part of their redevelopment proposals. Instead they have been asked to come up with a package of measures to improve the environment for those living near the ground, Councillor Simon Oelman, chair of Greenwich's planning and transport committee, said: 'Charlton Athletic say they want a stadium for the 21st century. But an area as congested and densely populated as Charlton is not the perfect site. The police will require streets in the area to be free of cars for long periods on match days. So what are local residents going to do? Parking on match days is not the only problem – the club have refused to rule out using The Valley for other events such as pop concerts, which cause all sorts of additional problems. Greenwich council believes Charlton need to make changes to their proposals. They need to concentrate on the football stadium, drop some of their other plans and make some compensation to the local people in the way of environmental improvements. We hope Charlton can rise to the challenge.'

In response, Charlton expressed their concern at the tone adopted by the council and published details of the statement in the programme for their match with Millwall. On the following Tuesday a press conference was called at the training ground where Mr Alwen made the following statement: 'I want to know if the council is putting itself in a bargaining position or if the truth is they don't really want us back at The Valley. No club can survive on football alone. We must have commercial use of the stadium and the banqueting suite would be a boon to local businesses and to the community as a whole. At the moment, the ground is an eyesore. Reference was made in the council's statement to pop concerts but we haven't at any stage mentioned them. We have user rights at The Valley but we haven't a hope in hell without commercial use.'

Suddenly, the fans' campaign was on again, only now their efforts would be aimed in the direction of the council rather the football club. This time there would be no factions; instead Greenwich would be met by a committed coalition of fans, directors, *Voice of the Valley* and the *Mercury*. In an opening salvo, both of those publications included a whole page with the single word 'YES', which people were encouraged to display, in a show of support for Charlton's return.

Meanwhile, Dave Picton surprisingly suggested that the club look again at the idea of building a new stadium on the Blackwall peninsular, only this time he did at least make it clear that this was his own personal view. In his opinion the club would be best served by a very modest redevelopment of The Valley, with a view to moving out once the new stadium was completed. Of course, given the club's financial constraints, and the fact that no suitable site had yet been identified, this was always a totally unrealistic suggestion.

The first actual confrontation soon took place when a group of fans disrupted a special meeting of the planning and transport committee, called to discuss the Jubilee Line extension. Interrupting from the public gallery they demanded to know why such a meeting had not been called to discuss The Valley planning application. In the circumstances, Simon Oelman was forced to suspend the meeting and face his antagonisers. And in response to the questions put to him, he said that there would be a special meeting to discuss The Valley proposals, held some time during the second half of January. However, what he had to say about the application seemed to indicate that the council's position was far from clear: 'We want Charlton back in the borough but for legal reasons I can't form a view on The Valley until we've considered all the opinions. If this was just about football then I'd have few qualms, but the club insist that pop concerts and other uses are essential to their finances. In my opinion, we're dealing with this application very speedily compared with other projects of a similar size.'

The council's repeated claim that Charlton were insisting on using The Valley for pop concerts seemed more and more absurd. According to Mr Alwen, this was never something that was seriously considered, and even if it was, it was of little concern to the planning committee since, in order to stage this type of event, a special licence would be required.

The special meeting of the planning committee was held on 31 January 1990 and, as a prelude, Greenwich gave an assurance that a decision would be given before the meeting was concluded. In the weeks leading up to the meeting, Laing Homes withdrew their housing application; Charlton insisted that any decision should cover outline proposals for all four sides of the ground, whilst Greenwich maintained they no longer considered the west side to be part of the application.

News of the approaching meeting was quickly announced in the *Mercury*, with a plea for fans to lay siege to the town hall in an attempt to put pressure on the councillors. The result, of course, was a huge turnout with standing room only in the hall and hundreds more left waiting outside in the rainy streets of Woolwich. Inside, the scene was set and ready, with a packed auditorium and the councillors sat at a long table on the stage, facing their audience.

As the evening's events unfolded, various individuals were asked to come to the microphone and give their objections or support. Most of the arguments against were irrelevant in terms of planning law, but instead talked about how a football stadium would be inappropriate in a residential area; how it would adversely affect house prices, and so on. There were even arguments offered based only on the rumour that Charlton were in discussions with Welling United regarding a possible ground-share arrangement at The Valley, which implied use of the ground week-in and week-out. But perhaps more significantly there was also a speech from Norman Adams, who once again raised the issue of the club wanting to hold pop concerts if the development was approved.

To most of those in attendance it appeared that the meeting was getting nowhere. As a result, a few began to drift away, shaking their heads in disbelief and soon this trickle of fans became a mass walk out. For some considerable time chaos reigned as hundreds tried to make their way through a single exit door, tossing their screwed-up 'YES' posters at the stage as they went. There were cries of 'fix' as several fans managed to grab the microphone to let the councillors know precisely what they thought of them.

The declared outcome was a 10–2 vote against the application: only Labour members Bob Callow and Jim Coughlin voted for, while Charlton fan Phil Graham abstained. The refusal almost certainly condemned Charlton to another season at Selhurst Park, only this time it was likely to be without first division football, since the team continued to flirt with relegation.

Not taking kindly to being treated with contempt by their elected representatives, the night's events would mark a significant turning point for the fans' campaign. The idea of contesting the local elections had first been suggested back in December. However, the worry was that if fans did take part, and failed to get a respectable share of votes, the result could be extremely damaging to their credibility. The idea had, nevertheless, attracted some local media attention; in particular the *Mercury*, but also the *South London Press* and, somewhat more surprisingly, *Thames News* and BBC 1's *Newsroom South East*.

And now, having been on the receiving end of the council's ruling, and with no palpable means of retaliation, the fans were ready to declare to the waiting regional TV cameras their intention to stand in the forthcoming local council elections. Thus, the Valley Party was born. The man selected to lead the new party was staunch Labour party member and supporters' club social secretary, Barry Nugent. Within a week Barry would appear on the back page of the *Mercury*, tearing up his party card beneath the headline, 'Vote Valley'.

With the aid of naïve exuberance, the recruitment of candidates was not a problem, and a decision was quickly taken to contest all seats across all wards within the borough, except for those currently held by Bob Callow and Jim Coughlin (the two councillors who had voted in favour of the club's planning application).

Among the fans who came forward at this time was Richard Hunt, an advertising executive with BMP DDB Needham. It was his invaluable contribution to the election campaign that gave real political credibility to the fledgling Valley Party. In order to agree a strategy on how best to win the sympathy of the electorate and thereby win their votes, there was some lengthy debate and careful consideration of a wide range of ideas as to the theme and tone of the campaign. Having completed this process, it took just over a month before Hunt was ready to present the work of his creative team to his new party colleagues. There were nostalgic poster designs aimed at the older generation, featuring much-loved ex-players such as Sam Bartram and 1947 FA Cup-winning captain, Don Welsh. There was one with the simple message, 'Let's send the council to Croydon and see how they like it', and another, obviously intended to appeal to mothers and sisters, showed a young boy watching a recent game at Selhurst Park; it asked the question, 'If you don't support us, who is he going to support?'

Somehow, with the help of Hunt's business contacts, the posters quickly appeared in 25 prime locations across Plumstead, Woolwich, Charlton and Greenwich, and soon after they were also reproduced in the *Guardian* and *Time Out* as well as all the local newspapers. The ubiquitous Valley Party posters were the most visible component of what was a very high-profile and professional electoral campaign. So much so, that local politicians and the general public alike suddenly sat up and took notice. The campaign would later win an advertising industry award for Hunt's team.

On 26 March, the Valley Party held a press conference marking its official launch. Although most of the national press were showing little interest at this stage, the *Guardian* was proving to be a real ally, carrying a detailed account of the launch on its back page. Local television, too, seemed to think that the story of a group of football fans contesting a local council election was newsworthy, and so the press conference was featured widely on the local BBC and ITV news magazine programmes that evening.

Saturday, 7 April was Grand National day, and Charlton were without a fixture due to their scheduled opponents Liverpool playing in an FA Cup semi-final against Crystal Palace. It was an ideal opportunity for Valley Party supporters to descend en masse to all of the shopping centres throughout the borough, in order to spread the Valley message, and try to get some measure of the political allegiances of the local electorate. Meanwhile, others set off for the Den where Millwall were playing host to Manchester City, to distribute a specially produced leaflet in the hope of securing the votes of Millwall fans living in the borough of Greenwich. The following day, the task of leafleting all 85,000 addresses in the borough commenced.

As was required by the terms of their lease agreement, Charlton had, by now, given Ron Noades two years' notice of their intention to quit Selhurst Park, and this period was due to expire in March 1991. At the same time. an agreement was reached that if they left before this date and Wimbledon stepped in as new tenants, anything outstanding would be waived.

The day of the election drew nearer, and as campaigning stepped up, *Thames Reports*, a weekly news programme for London, agreed to make a film explaining the relevant issues, Broadcast just two days before the election, it gave the campaign crucial impetus at a crucial time, serving almost as the Valley Party's very own political broadcast. Earlier that week there had been further welcome publicity with good, positive coverage in the *Sunday Express* and the *Daily Mail*.

On the eve of the election, around 250 supporters embarked on the final major undertaking, delivering a further leaflet to every address in the borough. It was not until the early hours of polling day, 3 May, when the last leaflet landed on a doormat somewhere in Greenwich.

Polling day dawned warm and sunny; perhaps a big turnout could be expected. For Valley Party candidates and supporters alike there was huge excitement as they looked forward to the day ahead. Not surprisingly, party HQ was the Valley Club, and it was from here that the day's work would be organised and allocated. As the day wore on, a steady stream of helpers turned up, but it was impossible to find tasks for all of them.

The polls closed at 9.00pm and candidates and supporters assembled at Woolwich Town Hall to await the day's results. Shortly after 10.00pm, Avery Hill and Sutcliffe wards were the first to declare. The Valley Party polled just 88 and 66 votes respectively. It was a huge disappointment, but nevertheless, this still represented close to 5 per cent of votes cast. By the time the last votes were counted the Valley Party had won 14,838 votes, or 10.9 per cent of all those cast. This represented about a quarter of those for Labour and more than twice the number for the Tories. It was a marvellous result and although no seats were gained, it was, nevertheless, a moral victory which sent a loud and clear message to the local politicians and reverberated around Labour's Walworth Road HQ, where there had long been concern regarding damage done to the party's image by the activities of some London councils.

But the real highlight of the night came when it became known that Simon Oelman's 1986 majority of 450 in Eynsham ward had somehow become a deficit of 300, despite a higher turnout. Charlton fans were ecstatic; whilst the former chair of the planning committee was in tears, as he left the town hall with the deriding chants of the Charlton fans ringing in his ears.

As expected, the team finished second from bottom and were relegated along with neighbours Millwall, and so the feared prospect of second division football at Selhurst Park would become a reality. Thanks to the terms of their tenancy, they would also be forced to pay half of the cost for the installation of seats in Palace's Arthur Waite stand, in order to comply with the Taylor Report.

The impact made by the election results very soon became apparent when, just eleven days later, Oelman's replacement, Norman Adams, contacted the *Mercury* to indicate his readiness to reopen negotiations with the football club. It took only two months for club and council to reach agreement on a revised scheme, but planning permission had to be granted and there still remained the problem of the safety certificate. It was hoped that planning consent could be obtained by October, but in mid-September the relevant council officers went on strike. NALGO knew that the high-profile Valley application would give their action maximum publicity, and so timed things accordingly.

By Christmas, time was running out if Charlton were to start the 1991/92 season back at The Valley, but still there was no progress. In fact, by the time Greenwich council finally gave the green light for The Valley, there were just four games left to play at Selhurst Park, but still the directors insisted that the ground would be ready for the new season.

Work began in earnest, but still it seemed that the Gods were against the return, when the main contractor went bust, causing significant delays and further expense. By the end of July with the ground nowhere near complete, the work came to a stop due to contractors not being paid; costs had soared.

At this point, Charlton had to seek another temporary home – this time Upton Park. In return for their hospitality, the Hammers would be paid £10,000 per game. Originally this arrangement was supposed to be for a handful of games, but ended up lasting for one and a half seasons.

In order to realise the happy return, the fans themselves would dig deep into their own pockets, raising nearly £1.5million towards the building costs in return for long-term season tickets and an elected seat on the board for one of their number.

In this way the happy homecoming was at last achieved on 5 December 1992 in a three-sided stadium with just over 8,000 seats. It was seven years and three months since the last game against Stoke City, and it was celebrated with a 1-0 victory over Portsmouth and tears of happiness and high emotion.

What a day that was!

John Barnes visited The Valley for the first time in 1964. The match on view didn't impress too much, it was the scale of things that engendered an excitement not previously known; so many people, such huge terraces, so much noise. Thus, like so many before him, he was hooked.

When Charlton left The Valley John refused to watch them play in the neighbour's back yard. And it wasn't until the club made clear their intention to a return that he once again became a regular follower, first of all at Upton Park, and finally, more than seven years after they left, back at The Valley.

CHAPTER THREE

AFC BOURNEMOUTH – COMMUNITY CLUB... OR CON?

BY DAVID WHITEHEAD

'BOURNEMOUTH WILL NEVER be a big club. It just isn't a football town. Round here, we don't take it seriously enough, you see...'

I was just eight years old, and my dad's cruel words hurt like hell. What was he on about? I took it seriously enough. Too seriously, I suppose. I used to lie awake at night, dreaming of great games against Liverpool, titanic struggles at Old Trafford, and best of all, the classic FA Cup Final victory over Arsenal at Wembley, with the winner in extra time from Ted MacDougall, a spectacular diving header.

I just couldn't understand what my dad meant. 'Not a football town... never a big club... don't take it seriously enough...' What on earth did he mean?

But as the seasons slowly rolled by, I began to understand. I recall, as a 12-year-old, one of my first away trips was to Luton, which was the closest I had been at that time to a northern industrial town. The back-to-back streets around the ground, just like the locals, looked a lot harder and meaner than the tree-lined avenues of Bournemouth. I could sense that in this grim little town, football somehow seemed to matter more. This was a tougher, harsher world, so unlike the relaxed, gentlemanly bonhomie of Dean Court.

Down at Bournemouth, home defeats were greeted with a good-natured shrug of the shoulders, victories with a sort of embarrassed awkwardness. Draws... well, who cared about draws? In a town buzzing with a hundred other attractions, who was bothered about the score down at Dean Court?

I recall, even more graphically, watching a group of Manchester United supporters on a rare trip down to Southampton in the early 1970s. These were battle-hardened veterans, and you could instantly tell by the way they walked, the attitude they exuded, that football meant a great deal more to them than a pleasant diversion on a Saturday afternoon. This was football red in tooth and claw, seething with raw passion and aggression.

I remember that one Man Utd lad had stencilled on the back of his parka the slogan, 'It's Not A Team, It's A Religion'. The look on his face as he pushed past me suggested that he took his football seriously enough. If someone at Bournemouth had done that, it would have been a joke. But this was the real thing.

And that was when I got it for the first time. These guys were professionals... we were only playing at it. This was a glimpse of another exciting world, an alien world I ached to be part of – but already I knew in my heart that at safe, comfortable Bournemouth, it was never going to happen.

I came to realise that Bournemouth was a bit of a joke team really. We'd never risen above the old Third Division in our entire existence, and showed little ambition of wanting to do so. It was almost as if, when God created football, He ordained that Bournemouth should forever occupy the same position bobbing around gently somewhere in the middle of the Third. That was the way it was, and like generations before us, we came to accept our fate. And nobody really minded that much.

So as the years crept by, one by one my boyhood dreams evaporated. Visions of appearing on *Top of the Pops*, of becoming the next James Bond, or of crazy celebrations after seeing Bournemouth scoring the winning goal at Wembley, gradually they faded away. Well, almost...

Fast-forward 30-odd years. It's the 19 April 1998, and I'm standing in front of the famous twin towers of Wembley, watching in open-mouthed disbelief at the thousands upon thousands of red and black-clad supporters advancing up Wembley Way. God, I can't take this all in. The colour, the noise, the flags, the crazy hats, and everywhere I look, there are thousands more converging on the famous old stadium.

I get inside, and there's a sea of red and black stretching more than halfway round the stadium. Someone tells me that we've sold over 34,000 tickets. What? Our average home gate is only about 5,000... who ARE all these people? I remember, as a child, dreaming about getting to Wembley but secretly fearing that we wouldn't be able to sell our ticket allocation, and feeling embarrassed at the wide open spaces at the Bournemouth end. But I needn't have worried – this has exceeded even my wildest dreams.

Then Robbie Williams comes thundering over the PA and those familiar red and black shirts emerge from the tunnel. The noise is just overpowering, the flags, confetti and balloons are everywhere. This is it, this is what we have been waiting for all these years. We have arrived!

Then amidst the ear-splitting inferno of noise, comes a

strange quiet voice at the back of my mind. Is this really happening? Is this really Bournemouth? And is this destined to be the glorious climax of an extraordinary year?

You see, just twelve months before, AFC Bournemouth was well and truly bust. Millions of pounds in debt, the wolves were at the door, and we were in the hands of the receiver. The game was up.

The details are of no particular interest, you could probably find a similar story at dozens of clubs around the country. Years of living on the edge, dodgy deals, shabby managerial incompetence, the usual tawdry tales. Decades of living beyond our meagre means had finally caught up with us.

But then something remarkable happened. At the time, it seemed like a miracle. The people of Bournemouth, who for decades had treated the club as nothing more than a vaguely amusing side-show, suddenly erupted in an explosion of passion, stood up and refused to let the club simply die.

It was truly astonishing what happened in that spring of 1997. Suddenly, just when it looked like the club was going to disappear, a massive surge of emotion seemed to sweep across the town, as if to say, 'No, we won't let this happen'.

There were countless stories of lifelong supporters digging into their life savings, of schoolchildren raiding their piggy banks, of marathons, sponsored walks, auctions, and every kind of fundraising activity. It was extraordinary to see the transformation that occurred within just a few days, culminating in a highly emotional public meeting at The Winter Gardens, where many thousands of pounds were collected in buckets, and grown men wept. We weren't going to lay down and die. Somehow, we were going to survive.

And then the hero of the hour emerged, a man who seemed to personify this new spirit of defiance. Trevor Watkins, a clever young lawyer who seized the moment, galvanised the supporters, and gave us leadership and a sense of direction.

Nobody can quite remember how or exactly when it came about, but the new buzzword was 'community club'. It was bold, revolutionary even, but we weren't going to let the club be wound up, and see the ground turned into another identikit retail complex. Neither would we let the club be sold to become the plaything of some rich businessman whom none of us had ever heard of, with no apparent affiliation to the town.

No, somehow we were going to sort out the bank and the creditors, raise the funds and take over the club ourselves: we were going to become a club owned by the fans, run by the fans: a community club! Never again would we, the supporters, allow our club to be run into the ground by a bunch of unaccountable businessmen.

What a beautiful, simple idea it was. It had always seemed to me that among the supporters of every club, you could find plenty of able lawyers, accountants, marketing experts, experienced professionals from a variety of backgrounds – in other words, people with exactly the skills and experience needed to run a football club. So why not do it for ourselves?

The fanzine movement from the late 80s onwards had given football supporters a platform, and up and down the country. The self-confident, articulate individuals emerged who were a complete contrast to the beer-swilling Neanderthal stereotype. In many cases, the guys writing in the fanzines appeared to be a great deal more intelligent and switched-on than your average club director. Football was in deep crisis in the 80s, and supporters began to challenge those who had mismanaged the game for decades.

People reacted with horror to the disasters at Bradford, Heysel and Hillsborough, looked at the run-down stadiums and the empty terraces, and thought, 'We could do better than this'. There was a feeling in the air that the game was stuck in a time-warp, and this new generation of confident, articulate supporters began to chip away at the football establishment.

The emergence of the phone-in culture, and in particular Danny Baker's *606* show, was very influential at this time. His cocky, irreverent attitude gave fans a growing self-belief that we didn't have to kow-tow to those in charge, and that, given half a chance, we could probably do a better job ourselves. I remember in the early 90s listening to Danny Baker mercilessly ridiculing the puffed-up pompous figures who ran the game, and thinking he had a real point. Why should we sit back and allow these incompetent fools to ruin the game we loved?

The advent of the Internet in the mid-1990s speeded that process up a hundredfold, and suddenly it became very easy to share information instantly, and to mobilise opinion in a way that would have been impossible back in, say, the 1970s. I am sure that the events at Bournemouth in 1997 were one of the very first instances where the Internet played a crucial role; one of the first examples of a grass-roots campaign that took off via the fans' websites, with the momentum maintained by e-mails and chatroom discussions.

We quickly realised that in order to mount a campaign and to spread ideas, you didn't need to spend time and money designing, printing and distributing leaflets, you didn't have to hire a public hall in order to address an audience of hundreds. Thanks to the Internet, new ideas could spread like wildfire, and lively, compelling debates could take place well away from the letters page of the local paper, without any of the usual restrictions.

The next few months passed by in a blur, the buckets kept on filling up with loose change, a Trust Fund was established to keep the club going while a solution was desperately sought. It was touch and go, and at one point we were supposedly just 15 minutes away from extinction, but eventually in the summer of '97, Trevor Watkins announced that a deal had been done, a new company formed with a new board composed of lifelong supporters, and there we were, proud to call ourselves the first community club in Europe.

We saw ourselves as a beacon of enlightened supporter democracy in the murky world of football. Trevor was our young, dynamic chairman and Bournemouth, yes Bournemouth, had shown the world of football the way forward.

Suddenly, we were THE club that everyone wanted to talk about. There were dozens of articles in the national press hailing our achievements, Trevor Watkins seemed to be on the radio every other day, and everyone was talking about us and our community club revolution down on the sunny south coast. We got emails every day from football supporter groups around the world, all wanting to know how we had done it!

Those were heady times indeed, and there was a sense of liberation in the air, a feeling of great optimism and togetherness. None of us had ever known anything like it. I imagined, somewhat fancifully, that maybe this was how it had felt in Paris in the days after the storming of the Bastille. I didn't think of extending the historical parallel any further...

The new season kicked off in August with high expectations, and things just seemed to get better and better. Amazingly, less than a year after the takeover by the fans, there we were at Wembley for the first time in our history, with tens of thousands of fans we never knew we had, infused with a belief and a passion that we'd never known before.

So as I stood there at Wembley looking at the scenes around me, I thought back to those Man Utd supporters I'd seen all those years before, and I felt that, at last, we had arrived in the big time. You could feel the power of what we had unleashed, and best of all, we had done it all ourselves. This wasn't the result of some millionaire pumping in his ill-gotten cash, this was the raw power of the supporters, unencumbered by a bunch of grumpy old men in the boardroom. I looked around again, and thought to myself, 'Yes, this is it. At last...'

By the way, we lost the game 2-1, but oddly, it didn't really seem to matter. The main thing was that we had survived, we had pulled back from the precipice, and now we were back in business, poised to enter an exciting new era. A golden future seemed to beckon... or so we thought.

It's difficult to say when the first cracks began to appear in our shiny new world but within a year or so of Wembley, the momentum had died away, and there was a subtle change in atmosphere. Perhaps it was disappointment that we hadn't marched on to promotion the following season, but had missed out on the play-offs by a whisker, in time-honoured fashion. We had thought that we'd left our tag as the 'nearly club' behind. Not so.

More likely, it was the gradual, uncomfortable realisation that in all the euphoria of the fans' takeover, and the establishment of the Community Club, nobody had remembered to check the small print. Most of us had simply assumed that the club would be set up on democratic lines, with members each having a vote, and the right to elect fans' directors to represent our interests at board level. It came as a nasty shock to find out that this was very far from the case.

Matters came to a head during the close season in 1999, when there was a massive 40 per cent increase in ticket prices. We were shocked. It wasn't so much that ticket prices had to go up to plug the gap – we could accept that– it was more the high-handed way the decision was announced as a fait accompli. Where was the consultation between the board and the supporters? Wasn't that what a community club was supposed to be all about?

It was all very well being a community club, but the flip-side was that the club seemed permanently short of cash. It became a bit of a standing joke that we were always being pumped for money, but that we had no direct way of finding out or influencing how it was spent.

Some of us began to ask questions about the actual set-up of the club, and how we could ensure adequate supporter representation so that similar PR disasters could be avoided in the future. It was all very well preaching to the rest of the football world about the virtues of being a community club, but when it came to democracy in action at AFCB, the reality fell a long way short of the rhetoric.

It transpired that the way the club had been re-structured was about as far away from fan democracy as you could get. In effect, Trevor and his fellow Trust Fund directors controlled two 'golden shares' that automatically gave them 51 per cent of the voting rights on any issue. This was in order to prevent any hostile takeover of the club, but the problem was, there was no mechanism for voting Trust Fund directors either in or out – so if the supporters didn't like what the Trust Fund was doing, there was nothing they could do about it. They could appoint new directors, they could even sell the club without having to refer to anyone. We shook our heads in disbelief; this wasn't what we had fought for.

When challenged, Trevor seemed to dismiss these concerns with an airy nonchalance that many of us found deeply unsettling. After all, we reasoned, we were the ones who had filled the buckets to keep the club going, we were the ones who continued to prop the club up with a range of fundraising activities. Why shouldn't we have a direct say in how the club was managed? We were the fans, this was a fans' club – so why not?

Trevor continued to appear regularly in the national media, and seemed to enjoy his new-found fame. It was well-known that he was an ambitious local politician, and some of us began to feel that this was grandstanding on an epic scale. People wondered if he was using AFCB to boost his own personal profile and further his political career. We weren't impressed.

Trevor published a book entitled *Cherries in the Red*, an account of the events of 1997, and how the club had survived. But the book was unfortunately sub-titled 'One Fan's Fight To Save His Club'. Hang on we thought... there was more than just one fan involved. There were thousands of us, young and old, ordinary supporters from every walk of life who had all helped in thousands of different ways. Sure, Trevor was the figurehead, and he did a magnificent job to hold the club together, but he didn't do it all by himself.

This wasn't how it was supposed to be. In the early days, Trevor had been open and approachable, but now he was becoming increasingly remote from us supporters. We thought we had left all that behind. Some of us started to mutter that this was beginning to resemble the Animal Farm of football: a noble, inspiring vision that had somehow gone badly wrong.

But what could we do about it? Without any formal rights to demand supporter representation on the main board, we were in a helpless position. Fans began to ask out loud if this community club tag was just a big con. It's only a community club, people sniped, when they want another bucketful of free money from us. The rest of the time, we could meekly stand on the sidelines, and not presume to poke our noses into matters that didn't concern us.

And so began a sort of sullen stand-off between the board and the supporters, where all the goodwill and optimism of 1997 soured into a series of bad-tempered exchanges on the websites and mailing lists. On the pitch, we continued to just miss out on the play-offs with depressing regularity. The minute any of our young players showed any promise, they were sold off with indecent haste. The never-ending appeals for yet more money to keep the club going just added to the feeling of gloom. The decrepit old stadium continued to crumble away before our eyes, becoming an unsightly, dangerous eyesore. It was beginning to feel like the bad old days all over again.

This was perhaps the time that the 'spirit of '97' should have reasserted itself. When it finally dawned on the supporters that the community club was in reality a bit of a sham, if at that point they had mobilised and demanded changes, then things might have turned out very differently.

But there seemed to be a meek acceptance that there wasn't much we could do about it, and that Trevor should be given the benefit of the doubt and allowed to get on with things.

I often joked that it must be the Dorset DNA, part of our collective genetic make-up, that we just didn't want to protest or to challenge those in power (with, of course, the honourable exception of The Tolpuddle Martyrs, and look how that turned out...). We were just too docile, too deferential. Go back a hundred years or so, and most of our ancestors would have been simple farmhands out in the Dorset villages, tugging their forelocks as the lord of the manor rode past in his carriage.

That's how it seemed at Dean Court – the general mood was that Trevor & Co. should be left to get on with running the club as they saw fit, and that it was no business of ours. Clearly, this flew in the face of the principles of the self-proclaimed community club, and it became increasingly clear that Trevor had little interest in discussing the finer points of supporter democracy or reform of the club's constitution. The passion and energy of just a few years before had all seeped away. No demonstrations, no protests, no boycotts... just a sour, resigned acceptance and a shrug of the shoulders.

Things took a turn for the worse a year or so later when Trevor Watkins resigned as Chairman – although he still retained control of the golden shares – to be replaced by a man called Tony Swaisland. This Mr Swaisland had previously been the Chairman of Brentford, and so far as any of us knew, had no personal links to the club of any kind. How could Swaisland, a Brentford supporter, become the Chairman of our community club? This was getting beyond a joke.

The answer was that apparently Mr Swaisland had a great deal of expertise in the construction industry, and that this would prove invaluable as we embarked upon the rebuilding of the stadium... oh, so that was all right then.

Dean Court was shabby, tired and hopelessly out of date for the 21st century, but the problem was, we simply didn't have anywhere near enough money to complete the project. The fans were urged, yet again, to dig deep, money was raised from the local council, sponsors and The Football Trust, but we were still several million short. However, we apparently had no choice but to demolish the old stadium, otherwise the ground would be shut down on health and safety grounds. Despite the gaping financial shortfall, in came the bulldozers and the project went ahead.

And so it was that in autumn 2001 we finally moved into our half-finished, three-sided ground (we didn't have enough money for the fourth stand), with a massive financial threat hanging over us. We had taken out short-term loans to help bridge the gap, but it didn't take long for a full-blown crisis to blow up.

In summer 2002, we were appalled to find out that the board was planning to sell the ground and lease it back as the only solution to our financial woes; we could see that if we went ahead with the sale and leaseback scheme and its punitive terms, then it was only a matter of time before we went bust again.

Besides, we were proud of our shiny new stadium. It might have had only three sides, and it might have been a bit short on luxury, but it was OURS. And we didn't want to sell it to some property developer so that five years later it could be turned into a Tesco hypermarket.

At long last, the old fighting spirit that we last saw in 1997 began to stir. There was talk of boycotts, supporters staged a walk-out during one pre-season friendly, and debates raged fiercely on every message-board. The feeling of growing anger was palpable and the dangerous whiff of revolution was in the air. The final straw was when we learned that Trevor Watkins planned to use the golden shares to push through the sale, in blatant opposition to the supporters' wishes. Was this going to be the final showdown?

At the last moment, in a curious echo of 1997, a figure appeared on the scene to galvanise our resistance and rescue the club from civil war and oblivion. This was Peter Phillips, just like Trevor Watkins before him, another lifelong fan whose moment had arrived. He came over as go-ahead, positive, and seemed to be a guy that fully understood the situation from the supporters' perspective.

Peter managed to persuade the board that he would be able to mobilise enough support and raise enough money so that we could somehow stave off the encircling creditors.

And he did it too; on a massive wave of popular enthusiasm, Peter was appointed Chairman with the pledge that we would reject the sale and leaseback agreement, and that we would find another solution to our problems. It was just like the great days of 1997 all over again – there was a real feeling now that it was one of us that was running the club, a guy who would fight for our interests, and would honour the ideals of the community club.

And just like his predecessor, Peter Phillips was a media natural, seldom missing an opportunity for a photocall in his trademark fedora. We quickly nicknamed him The Man with the Hat. One of the first things Peter did was to erect a massive sign behind the goal at the home end bearing the slogan, 'Stadium Not For Sale'. We thought that was just great.

Within a few months, to popular acclaim, Peter launched Cherryshare, a scheme whereby supporters could invest in the club, and this raised over half a million pounds. He also amended the club's constitution so that there would be some direct fan representation on the board. At last, we felt, we were getting somewhere!

On the field, Peter's first season ended on a euphoric note: a year before, in 2002, we had been relegated down to the bottom division, but the team responded well, and fought through to the play-off final in Cardiff, where we thrashed Lincoln 5-2 with a breathtaking display of adventurous attacking football.

Now, wouldn't it be nice if life was like a Hollywood film, and we could end the story right here? We had put our financial worries behind us, the stadium was still ours, we had a popular Chairman who seemed able to reach out to the fans in a way that Trevor Watkins no longer could, and the team had just given us one of our best days ever. Admissions at the gates were up, life seemed good again, and we could look forward to the future with renewed confidence. But as we all know, life isn't like that, and sooner or later reality intrudes...

Although on the face of it, things appeared to be going well, there was a constant exodus of our best young players, often for derisory fees. We couldn't quite understand it. If the financial problems had been largely resolved, then why couldn't we keep our best players and build a winning team?

Peter regularly reassured us that everything was going well, but we lost a lot of money on an ill-advised attempt to break into the concert business, and nobody was quite sure who was going to pick up the tab for that, although we could hazard a guess. Sure enough, the never-ending demands for yet more money from the hard-pressed supporters continued.

To go to a game at Dean Court, you had to run a gauntlet of supporters outside the ground, each shaking a different bucket in your face for a variety of fundraising causes. The match programme would be filled with appeals for cash, while the tannoy announcer would regularly cajole you for yet more of your hard-earned. But donation fatigue had well and truly set in by now, and we felt we were being milked dry.

Supporting AFCB became a bit like having a mate who was always down on his luck. The kind of mate who, if you met him for a drink, would spend the whole evening going on and on about his money worries, his job troubles, his relationship problems, a never-ending list of woes. The kind of mate too, who would always somehow manage to dodge his round, then try to borrow a tenner off you at the end of the evening. We looked back fondly to the long-lost days when going to football was just a bit of a laugh – this wasn't much fun at all.

It all unravelled in 2005. With a talented squad, the team seemed to freeze just as we were on the verge of the play-offs, and once again, we missed out. Cynicism was rife. Unsurprisingly, we promptly lost three of our young stars who left in search of success at a higher level.

Then there was the deeply disturbing 'Noonangate' affair, the strange case of Andrew Noonan, the former Company Secretary and founding director of the 'community club' back in '97, who in summer 2005 issued a winding-up order against AFCB for non-payment of over £250,000-worth of invoices for services rendered in relation to the rebuilding of the ground.

We were gobsmacked that that a so-called community club director had apparently invoiced the club for such astronomical amounts when hundreds of ordinary fans had happily given their time for free. How could such invoices be justified? Had the work been put out to competitive tender? Who had agreed these fees? The questions kept on coming, we were shocked by what had apparently been going on behind the scenes, and the official explanations left us baffled.

Eventually, the matter was settled in the High Court, the club was ordered to pay just over £81,000 to Noonan, and ordinary fans reacted with a mixture of anger and bewilderment. Over the years, the supporters had raised hundreds of thousands of pounds, often making sacrifices that they could ill afford, just to keep the club alive. Was this what local children had emptied their piggy banks for? Was this why older supporters had dipped into their precious life savings? We wondered what else might have been going on at the community club, as confusion turned to anger.

Then came the final bombshell. In late 2005 it was announced that unless the club went ahead with another sale and leaseback deal, then we were going to be wound up by the Inland Revenue, who were owed a vast sum in unpaid NI contributions. The club president wanted his personal loan repaid, other angry creditors were banging on the door, and sale and leaseback was presented as the only possible way out. This was particularly hard to accept as the man who was now urging sale and leaseback as the only solution was none other than Peter Phillips, the same guy who had swept to power just three years before, promising to defend the club against any such scheme. Surely, if it had been wrong in 2002, then it was just as wrong in 2005.

REBELLION

We felt stunned, sickened by the whole situation. True, if the financial picture was as bad as we were now told, then it was difficult to see another way out. But why had things been allowed to get so bad? Why hadn't we been told earlier that the situation was deteriorating, so that we could have tried to find another answer while there was still time?

It felt like a gun was being held to our heads, and reluctantly, the majority of supporters went along with the deal, accepting that this was the best we could hope for in the circumstances. What was the alternative? There was an attempt to persuade supporters to put their personal pensions into a fund to buy the ground, but given the recent financial history of the club, most of us felt that was one step too far. Nobody had any real answers this time round. Just an overpowering sense of resignation to the inevitable, as ownership of the stadium passed to a London-based property development company. The smiling, waving Man in the Hat was no more. In AFCB history, Phillips will forever be remembered as 'The Man who Sold the Ground'.

May 2006 saw the end of yet another frustrating season during which the team were too good to be relegated, but lacking the talent and ambition to make a bid for promotion. Marooned, as we always seem to be, somewhere around the middle of the division.

Off the pitch, things looked bleak. Despite the deal, we were still apparently millions of pounds in debt, except that we had sold our biggest asset, and our new landlord's monthly rent demand looked ever more onerous. Those who claimed to be in the know hinted darkly that we couldn't carry on for much longer. And yet again, we were urged to dig deep, to bail the club out of this latest mess. We want donors, not moaners – that was the message coming over loud and clear. In other words, stop trying to meddle in matters that are way above your heads, let the 'professionals' get on with the job of running the club, now run along and sell a few raffle tickets, there's a good fellow.

Rumours swirled around of strange goings-on in the boardroom, of players and staff being paid late, of an ever-growing queue of creditors, and the Internet whispers grew louder every day. The board of our so-called community club retreated into its bunker, secretive and suspicious, and our supporter representatives seemed to find it impossible to enter into any kind of meaningful dialogue with them. Except when they wanted a little fundraising done, that is. They're always happy to talk about that. And somehow the club staggers on, lurching from crisis to crisis.

But where are the protests? Where are the sit-ins and the boycotts? Where is the wave of anger at this sorry debacle? How long will it be until people finally stand up and shout, 'Enough is enough?'

Well, I guess you know the answer to that already. You know how it goes: Bournemouth isn't really a football town, the people just don't take it seriously enough, no real passion.

And yet the time may well come again, just like '97, when the club finds itself on the brink of collapse, and perhaps that's what it will take to make the long-suffering supporters of AFCB finally rouse themselves, take matters into their own hands and do something about it. We did it before, and we can do it again.

You know, football clubs are funny things: how do you define exactly what a football club is? It's not the players; they change with every season, and it's certainly not the directors and managers who come and go over the years. Thinking about it, the only constant is the fans, who will always be there, because they have no other place to go.

Take away the supporters, and there is no club left at all, just an empty, meaningless shell. When the supporters realise that they ARE the club, that's the day when things will really start to change. And maybe that's when the dream of a community club, run by the fans for the fans, finally becomes reality.

David Whitehead was taken to his first Bournemouth match as an 8 year old in 1964, and was instantly hooked for life. He still hasn't forgiven his dad for inflicting a lifetime of heartbreak and disappointment on him in such a thoughtless way. David often wonders how much happier his life would have been if he'd been taken to the cinema instead on that fateful afternoon...

These days, David runs a media promotions agency in Essex, is a regular contributor to various fanzines, occasional poet, and an enthusiastic – though strictly amateur – musician. His ambition is to write a best-selling book about growing up miserable in the 1970s, but the problem is, apart from the football, it was mostly quite a good laugh.

CHAPTER FOUR

BRIGHTON AND HOVE ALBION FC – THE BRIGHTON STADIUM MYSTERY

BY TIM CARDER

PREPARE YOURSELF FOR a saga of deception and determination; an anarchic journey from crumbling terraces to Downing Street with more twists and turns than a Stanley Matthews dribble.

This is the scarcely credible – and hugely abbreviated – story of how Brighton & Hove Albion's Goldstone Ground was sold, how supporters fought for the soul of the club, and how the battle for a new stadium still continues eleven years later. It's a struggle that took over the life of this ordinary football fan and is told from my perspective – but happily I have been far from alone in this ongoing tale.

At 7.30 am on 7 July 1995, I had no idea I would spend the next decade and more becoming something of an expert in council procedures, planning law, registration of political parties, public inquiries, arranging marches, analysing petitions, organising leafleting, and host of other unlikely activities. But as I awoke that Friday morning, the local radio reported, 'Brighton & Hove Albion Football Club will be playing home games at Portsmouth from 1996.'

'WHAT?' *My* football club moving 48 miles away? There had to be some mistake.

The story had come from the local *Evening Argus* newspaper. Someone at Fratton Park had leaked a request by the Albion board for a ground-share – because the club's Goldstone Ground had been sold.

The roots of this tale stretch way back into the early 1980s when the club, then in the old First Division, spent serious money that it didn't have as record-level gates fell rapidly. In 1983, Albion reached the FA Cup final – 'And Smith must score!' – but were also relegated. The debts accumulated, and by the early 1990s winding-up petitions were brought by the Inland Revenue, a scenario familiar to followers of many other clubs.

The long-term solution was the provision of a new stadium with much greater earning power, but here the tale diverges from the norm. Brighton & Hove is a city of 250,000 people constrained by the wonderful South Downs to the north and east, and the sea to the south. In fact, in the early 1980s the two towns had separate councils. A single unitary council came into being in 1997 and city status was granted for the millennium. Residential areas stretch westwards to form the tenth largest urban area in England. There is little 'brownfield' development land available – no former coalmines or derelict steelworks in Sussex! And therein lies the nub of the whole problem: there is no ideal site for a new stadium, an issue to which we'll return.

But faced with insistent creditors, Albion also had a short-term plan: to borrow more money secured on the Goldstone Ground, the club's somewhat ramshackle but loveable home since 1902, *with its value enhanced by gaining planning permission for a retail park*. It was just a paper exercise, we were told. For instance, managing director Barry Lloyd wrote in the programme, 'I can assure all our supporters that there will be no question of any move from here until a new location is found that is suitable in every way to all of us and, in particular, suitable to you all, our supporters.'

There was even a modest fans' campaign of support: 'STAN' (Save The Albion Now). I got involved delivering leaflets and attending council meetings. 'What guarantee is there that the ground won't be sold?', asked opposing councillors. 'Don't be stupid and stop trying to destroy the club,' I thought to myself. Hove Council eventually granted permission to sell the ground [?] when it realised it couldn't win an appeal.

More petitions followed. I went along to one hearing in the High Court, but otherwise had to listen to the radio for news from London, a heart-stopping affair of extended deadlines and last-minute deals – but we survived.

Amid this chaos, the club was taken over in 1993 by two of the directors: Greg Stanley, then chairman of Focus DIY, and his managing director Bill Archer, whom he had introduced to the Albion three years earlier. They brought in new money to pay off the immediate debts and appointed David Bellotti, the former Lib-Dem MP for Eastbourne, as chief executive. He was known to have supported the club and, as a county councillor, was perhaps considered to wield influence in the corridors of power. Stanley became club chairman. Bellotti started to make swingeing cuts. It was just what we needed – a leaner, fitter club finally cutting its cloth according to its means. The crisis appeared to be over. Lloyd was sacked and the great Liam Brady was brought in as manager.

So back to July 1995, and the local paper, the *Argus*, did not make good reading. The Goldstone had been sold, it said. The club would play at Portsmouth until a new stadium was developed at Waterhall, a former tip to the north of Brighton used for playing fields, with funding generated by a new shopping centre nearby at Patcham Court Farm. In a hurried statement, Bill Archer called it an 'exciting new venture'. But that didn't seem right at all, because Brighton Council opposed development north of the bypass. I knew that. I had a letter from council leader Steve Bassam when I'd written to him about a stadium at Waterhall a couple of years earlier. As a member of the public I'd even asked the question at a council meeting and been met with a stony response. Sure enough, the *Argus* also asked the council and got the same answer: Waterhall and Patcham Court Farm were 'no-goers' – and the club had known for two weeks.

Bellotti was abroad when the story broke. 'It'll get sorted when he returns,' I thought. It didn't – things got worse. First of all he denied the ground had been sold – perhaps technically he was right, as only a conditional contract then existed, but it was disingenuous – then he insisted that Waterhall was a still a possibility. But the deal to sell was exposed when, in conjunction with the *Argus*, supporter Paul Samrah, an accountant, found the answer at the Land Registry. The Goldstone had been sold to property developers, Chartwell Land, for £7.4 million.

Companies House records showed that Archer and Stanley had taken over the club in 1993 by introducing an £880,000 loan from the Co-op Bank. The other directors had surrendered their shares to a new, off-the-shelf holding company set up by the pair in return for having their loans repaid in 1996. The share capital of the new company was just £100. Archer, who had never put any money into the club, held the majority of the shares; his control of Brighton & Hove Albion Football Club cost him just £56.25!

But there was more. Paul Samrah, who headed our campaign team, also found that the club's constitution had been changed during the takeover. A clause had been removed which required that, in the event of the club being wound up, any surplus remaining after the settling of debts and repayment of share capital must be given to a sporting club or charity in Sussex. Without this 'no profit' clause the club could be shut down, the debts paid off, and the ground sold (with its permission for a retail park) with the shareholders netting a healthy profit.

Cue alarm bells! The club described the removal of the clause, which is a requirement of the Football Association, as 'an oversight'. The FA hadn't been informed of the changes – a clear breach of its rules – but merely rapped the club's knuckles and demanded the restoration of the clause. The 'guardians of the game' would surely have sufficient grounds to bring disrepute charges before the end of this sorry saga, but they never had the backbone to try it.

But still there was more. Bellotti, in his programme notes, said the club had to repay more than £6 million at the end of the season. The figure was questionable and seemed to change week by week, but in any case, Paul's examination of the accounts showed that only £915,000 had to be repaid in 1996: a £715,000 mortgage and £200,000 due to Greg Stanley. (The other directors were prepared to leave their money in the club.) So why did the club not attempt to reschedule these relatively minor debts while it worked with the councils towards a new ground?

In fact, there was another sum linked to Stanley, a

£600,000 loan from a trust fund administered by Archer. This was accruing interest at around £45,000 per annum – but because the club failed to service this interest it had incurred a penalty of £250,000! Surely there was a conflict of interest here; Archer had a duty to the trust fund *and* the football club. Stanley quickly resigned as chairman and Archer, much the stronger character, took over. Hit by the sudden furore resulting from these worrying revelations, the new chairman hastily looked into buying Hove's greyhound stadium but was rebuffed.

So the truth was that there was *no* arrangement for a homecoming after a sojourn in Portsmouth. The club would move to the next county with no firm plan to return – and that obviously meant its future was in severe doubt. The ground had been sold for what looked outwardly like dubious reasons. Why had there been no exploration of other options like rescheduling? The club said there had been no interest from potential investors for two years – but why didn't they try to strike up a meaningful relationship with the councils? And why was it all done so secretively? The kindest way of looking at it was that they believed the 'emotional blackmail' of exiling the club was the only way to force the councils to grant permission for a new stadium. But there was no doubt in my mind – we'd been sold down the river. And what was Bellotti's comment in the club programme? 'Stop whining!' Is it any wonder a lot of people were very angry?

The councils appealed to the club to stop the sale, but it was too late. They offered to buy the freehold of the ground and lease it back, but the club wasn't listening. They tried to strike up a transparent relationship with the board but nothing came of it. They called in the FA who had a dossier of revelations, but the club was given a clean bill of health financially. The councils stuck to their principles: no development north of the bypass and no out-of-town retail parks, and to find a basis for a solution they commissioned a report to examine all possible sites for a new stadium.

However, the Albion board ignored any suggestion of partnership and carried on regardless. In December 1995 the club submitted a planning application for a 30,000-seat stadium at Toad's Hole, an undeveloped valley *south* of the bypass which Hove Council had already rejected as a stadium site in its Local Plan. The scheme included the inevitable 200,000 square feet of retail and office development, giving it no hope of success. Archer and Stanley would, it was said, invest a great deal of money towards the £32 million cost. The Government directed Hove Council to reject the scheme on traffic grounds, but still Bellotti insisted: 'Make no mistake, subject only to planning consent, this site at Toad's Hole Valley is going to be our new home.'

Did anyone at the club really have the desire to develop a stadium?

What could the ordinary supporter do about this? Well, I wasn't prepared to stand by while the club I had supported for 30 years went down the pan, and neither were many others. There were meetings between fans' groups, past rivals now united against the common enemy. The fanzines became essential reading, with analysis of the situation and news of events. There were demonstrations and protests at matches, and there were letters, hundreds of them sent in uncoordinated fashion by individual supporters to anyone who might wield the tiniest amount of influence. For my part I wrote to Chartwell, the property developers, and to Sir

Geoffrey Mulcahy (chief executive of Chartwell's parent company, Kingfisher) who promised to discuss the matter with Chartwell – but there was no obvious movement from the firm buying our football ground.

At the Goldstone the demonstrations were mostly against Bellotti – 'Target Archer,' I thought – and quickly intensified. On 2 September a group of lads staged the first sit-down protest in the centre-circle at half time before being persuaded to leave by the equally-frustrated manager, Liam Brady, who told them he didn't know what was going on. Bellotti responded by closing sections of terracing to keep demonstrators away from the main stand. A televised game at Bournemouth saw the 'Brighton Beach' end a sea of banners. In the second half, a hundred Albion followers ran onto the pitch, but many of them were just old-fashioned hooligans who abused home supporters, stewards and police. What a waste! Hooliganism has always been utter folly; on this occasion the morons were aiding the destruction of the club they professed to follow. It was depressing stuff.

By this time I'd joined the committee of the Supporters' Club in an effort to help. The aim was to keep the Albion in the local area, and the first glimmer of hope came when Ivor Caplin, leader of Hove Council, negotiated a deal with Chartwell for another year at the Goldstone if permission for a supermarket was granted in place of the retail park. In fact the permission never came, but it at least showed there might be room for manoeuvre.

At the end of January 1996, a number of us met David Bellotti at the Goldstone, but his attitude to our very real concerns was cavalier. I followed up with a letter seeking to establish some trust between worried fans and the board.

Would the club agree to a joint account, as suggested by the FA, for the proceeds of the ground sale? Would the club issue a statement of simple promises to reassure supporters? Would it heck – but at least I tried! I analysed the travel arrangements for 30,000 fans at Toad's Hole, reckoning on at least 1,300 cars cruising the streets of northern Hove looking to park. 'Many more buses,' was Bellotti's curt reply – but I'd allowed for 50 *full* double-deckers, 4,000 people! His planning application was nonsensical, and his refusal to discuss it merely emphasised a siege mentality.

In March came the best news yet. Chartwell would lease the ground back for one more season for £480,000. 'No deal,' said Bellotti, but Ivor Caplin produced a leaflet explaining the economic sense of accepting the offer. Albion's chief executive was incensed. An elderly lady distributing the leaflets outside the ground was intimidated, and Liz Costa, the Supporters' Club vice-chairman, was literally hauled before Bellotti, who went into a rage at one of the club's most dedicated fans. He was losing it.

Bellotti claimed Caplin's figures were wrong – but refused to reveal the rent at Fratton Park, citing 'commercial sensitivity'. Instead, the club made an offer of £200,000 for the extra year. Bellotti said, 'We've taken the views of our supporters on board and want to show our sincerity in wishing to stay at the Goldstone for another year.' Codswallop! Chartwell responded: 'Not negotiable' – and set a deadline of midday on 30th April for the club to accept.

So as the last home game, on 27th April, approached, we didn't know if it would be the last-ever at the Goldstone. Greg Stanley, who in this appeared to be influenced by Archer, attended a public meeting in the week before the game, but he rambled and failed to give a clear indication that the deal would be done. However, he did reveal that he'd been approached by a mystery consortium – at last, something to pin long-term hopes to, perhaps.

Tensions were now boiling over. The previous home game had seen several hundred fans invade the pitch at the final whistle, with a fair number climbing into the main stand in an attempt to storm the boardroom; the siege was ended after 35 minutes by the arrival of police reinforcements. In midweek, Albion were relegated to the bottom division of the Football League for the first time in 31 years – but it really didn't seem that important with the club's existence at stake. I arrived around 2 pm for the final home game, against York City. 'SACK THE BOARD' had been carved into the pitch. The directors, for their own safety, stayed away.

Rumour was rife that the game wouldn't end, and on sixteen minutes, as the North Stand chanted 'Shit board, no ground!' a small group of fans ran onto the pitch from the South West Terrace. Very quickly the playing surface was swamped and the crossbars were broken, ensuring that the game would not resume. The police and stewards stood to one side as the masses demonstrated in front of the West Stand. There was a handful of violent thugs in the crowd who later received prison sentences and a fair number probably came just to see the anticipated trouble, but the overwhelming majority of the pitch invaders were peaceful protesters who had simply been driven to the brink. And the York fans, who'd come all that way for 16 minutes of play, were superb; dedicated supporters themselves, they understood.

I remained on the East Terrace, where I had stood for 31 years, watching this scene for about 45 minutes. The destruction of the goals was traumatic to witness – such a potent symbol of a football club wrecked. That day a 38-year-old man wept. He was far from alone.

The abandoned match was the lead on national television news. Everyone now knew something bad was happening down in Brighton, so perhaps 'direct action' was the way to make things better. The tabloids highlighted a riot but the broadsheets began to explore the causes. The club was eventually punished by a *suspended* three-point deduction. The game was replayed at 11 am on a Thursday morning – a surreal experience. The following day the mystery consortium was represented at a press conference in Hove Park by Liam Brady, the former manager who had resigned in November. He insisted that the club would die unless the lease-back was signed. He also revealed that the London businessman behind him had local connections and was prepared to invest in the club and work with the councils to find a permanent solution – but only if Archer and Bellotti stood down.

Now supporters finally had someone to rally behind. Here was a real football man – not a politician or a DIY magnate – with someone of substance behind him willing to take on the board. But, of course, the reply from Archer and Bellotti was that they were not about to step aside. The following Tuesday was decision day. Would Chartwell's deal be accepted, or would the club be consigned to history? The statement was promised for 10 am, so I took an early tea-break with my radio, but it wasn't issued until 11.03. The club had decided to stay, and the papers were signed at 11.55, just five minutes before the deadline. I felt absolute relief – but also anger at the way the board had toyed with my emotions.

Bellotti was defiant, laughing at suggestions that he might resign. Why did the decision go to the wire? 'Delicate negotiations' apparently – but the £480,000 asking-price remained. He even asked for 'some credit' for keeping the club at the Goldstone! The Supporters' Club AGM was dominated by ideas to get rid of Archer and Bellotti. I'd already tried one of my own when I wrote to Archer in May with a cheque for £56.25 – the only money he'd put into the club. I offered to buy back his shares and work with the consortium, the councils, the supporters and any other genuinely interested parties to secure a new stadium – the exact opposite of his plan! The cheque was not cashed.

At the end of July 1996, supporters' representatives met the board, the first of a series of meetings promised as an olive branch. Archer referred to David Bellotti, who was present, as a 'defunct voice-piece'! He went on to say that he would step aside if any group could satisfy him that they had the expertise to build a new stadium; that they had the funds to repay loans; and that they could 'deliver the future'. But even though the consortium provided plenty of information on those conditions, it was not enough for Archer, who went on to demand to know what site they had agreed with the councils. When the news broke that Alfred McAlpine Ltd were involved in the consortium I was elated – this was serious stuff indeed. McAlpine's, who had built Huddersfield's magnificent stadium, were interested in the Albion!

Archer wanted McAlpine's to work with him, but Dick Knight, the consortium leader, was having none of it. Knight, an advertising millionaire who had supported the Albion for 50 years, had been sought out by Brady – who had since accepted a job at Arsenal – to save the club. The consortium remained solid and demanded access to the club's books, as had been promised. The supporters' reps pulled out of the next meeting, although I thought this was slightly premature as Archer had indicated that supporters would have the final say on who would take the club forward.

At the end of September, the FA's Graham Kelly invited the parties to London for talks. A small group of us waited outside all day for news, which eventually came from Kelly himself, but it was not what we wanted to hear. Both sides were insisting on complete control – the positions were irreconcilable.

The following night, Albion played Lincoln at home. With tensions at breaking point again, Liz Costa asked the Football League to postpone the game, but to no avail. Before kick-off Archer inflamed the situation further by issuing a statement rejecting the consortium's approach; the club would persevere with Toad's Hole and share Fratton Park in 1997/98.

Lincoln's first goal was the cue for a hundred supporters to run into the centre-circle and stage a sit-down protest. With a suspended sentence hanging over us, the crowd knew the consequences – we were eventually docked two points – but when they left the pitch after seven minutes the invaders were applauded as heroes. The protest *had* to be made, and the demonstration outside the main stand after the match was particularly well supported.

The following Saturday, Albion travelled to Wigan, near enough to the Blackburn home of Bill Archer for a demo – yes, our chairman lived in Lancashire! My girlfriend asked me not to go; her boss had told her everyone would be arrested. I wrote a letter to Mrs Archer, explaining why we were protesting, and delivered it personally on the Friday night. On Saturday morning I helped deliver leaflets around the village of Mellor explaining why we were there, then went off to the match. Defeat sent us to the bottom of the table. We were now in danger of going out of the Football League even if we survived.

That evening about two hundred of us gathered at the friendly Traders Arms. There was talk of storming Archer's house, which left me seriously concerned, so I phoned the police to make sure they were prepared. I needn't have worried – there was a massive turnout from Lancashire's finest. We marched from the pub to the house with our banners and sang our songs. A couple of youngsters made a dash for the house, but I pulled them back before they were arrested.

The Archer family had gone away for the evening, leaving the police in charge, and they did a good job. Our protest was brilliantly handled by Attila the Stockbroker, our resident 'punk poet', who made a brief speech, played the club song 'Sussex by the Sea' on his violin, and delivered a letter to the house. A tabloid newspaper reporter offered £20 to a couple of fans to 'kick off', but he was disappointed.

How could we get out of this mess? I came up with a possible solution: arbitration. Archer insisted his proposals were best for the club, so why not put them to the test? A three-man commission comprising a neutral chairman – Sir Bobby Charlton, for instance – and two people trusted by Albion fans would look at the rival proposals and judge the matter. I copied my letter to everyone of influence and got some good feedback. I went on Meridian TV to promote the idea. But all I received from the club was a standard reply.

The next big event came against Hereford. It had been publicised with leaflets – an 'unmistakeable signal' would occur fifteen minutes from time. At the prescribed moment, a brilliant rocket firework lit up the Hove night. We were 1–0 down and seeking an equaliser, but on the signal most of the ground emptied, about two-thirds of those present walking out of the Goldstone to stage another demonstration outside the West Stand. The mass exodus during a match was quite stunning to witness.

Around this time, the proposed Portsmouth ground-share fell through, so the board made a new arrangement – with Gillingham, 70 miles away! The demonstrations kept coming.

For Fulham, we marched from Brighton Station through the shopping areas to the Goldstone. The game was played in the usual hostile atmosphere with David Bellotti in the directors' box. No one could concentrate on football; attention was focused on the chief executive and the endless abuse hurled at him. And unbelievably, he always brought his wife as well! But then a firework was thrown in Bellotti's direction and he was asked to leave in the interests of safety. He did so, to the most triumphant roar, as if a goal had been scored. In fact, it was as good as a goal as the atmosphere completely changed, the crowd feeling free at long last to get behind their team which forced a draw against the league leaders. If only he'd stay away!

Then to Rochdale via Crewe, where Andy Naylor of the *Argus* delivered a 6,500-name petition to Focus DIY headquarters. The staff locked the doors and cowered inside the building – I don't quite know what they were expecting – so the petition was left on the doorstep while we pinned notices to the walls.

That evening at Spotland the warmth of the Rochdale fans was fantastic – they sang our songs and joined in with our anti-board chants. OK, they were 3–0 up at the time – but the message was spreading. It was a real 'love-in'. They joined in a picket of the team coach which was due to carry Bellotti home. In fact, he remained in the ground and the coach returned for him once we had dispersed. His response was to stop supporters' coaches booked through the club. Fine! We ran our own, better service thereafter, which continues to this day.

The next step was a match boycott, a highly controversial move. The initial call to stay away from *all* remaining home games – to force Archer out by starving the club of money – failed at a public meeting at which the consortium members introduced themselves. Instead we voted to boycott the fixture against Mansfield, and wrote a letter to the team to explain.

I got to the ground to find that picket lines had been set up, handing out the leaflets I'd supplied. (I worked for a printing company, a very useful trade to have when campaigning.) The 'ultimate gesture', I'd called it. I strode through the North Stand picket, only to tear my ticket up theatrically at the turnstile to loud cheers; but it wasn't pleasant trying to persuade fans not to go in. 'I'm here to support the team,' was the reasonable protest. 'There won't be a team to support unless you make a stand,' we retorted. The official gate was a somewhat dubious 1,933, the club's lowest-ever for a Football League game.

After half an hour a handful of fans scaled a wall and a gate opened, allowing 500 supporters on to the forbidden East Terrace. At half time there was a pitch invasion, with fans of both sides sitting together in the centre-circle. Then the protesters dispersed, but many made their way into the West Stand seats. The tannoy said the match would be abandoned if they remained there, but the players and officials emerged to resume the game – no one was on the pitch! Bellotti was forced to remain in the boardroom for the second half, and the match continued in relative peace with vociferous support for the team. For an hour the ground was reclaimed by the people, but I chose to remain outside. I could have gone in, but I didn't want to be a trespasser. I wanted to be welcomed back.

Then another march, this time in London before the Fulham game. Around 800 Albion fans walked from Victoria to Marble Arch, headed by three clowns representing Archer, Bellotti and Stanley. A delegation presented a 5,726-name petition to the FA calling for disrepute charges to be brought.

On the tube to Fulham I remember suggesting to Tony Foster, Supporters' Club chairman, the setting-up of another club *if* Albion were forced to play Conference football away from Brighton under Archer, a scenario that was only too feasible at the time. In those circumstances I couldn't see any way that the club could regain its league status, because the councils could not work with Archer towards a new stadium. *My* Albion would effectively be dead, its heart and soul ripped out by those entrusted to care for it. But there would be continuity for supporters by starting our own club at a lower level (like AFC Wimbledon did later). What's more, it would remove Archer's trump card: control of the club which belonged emotionally to the people. I wrote to Archer again and told him.

But fortunately it never came to that. The FA, mainly through the efforts of David Davies, suggested the use of professional mediators at the Centre for Dispute Resolution (CEDR) – and, much to my amazement, Archer agreed, though he emphasised that total control was not on offer. In a letter to Attila (following a second, much smaller visit to his Lancashire home), he condemned supporters demonstrating against him – 'hoodwinked by the propaganda', apparently, and 'destroying the very club you love' – but he also said he was prepared to talk to any consortium with proposals to assist the Albion.

Why did Archer agree to mediation? It can only be that he finally realised he couldn't win. He couldn't achieve whatever it was he was trying to gain from this situation.

The talks lasted for four frustrating months. CEDR got the two sides together and also asked the views of supporters. At times it looked as though the negotiations had broken down, but CEDR kept going with a demanding, professional effort which eventually produced the result we so desperately needed. But in the meantime, until we got that result, we kept on demonstrating. We had to.

Tuesday, 3 December: the visit of Darlington, and it was noticeable that the pitchside Focus DIY advert had disappeared! I was one of just half-a-dozen supporters on the West Terrace North. As was his custom, David Bellotti took his seat a couple of minutes into the game, signalling the usual, raucous protest in the West Stand. A minute later, fifty to a hundred fans ran across the corner of the pitch from the North Stand into my area to hurl abuse at the chief executive. Bellotti, just 90 seconds after his appearance, was forced to retreat to the boardroom once again. Oh joy! And it turned out to be an even more significant victory, because the stewards voted to walk out if the chief executive came to any more home games.

But defeat left Albion nine points adrift at the foot of the League – eleven when the two points were docked. There were violent scenes as some frustrated fans turned on beleaguered manager Jimmy Case, with some damage to the buildings. The club responded by sacking Case, but also by trying to rearrange an Auto Windscreens home match against Fulham for another venue on safety grounds, possibly Orient or Gillingham. Some fans believed it was an attempt to move the club eight months early, but a call to the Football League ensured the game went ahead in Hove.

We needed a new manager, but who would work for Archer and Bellotti? Many supporters didn't want anyone to apply, but that was unrealistic. We now had hope in the form of the mediation, and we needed the team to do its bit to save league status. We needed a good manager, and there was a queue of people willing to do the job. The man chosen was Steve Gritt, who was greeted by hostile graffiti on the walls of the Goldstone merely for taking the job.

The disgraceful treatment of the new manager got worse. Gritt's first game in charge was Hull at home and there was a shameful crescendo of booing as he emerged from the tunnel. There was also an organised attempt to force a peaceful abandonment of the match – with whistles. The whole game was played in a continental-style cacophony of whistling, but the canny referee used hand signals most of the time, and when he did blow his whistle it proved to be much more shrill! At half time one fan handcuffed himself to the north goal, but was quickly freed and led away. The team responded to Gritt's arrival with a 3-0 win, the first home victory for three months.

The match at Orient was Peter Shilton's 1,000th league game and was live on Sky. My A3 sheets – 'Archer Out', 'Bellotti Out', 'Stanley Out' – were confiscated at the turnstile. Dangerous weapons, apparently. At the end of the game we remained peacefully in our seats for 45 minutes where we were joined by a lone Southend supporter who unfurled a banner: 'Southend – United in Football'. There was then a lull in major match-day protests – three months of such intensity was gruelling – but plenty of initiatives were happening in the background.

There were little things, like 'demon eyes' postcards of Archer sent to his home in Lancashire; and hundreds of Christmas cards signed by Albion fans (but posted to him from towns in the north). Well, he'd ruined our Christmas! An effigy of Archer was exploded in Hove Park the day we did the Christmas cards. There were also postcards to Mrs Stanley, urging her to get her husband to act. And we encouraged fans across the country to boycott Focus DIY, the source of Archer's wealth – hit him where he might feel it, in the pocket!

We took legal advice from sports law expert Edward Grayson QC on forcing the FA to charge the directors with misconduct. Mr Grayson, who had written to the *Daily Telegraph* on the matter, was convinced the Association had the power to remove them and we sent a couple of solicitor's letters to that effect, but our action would eventually be overtaken by events.

There was an attempt to organise the abandonment of a game at Gillingham, which was apparently to be our home in 1997/98, but this was sheer lunacy. We were trying to win friends to help us, and such action would do exactly the opposite. Happily, those arguments eventually won the day.

Then there was David Bellotti's political ambition. A former MP, he was still a county councillor in Eastbourne and a member of the Sussex Police Authority. Back in September we'd demonstrated against him outside the Lib-Dem conference in Brighton, much to his annoyance and that of his party. There were also regular activities outside his house in Eastbourne. In January 1997 he was de-selected as a candidate because of the furore, to jubilation from Albion fans waiting outside the hall. Three supporters who'd written to the selection committee received solicitor's letters alleging libel. Two of the three were very worried, but the third simply highlighted dozens of grammatical and spelling errors in the solicitor's letter and sent it back; nothing more was heard! Bellotti, though, moved on to Pevensey & Westham where a supporter, Norman Rae, wanted to stand against him, but the Tory candidate persuaded us to let him have a free run and he trounced the object of our derision. To be honest, this part of the campaign did little for our cause – but it was satisfying.

In 1996 the Internet was not yet ubiquitous. Luckily I had access at work and found the main Albion discussion site, set up by Gary Crittenden from the Isle of Man. I'd also been in touch with supporters of other clubs via the new medium and found them to be hugely supportive, wanting to know more. Together, Gary and I developed a campaign site which detailed the history of the crisis, information on the principal 'players', suggestions on how to help the campaign, latest news, etc. We provided a simple, copyable logo link which rapidly appeared on dozens of other websites.

I also suggested a 'campaign guestbook' which quickly filled with the most heart-warming, supportive comments from across the country. Whenever we ever needed a lift, a quick look at that guestbook was the answer. One message, from 15-year-old Plymouth fan Richard Vaughan, particularly grabbed Albion supporter Warren Chrismas. Richard suggested a day when fans of all clubs, wearing their colours, would descend on the Goldstone to show their disgust at what was happening. Warren developed the idea and thus 'Fans United' was born. It quickly took off via the Internet and some brilliant marketing.

Saturday, 8th February, was the chosen day. I printed fifty of the best messages, real tear-jerkers, and posted them on the railings in Hove Park. But would anyone come? We were not disappointed. By lunchtime, Hove was heaving with every league club represented; there were non-league and foreign clubs too. The day was an outstanding success – no one who was there could ever forget it. It was emotional and inspiring – supporters of other clubs really did care that Brighton & Hove Albion had been endangered. We were supposed to organise a human chain around the ground before kick-off, but the numbers were overwhelming. It didn't really matter.

Fans United will go down as one of my all-time great Albion occasions. And to top it all, we thrashed Hartlepool 5-0. Craig Maskell scored a hat-trick and kicked his match-ball into the North Stand – he was giving football back to the people.

We blitzed the FA with faxes and phone calls for the next few days, begging for more positive action, but understandably, they relied on the mediation process that was continuing. On Meridian TV there was a studio debate which was essentially hijacked by Bill Archer, but we also let ourselves down with a lack of potent questions – it was a bad day in our campaign.

With no directors now attending home games, we were able to concentrate on football. The team, now looking organised, was unbeaten at home under Steve Gritt and showing signs that a great escape was just possible. Home gates nearly doubled after Fans United as supporters rediscovered the joy of watching their team once more.

There was just one hiccup at the Goldstone: Orient.

The game saw Albion take a 2-0 lead, but the visitors fought back to make it 3-2. An equaliser was followed immediately by Orient's fourth and a number of gestures to the crowd. Shamefully, five idiots could not handle the tension and ran onto the pitch where they attacked the visiting players. This was no on-pitch demo, this was thuggery, and it did nothing for the club's position considering we'd already been fined two points. The booing said everything. One of the miscreants jumped back into the packed crowd near me and was mercilessly pummelled. I have never been so angry at a match and had I been nearer I might well have joined in.

We drew 4-4, but I was deeply depressed and distressed. Surely we hadn't come all this way just for these morons to destroy everything? Fortunately the FA showed considerable mercy and imposed no penalty beyond a warning, but the tabloids had another field day. It's a sad fact of life that five people behaving badly generated more publicity than when 8,000 came together peacefully for Fans United.

Four days later, 12 March, came the news we had prayed so hard for. The mediators announced that an agreement had been reached between Archer/Stanley and the consortium, although no details were released. We wanted to know more.

Amazingly, I was in the car-park before kick-off at Chester when Archer arrived. It was, I think, his first Albion match for 16 months. As he walked by, I wondered what to do. Should I thump him? Should I shout at him? Should I abuse him? No, I thought I'd ask him a polite, civilised question and try to glean some information: 'When are we going to hear something?'

'What's it got to do with you?' came the abrupt reply, not even adjusting his stride. It had everything to do with me, and thousands like me. I should have thumped him! It also told me he was seriously rattled.

But as the season came to a head, there was still no news. Graham Kelly pleaded with the two sides to sort it out before the last game at the Goldstone, and finally a press conference in London confirmed that the present owners would share control with the consortium, with two FA-appointed directors resolving differences. Dick Knight would be the new chairman, a new temporary venue would be investigated for next season, and there would be a planning application for a new stadium in the next three months. Archer expressed regret: 'With hindsight, I would like to apologise for all the trauma, all the distress which I have caused, as an individual, by my actions.'

And so to the last-ever match at the Goldstone. The Supporters' Club issued its own programme because the club couldn't be trusted to produce a fitting publication. I contributed a statistical and historical piece – I had co-written a club history book in 1993 – and sold them outside the ground. Demand was unbelievable, and it was actually quite frightening being swamped by hundreds and hundreds of fans clamouring for a memento of the day.

Knight took his place in the directors' box to huge applause. Albion won a tense game 1-0 against Doncaster Rovers and moved off the bottom of the table for the first time in almost seven months. But my abiding memory is of the aftermath. There was no civilised send-off for the Goldstone Ground, no parade of former heroes. Instead, as I took my piece of turf, all I heard was the sound of wrecking as supporters grabbed whatever they could. It made sense –

the place would be bulldozed in a few weeks – but it wasn't the most peaceful funeral for an old friend I had known since I was seven.

The Goldstone Retail Park was developed over the next year, but I have never laid eyes on it. In my mind's eye the football ground where I spent much of my life is still there. I will go back and have a look, but not until the new ground is well on its way.

But we couldn't dwell on the demise of the Goldstone because there was one final hurdle: Hereford. Fate had decreed that we should play the only team now below us in the last game of the season. The losers – or, if it was a draw, Hereford (because they had scored fewer goals) – would be relegated to the Conference. In fact, the success of the mediation had slightly reduced the significance of the fixture. We were playing for league status, but now, even if relegated, the club stood a chance of surviving under Dick Knight. Had the deal not been done, the match would undoubtedly have been for the club's existence. Nevertheless, if Doncaster was tense, Hereford was ten times the tension.

I remember sweating nervously and profusely throughout, and also shouting the most vile abuse at the referee when he gave a minor decision against us, something I would not normally have done – but this was anything but normal. I lost it, and I never want to go through an experience like that again.

When Kerry Mayo put through his own net, grim reality stared us in the face, but in the second half a journeyman player called Robbie Reinelt became an Albion hero forever when he scored the goal that kept us in the Football League. At the final whistle Edgar Street was a ground of two halves: blue-and-white joy at one end, black-and-white desolation at the other, divided by a line of riot police. While totally elated, I could not help feeling for the home fans – my mind drifted back to the walk-out game in October and the Hereford supporters who joined us that night. And now Steve Gritt was a hero, having come a long way since that shameful greeting.

We celebrated in the car-park but the journey home was largely silent – everyone on the coach was simply exhausted!

So, we held on to our league status, Dick Knight was the new chairman, and plans were being made for a better temporary home and a permanent stadium.

By now you should have realised that nothing in this story is straightforward! First there was the 'bond saga'. The Football League board allowed the club to share Gillingham's ground – the only offer on the table – on payment of a £500,000 bond which would be refunded if the club moved back to Brighton within three years. However, the League's paperwork was very late and too loosely drafted; it was unacceptable. The League also had to deal with Bill Archer, as he was still legally the chairman.

Frantic efforts to sort the wording followed, but the League board, to their shame, opted to try to expel us. I remember Liz ringing me in tears saying we'd been expelled, but I reassured her it had to go to a vote of the clubs. On behalf of the Supporters' Club, I wrote to all 71 other clubs explaining why we deserved a break. It would have been so cruel to kick us out after the two years we had just endured.

The clubs voted not to expel us, but the 47–17 margin (eight abstentions) was a severe warning. Eventually the bond was lodged to the League's satisfaction and the Gillingham ground-share approved. One of the conditions was to have plans for a return, so the club submitted a minimal outline application for Waterhall. This really was a paper exercise with a hint of 'testing the water', but the outcry from councillors was as expected.

Then there was the club's restructuring. The issue dragged on through the summer and Tony Banks, the Minister for Sport, joined the FA in calling for a resolution. Eventually the deal was done, but not before Albion started playing at their new 'home' 70 miles away in Kent.

In fact, the incoming board had tried to arrange a more convenient ground-share. Crawley Council turned us down, but Millwall, a convenient rail journey, were amenable only for the Metropolitan Police to veto the idea. There was also a look at Woking, but in the end we were left with Gillingham.

I refused to go to Priestfield at first – plenty of Albion fans never went at all. A club still controlled by Bill Archer and playing in the next county was not one I wished to support, especially with Bellotti turning up again in the directors' box. Happily, that situation did not last long. On 2 September 1997 the new board finally took control. I remember the date well: it was my 40th birthday and this was the sweetest of presents. The following night we were playing Peterborough, so I booked a place on one of the Supporters' Club coaches – the only organised transport from Brighton to Gillingham – and enjoyed a 2-2 draw.

As part of the restructuring, Archer invested £1.3 million in the club and remained a director for another year, albeit a passive one. In May 2002 he accepted £700,000 for his shares and finally left the club. He is still chairman of Focus and has a fortune estimated at around £150 million. Greg Stanley was repaid and left the club upon restructuring, preferring to watch Chelsea. No longer involved in Focus, he is said to be worth around £135 million. David Bellotti, who deflected much of the flak from Archer, was immediately sacked. He is now a Lib-Dem councillor in Bath & Northeast Somerset.

They may all be gone, but it will be a long time before they – and their deeds – are forgotten. Even now the occasional nostalgic chorus starts up: 'Build a bonfire, build a bonfire. Put Bellotti on the top. Put Bill Archer in the middle, and we'll burn the fucking lot!'

The new board proved to be supporter-friendly. Regular meetings with supporters' representatives and fans' forums have sorted out problems, and relationships have developed into trust on both sides. The directors are approachable and know many supporters on first-name terms. In fact, they're all supporters themselves, and we have the same aims and ambitions. Cooperation is now the theme as we, the supporters, work jointly with the directors and management in the closest relationship the club has known in modern times to secure the future we all desire.

In the autumn of 1997, however, things looked bleak. On Bonfire Night the gate at Gillingham fell to just 1,025, so the football club started to lay on buses. It worked to a limited extent, and by the end of the campaign the average was 2,328. But the football was dire. Gritt was regrettably sacked – he remains a hero – and Albion finished 23rd again only because of the ineptitude of Doncaster.

We did, though, form a bond with the Rovers fans. On our visit to Belle Vue in October 1997 we galvanised the waning home support and drove Ken Richardson and Mark Weaver from their seats, just as we had with Bellotti. In February 1998 we hosted a second Fans United event against Rovers to highlight the problems; it drew 6,339 fans to Priestfield, by far the biggest gate in our time there. We haven't played each other since, but that bond will now be strengthened in 2006/07.

We've learned that there is strength in football fans standing together, whatever happens on the pitch. Knowing how we needed support in 1995–97, we've backed many clubs in times of adversity since – Chester City, York City, Portsmouth, Wimbledon, Crystal Palace, Wrexham, Cambridge United and Bury come immediately to mind. The troubles of football clubs are so widespread that, in 2001, I dreamed up *ClubsInCrisis.com*, a website for fans of any club in trouble to ask for assistance. It's run on behalf of the Supporters' Club by Clive Moon, Clive Tinkler and Jan Merritt, and has helped many sets of supporters – not least those of Brighton & Hove Albion as we shall see!

But there was no future for the Albion at Gillingham. The club had to come home as soon as possible, to a temporary venue while the perennial problem of a permanent site was resolved. After a considerable search, the club concluded in November 1997 that the only viable option lay in converting a somewhat run-down athletics arena, Withdean Stadium. The main problem was that it lies in a quiet residential area. Thus began a bitter new battle on the home front – literally for me, as I am a Withdean resident.

Fans launched a new campaign, Bring Home the Albion, with a blue-and-white ribbon motif and fronted by Adrian Newnham. Support was elicited from businesses in Brighton – it was estimated that the club's return would pump £4 million into the local economy – and the *Argus* newspaper was brought on board. There were posters, car-stickers and the like.

Initially it was hard to find a group of residents, apart

from councillors, with whom to have a dialogue. We tried. We invited residents to meet us at the stadium, but just one turned up. But in March 1998 a handful of activists formed SWEAT (Save Withdean Environment Action Team). Their alarmist predictions, in a letter distributed throughout the area, ranged from mass urination in gardens and residents cowering behind bolted doors to a mini Hillsborough at nearby Preston Park Station – insulting to say the least.

All of SWEAT's concerns were answerable; they actually helped the club alter its planning application which was submitted the same month. Temporary permission for two years was sought for a 6,000-seat stadium with improved floodlighting, security, changing-rooms, and so on. The application also included an innovative transport package, with every match-ticket bearing a voucher to allow free travel on buses and trains. A no-parking cordon would be stewarded and monitored, with the club fined if the number of extra cars exceeded targets.

We launched a petition to support the application. 'But we only get 2,500 at matches – not many signatures,' moaned one seasoned campaigner. 'Don't get signatures at matches, just hand supporters the forms. Let them do the rest – they want to help,' I replied. It worked. In seven weeks we got 32,355 names – nearly fourteen times the average gate at Gillingham!

With my mum's help, I analysed where the signatures came from and found more than 1,300 in the Withdean area. SWEAT submitted a petition of around 2,000 signatures. We also asked supporters to write to the council, but when we heard we were being 'out-written' we brutally told them that they were killing the Albion if they hadn't done their bit. It helped, but in the end we handed out 4,000 pre-stamped envelopes with pre-printed letters. That took the total to over 8,000 letters of support with 1,400 against in the numbers game. We held public meetings to explain the plans. The club's general manager, Nick Rowe, manned an exhibition at the stadium for four evenings.

To show that the whole of Withdean was not against the Albion we also formed WISH (Withdean Invites the Seagulls Home), the brainchild of supporter Paul Whelch. As a Withdean resident myself, I helped leaflet the area and distributed posters to known supporters. We held a meeting at which I displayed a map of the locations of the 1,300 local residents signing the petition, all within a mile or so of the stadium. SWEAT also kept up their offensive with a 300-person rally in May when Lord Steve Bassam, the council leader, visited Withdean.

Brighton & Hove Council took its decision in June 1998 – and it was positive, the planning vote going 10–2. The Government didn't call the scheme in. Football was coming home!

It was hoped to have Withdean operational by October 1998 and season tickets were sold on that basis, with the club providing free buses to Gillingham in the interim. In the event, the (eventually withdrawn) threat of a judicial review from SWEAT and contractual delays with Ecovert, the council-owned stadium's managers, meant that the timetable continually slipped, and in the end the club could not return until the start of 1999/2000.

We played our last game at Gillingham in May 1999 in a carnival atmosphere, with the buses decked out in colours. (The *only* benefit to come from playing games 70 miles away was the fraternity that developed between supporters on the trips there and back.) But, to be fair to Gillingham, the use of Priestfield kept Brighton & Hove Albion alive, albeit at the cost of £300,000 for two years. Paul Scally, the Gillingham chairman, was heavily criticised by many Albion fans for dealing with Archer and Bellotti, but the fact is that he and his club gave us a home when we had no other. Without Scally and Gillingham, my club would be dead. We should be grateful.

Withdean Stadium opened as a football ground in July 1999 with a friendly against Nottingham Forest. Two weeks later Albion won their first league game there 6-0 against Mansfield. Readers familiar with Withdean will know that it is still essentially an athletics track with mostly temporary stands. Even the North Stand, the only one with a roof, hardly provides protection during inclement weather. (The club has dispensation from the League on covered accommodation pending the opening of the permanent stadium.) But for someone who'd spent most of his life in Withdean, growing up with the stadium, it was an amazing transformation.

Of course, the dire predictions about the problems arising from a stadium at Withdean never came true. The parking cordon is generally respected, and the park-and-ride sites work well. Around half the fans arrive by monitored means of sustainable transport. Post-match litter-patrols keep the area tidy; I organised them for a year and still pick up litter on my route home after each game. And the club receives an average of one complaint on the residents' hotline each match.

In fact, those most affected by the Albion's presence are the club athletes who lose a training night every time there is a midweek game. I have every sympathy for them – but even they now have use of much improved facilities.

However, some continue to plague the club, doing all they can to end Albion's time at Withdean with or without anywhere else to go. As I write, there is a case in the High Court in which a local resident – who moved into the area *after* the club – is challenging not just the recently-implemented expansion to 9,000 seats, but the whole concept of temporary permissions for use of the stadium.

Withdean doesn't work very well as a football stadium – many Albion fans hate it, and all yearn for something better – but it has kept the club alive while the permanent stadium is resolved. And that brings us to the third and much the longest part of this saga. You will have read that permission was sought at Withdean for two years. How laughable that seems now, after seven years in our temporary home. We don't yet know when or how this final part will end, but my optimism remains high.

The club started looking for a permanent site in 1998 and all the old favourites were included – Waterhall, Toad's Hole, Greyhound Stadium, Shoreham Airport and Withdean – but the best one in their sequential analysis proved to be on the northern side of Village Way, Falmer. It, alone, was considered large enough, accessible enough and affordable.

The Falmer site occupies part of the University of Brighton campus and part of a ploughed field. Falmer Station is adjacent, beyond which is the six-lane A27. Across the main road is the University of Sussex, which will provide most of the car-parking; only 150 dedicated parking-spaces are envisaged at the stadium, minimising land-take. Essentially, the area has been urbanised. The stadium would be wholly within the city boundary, but a bus-and-coach park, a vital hub of the transportation strategy, would lie within neighbouring Lewes District.

The club proposed a 22,000-seater stadium with major benefits for the community in terms of employment, education, skills-training, etc. The £50 million needed would come principally from sponsorships, commercial rights, grant funding, private investment and money borrowed on future season-ticket sales. There would be *no* retail park. But not everyone was happy. Falmer village lies nearby, outside the city, and most of the villagers were very much against the stadium. They were backed by Lewes District Council – and they had one crucial plank on which to base their opposition.

The entire area – including the universities – lies within the Sussex Downs 'area of outstanding natural beauty', a national designation dating from 1966 which essentially prevents major development except in the national interest. As mentioned, the site had already been adversely affected by development and was soon to be reviewed as a fringe area for the likely designation of a new South Downs national park. But until the national park comes into being, the legal position remains as it has been since 1966.

The problem for the club, therefore, has always been to convince the decision-makers that the socio-economic benefits of the stadium outweigh any environmental impact, and that it is in the national interest.

Once Falmer had been positively identified, campaigning began, also in 1998. Supporters had already written to Lord Bassam, asking for a site to be chosen. They now had the chance to influence that, in the form of the new Local Plan for Brighton & Hove. Now chairman of the Supporters' Club, I handed out leaflets on the fans' buses and at Gillingham asking supporters to write to the council in support of Falmer. Adrian Newnham and I were invited to meet Bassam, who told us he intended holding a referendum on the matter. I said to Adrian, 'I think we can win it – but it's going to be hard work.' There were two questions put to voters: in essence; should the Albion have a permanent home in the area, and should the council support the club's bid for Falmer? We wanted a resounding 'yes' to both questions, so 'Yes Yes' was the slogan.

We launched another supporters' campaign, chaired by Ian Morley, in March 1999 and held a public meeting to explain the plans. There was a debate at the University of Sussex to which the Falmer residents were invited. I organised a two-leaflet mail-drop to every home in Brighton & Hove. Given enough money, we could have employed the Royal Mail, but supporters *wanted* to help so we used the mail only for difficult areas. I provided maps for hour-long rounds together with the number of leaflets needed. Sunday mornings were spent weighing leaflets – much quicker than counting – for our volunteers who delivered over 120,000, a phenomenal effort. Joining us was director Martin Perry, then of McAlpine's, who got a real buzz from being part of this immense communal effort. The brains behind Withdean and Falmer, he is now the club's chief executive – and the best in the country.

In the week of the referendum, we toured Brighton & Hove, promoting the cause with a portable display. On the Wednesday we took the players on an open-top bus tour, with Adrian manning a loud-hailer. Then, overnight, we tied 5,000 'Yes Yes' balloons to lamp-posts.

I spent the day of the referendum, 6 May 1999, on the phone liaising with campaigners on the streets. 'Mr Jones doesn't know where his polling station is.' I'd look it up and relay the answer. Another vote secured! I also answered queries from the public and was called a fascist for promoting a stadium a couple of miles from where one caller lived. 'No sir, a fascist is someone who won't tolerate other opinions.' I remained calm, but it was not nice.

The result? We won! Eighty-four per cent of voters were in favour of a permanent stadium, and 68 per cent thought it should be at Falmer. That was enough for the council to work with the club and they have been enthusiastic backers ever since, enjoying a close relationship – but the planning battle for the stadium had not yet begun.

We supporters did our bit – sending in our letters for the Local Plan and the national park, and lobbying our councillors – but we waited an age for the planning application. If there's one criticism of the current board that sticks, it's getting its timetables badly wrong. But then there were major hiccups along the way. Firstly, the new council leader, Ken Bodfish, pronounced against Falmer – he seemed to be after a site where he could tag on a city-centre park-and-ride as well – but he was soon persuaded by Labour colleagues and came on board.

A more worrying obstacle came from the University of Brighton, which owned land required for the stadium. The university demanded assurances over the integrity of its campus which took two years to resolve. It smacked of academic elitism over us rough-and-ready football types.

The application was submitted in October 2001. I remember it well. You will recall I was in the printing trade – I printed most of the 130,000 pages! We started to lobby councillors again and organised another petition. In May 2002, I presented the completed petition – all 61,452 names of it – to Bodfish. I also got volunteers to type in the postcodes for analysis. The most significant fact of all was that the deprived Moulsecoomb & Bevendean ward, where the stadium would actually be situated, had the highest number of signatures of any ward in the city. In stark contrast to the residents of Falmer village, the locals in the city really did want the stadium on their doorstep.

In June, the planning committee passed the application 11–1, but, as expected, the scheme was called in by the Government for determination at a public inquiry. It opened in February 2003 and had a further session in October to deal with road access.

I attended as much as I could. It was fascinating – well, noise and lighting analysis was a bit dull, to be honest! But I learned so much about the application and, incidentally, about planning law and procedure. The professionalism of our team and the detail were stunning. I was happy to help in any way I could and supplied attendance statistics to back the case for 22,000 seats.

When the inquiry closed we thought we had made a good case. We didn't take any chances, though, and asked supporters to write letters to the Deputy Prime Minister, John Prescott, who would make the final decision. I assembled them into binders which were delivered in December 2003 to Downing Street. There I was, in my Albion shirt, standing outside no.10 alongside celebrity fans Des Lynam and Norman Cook (aka Fatboy Slim) and other campaigners. Bizarre! We took the binders inside, then went for tea in the Commons as guests of Ivor Caplin, by now MP for Hove.

We sat back, waited and prayed. And for two months I enjoyed my time away from the campaign – until the brown stuff hit the fan.

The government inspector looking into the Local Plan,

who sat through the whole of the public inquiry almost silently, released his report in February 2004 firmly against the stadium. His report was superficial and smacked of elitism – he considered it all right for the universities to use the Falmer site as a last resort, but not the city for a community stadium. I wrote a long, detailed letter highlighting the inconsistencies and deficiencies in the report and sent it to Prescott.

But the likely scenario was that John Collyer, the planning applications inspector, would come to the same conclusion – and John Prescott would reject the proposal. If that happened, we were finished – because there is no other stadium site.

All we could do was to emphasise the desire and need for the stadium and the legitimate reasons why it should be given permission, but as we didn't know how long we had we went for a seven-day blitz.

I emailed a message to all my football contacts across the country, asking for help and for messages to be sent to the Office of the Deputy Prime Minister. The message was passed on like a chain letter and the Prescott email system was temporarily suspended because of the traffic! We used our own *ClubsInCrisis.com* to ask for assistance for our cause, a somewhat ironic turn of events.

With the cooperation of the authorities, I arranged a post-match sit-in at Wycombe, the next game, to highlight the situation. Then, because Valentine's Day was imminent, we arranged for 91 bunches of flowers to be delivered to Whitehall, each bearing a message of support from the other league clubs. And on 14 February itself we travelled to our match at Grimsby via Hull, where we delivered a giant Valentine card to Prescott's constituency office. It had a romantic ditty, plus ten good reasons why he should approve the stadium; he is said to have greatly enjoyed it. That marked the end of the seven days, but the campaign kept going. We went on phone-ins, encouraged more letters and emails, and took the message around the country to other clubs on 'National Falmer Day'. I created a four-image, seaside-style postcard, linked to a special website, with which people across the country could lobby their MPs very easily. As the MPs started to receive the cards they asked about the scheme, and many signed a Parliamentary motion calling for the plans to be approved. I wrote letters to all those MPs who had not yet signed, and with other supporters keenly lobbying as well we drove the total up to 145 MPs of all parties. Our motion was in the top 5 per cent of all 'Early Day Motions' in the session.

When we reached the play-off final in Cardiff, we printed 16,000 more picture postcards to hand out with tickets so supporters could send them to Prescott at his Whitehall office. They said, 'We're pleased to be here [the Millennium Stadium] but we wish we were here [new stadium at Falmer].' Cardiff was an eye-opener. Albion sold over 28,000 tickets, four times the capacity of the club's temporary home. If proof was still required of the need for a new stadium, that was it!

All the lobbying was friendly and light-hearted, which was appreciated. But would it do the trick? At the end of July 2004 the announcement came: the public inquiry would be reopened to look at alternative sites even though the inspector had, as we had anticipated, come out against the stadium. At first there was some considerable confusion, especially when the BBC's regional station broadcast 'It's no to Falmer'; but it soon became apparent that it was in fact an amber light, albeit with more delay attached.

That was the day I knew we would win the battle for Falmer, although it lumbers on still. The only reason the Deputy Prime Minister would want to know about other sites was if he was prepared to give us Falmer, provided it was shown that no other site was suitable – as we knew it would be.

Still, the resumed inquiry was some months away. In the meantime, the Labour Government was coming to Brighton in September for its conference, signalling a week of frantic campaigning. We printed cards with the club's pledges on community benefits to hand to delegates. We commissioned blue-and-white striped Falmer seaside rock. And we had banners printed which we hung from city-centre buildings and seafront railings.

I got a huge lift from lobbying Labour delegates as almost all the feedback was supportive. We held a fringe meeting to explain the proposals, and I spoke at another fringe meeting with the Minister for Sport, Richard Caborn, present. Paul Samrah, the chair of our campaign team, and I also bumped into Tony Blair. 'Prime Minister, can I give you a seaside postcard from Brighton?' I said, thrusting one of the four-image cards into his hand; 'It's about the new stadium at Falmer.' Cherie asked, 'What exactly is happening with the stadium?' to which Paul whispered, 'It's with John Prescott at the moment.' Tony murmured, 'Ah, ministerial decision,' and moved off into the function room!

But the highlight of the week was a friendly march along the seafront to the conference hall, with about 4,000 taking part on a Monday afternoon. The delegates liked that; it made a change to confrontational protests.

In January, my singing talents were featured along with

those of other campaigners on 'We Want Falmer', a CD single. The brainwave of Attila, it was released when record sales are traditionally at their lowest and reached number 17 in the BBC chart for one week!

The inquiry reopened in February 2005 and I attended as much as I could. There were nonsensical suggestions from opponents. The lady from the Regency Society, for instance, thought it would be too difficult for supporters to get off a bus in the middle of Brighton and walk ten minutes to the railway station for Falmer – but they wouldn't mind walking five miles along the seafront to one of the other, less accessible sites. The more I listened, the more I knew Falmer was the only choice – and the more confident I became. The inquiry finished in May, making 62 days in total of detailed public examination of the Falmer plans. Again we waited.

In August we played at Hull – cue giant postcard to Prescott's constituency office! This one highlighted that city's excellent KC Stadium: 'Please can we have one too, Mr Prescott?'

In September, Labour was in town again so we had another march, this time with around 7,000 participants. Prescott mentioned us in his speech: 'Once again, we're delighted to be in Labour Brighton & Hove at our conference. I know many in this city want a new football stadium. They'll be demonstrating tomorrow in their usual good-mannered way. Can I say to them, this announcement will be made by the end of this October.' It sounded hopeful. Why mention it if you were about to disappoint all those people in the city?

The decision finally came on Friday, 28 October 2005, confirming that the club had been granted planning permission for Falmer. Prescott disagreed with his first inspector on the already-urbanised nature of the site at Falmer and the national importance of the stadium's powers of regeneration in the deprived Moulsecoomb area. He, therefore, judged that the benefits outweighed the damage of the stadium's impact. And the second inspector found, as we had anticipated, that there was no alternative site capable of gaining planning permission.

I was, of course, elated – but it was what I had expected. A day of champagne, news conferences and photos followed. There was even champagne for all supporters – including Ipswich fans – at the match at Withdean the following day.

But when the celebrations ended, I read the decision letter, all sixteen pages of it – and I saw a factual error (concerning the boundary of the 'built-up area' in the new Local Plan). After all the waiting, the Government had messed it up! The question was: what would the stadium's opponents do about it?

A month after the decision was made, Lewes District Council, backed by Falmer Parish Council and others, challenged the decision on that point and on *fifteen* others. You cannot know what a kick in the teeth that was. We had spent over ten years to get to this point – and now it could all be taken away again. To add insult to injury, the decision was made behind closed doors and the details were not released for another week; councillors were gagged as Lewes adopted a siege mentality.

But we didn't get this far by lying down. We asked supporters to write to or email the council, and we organised yet another petition. In one week we gathered 5,165 signatures from residents of Lewes District – roughly 4,000 more than on the council's own petition against an incinerator! I asked pertinent questions at a council meeting and managed to get Lewes to commit itself to a swift process – but that might be easier said than achieved. We produced evidence that pro-stadium residents vastly outnumbered those against it. We accused the council of trying to delay the process in the hope that the club dies. But Lewes would not back down, claiming a democratic mandate to protect the countryside – yes, including part of one ploughed field in an urbanised environment – through their Local Plan process.

Will the issue be resolved in the High Court? Well, in April 2006, the Government admitted its mistake on the boundary issue, but did not concede on any of the other points raised. As I write we await the outcome of discussions between Lewes and the Government. It may still go to court, or it may be referred back to the new decision-maker, following John Prescott's fall from grace: Ruth Kelly, Secretary of State for Communities and Local Government. If it is, Lewes has the right to challenge again. We must hope the Government gives them no grounds to do so – but we must also make it clear that it is not in the public interest for them to do so either.

The issue will eventually be resolved – and in our favour, I'm sure. In the meantime we have now formed The Seagulls Party – it's just been registered with the Electoral Commission and I am party secretary – to provide a political challenge to our opponents, in the way Charlton and Brentford fans have done in the past. We are looking to contest the 2007 Lewes District Council elections, but we will make certain our existence is felt long before then. (In fact we have used the electoral power of supporters before, by publishing surveys of candidates at the most recent city council and general elections.)

And that, dear reader, is the situation at the end of May 2006. Eleven years after the Goldstone Ground was sold, we still await confirmation of a permanent stadium which will, we hope, now open in 2009.

I would not care to calculate how much time I have spent on this saga – it would be too depressing. But you will realise from the story above that others have spent similar chunks of their lives on it. And when future generations look back and read what this generation did to keep our club – their club – alive as they wend their way to the community stadium at Falmer, they will surely be grateful. I hope too that our hard-learned lessons will be taken on board by supporters of other clubs.

Would I have had it any other way? You bet! Oh, what I could have done with all that time again. I could certainly have made more of my interest in Albion history. (I am also chairman of the club's historical society, formed in 1998 as a result of an exhibition to enthuse supporters while the club was playing at Gillingham.)

There has barely been a single day when I have not worried over the future of my football club. I have merely brought what skills I possess to assist the ongoing battle to save it, for it remains in crisis until the day Falmer is confirmed. But what I would not change is the fraternity between supporters that the 'troubles' stimulated. Firm friendships have arisen over the years, relationships which have stood the test of time.

Sometimes it's interesting to look back and imagine what would have happened if the Goldstone had not been sold. We would probably not have the dynamic club led by Dick

Knight and Martin Perry we now enjoy. We would probably not have the fraternity among supporters mentioned above. And we would probably not be within touching distance of a 22,000-seater stadium fit for the 21st century.

With fraught difficulties over finding another site, the council would probably have insisted we stayed at the Goldstone. Neighbouring businesses might have been relocated to have enabled a hybrid stadium to expand up to, say, 16,000 seats, but the club would still be inhibited by an inadequate ground on a restricted site.

When the restructuring deal was announced Archer commented on the mayhem he had caused: 'I felt it was a price worth paying to get us into a position where we can build a brand new stadium. We knew we wouldn't win friends and influence people but I believe my actions will ultimately be proved right.' And that makes me worry. Where would we be if Bill Archer had never become involved?

Tim Carder has supported Brighton, his home-town club, since the age of seven. He co-wrote a club history book Seagulls! The Story of Brighton & Hove Albion FC *in 1993, two years before one of the most bitter battles for control of a football club erupted. A second book,* Albion A-Z: A Who's Who of Brighton & Hove Albion FC, *followed in 1997 when the dust had settled.*

In 1998 he founded Albion's Collectors' and Historians' Society to preserve and promote the history of the club, and also became chairman of the Supporters' Club, a position he still holds. A member of the supporters' team working with the club to secure a new community stadium for the city, he

REBELLION

was one of the founders of The Seagulls Party in 2006 to carry the battle into the political arena.

But all he really wants to be is an ordinary fan with a passion for his club and its history – and watching his team in a modern stadium!

CHAPTER FIVE

WATFORD FC – PETCHEY OUT!

BY PETER FINCHAM

AT THE TIME it felt like the right thing to do. For a while, it even felt like a real-life demonstration. But, looking back, it was comical and was remembered only by those who took part and perhaps the man it was aimed at. Rather than a planned activity, it was just an instinctive reaction to the nadir of a decade in decline, kick-started when Graham Taylor left for Aston Villa, culminating in years of under-investment which followed the regime of Dave Bassett. Follow-up shows headlined by Steve Harrison, Colin Lee, Steve Perryman, Glenn Roeder and, finally, Kenny Jackett had failed to lift the club and here we were losing 2-0 at home to Plymouth in August 1996, where the fans website recorded the following: 'I'd rather not try to remember the last time I saw a Watford side look so utterly and completely devoid of ideas!'

The relegation from what should be called Division 2 a few months earlier had been expected for several seasons. Had it not been for an unbelievable 40-yarder from Gary

Porter at Norwich a week before the end of the season, it would not have gone to the final game. At least we finished above L*ton, but it was hardly compensation for what had been a horrible season, made palatable only with the return of Taylor in the February. He had given us a bit of hope.

But with Jack Petchey still running the show, things were unlikely to improve. There had been the on-pitch demonstration after a home defeat to Grimsby a few years before, but it made little difference. He had stepped down as Chairman having suffered the ignominy of 'His' Directors' Box being stormed by the disaffected masses. Following the attempt at a Vicarage Road revolution, changes were made; although a new Chairman was appointed Petchey retained too much influence over the club.

What he was trying to do was fair enough and not exactly revolutionary – run a club like a business. What goes out, must come in first. It was fairly straightforward and to any other business that was not lower league football, it was fair enough. Petchey would point to the fact that Vicarage Road boasted two-and-a-half new stands from his stewardship, ignoring the fact that we sold virtually any talent that showed itself at the club whilst also receiving generous grants from the body set up to oversee ground improvements following the vile Taylor Report. Crowds were plummeting, however. Morale was at a 20-year low. We were crap.

While the staff of the club deflected all attempts to have a meeting with Petchey, it was evident that not even the God-like presence of Graham Taylor could change things off the pitch. Petchey had to go for things to improve, but what could we do?

I guess at the time I thought it might make a difference, but that was not really what kicked things off. As the second goal went in 11 minutes from the end, I just had had enough. The choices were go back to the Estcourt for a beer, or go and make a noise somewhere. The crowd which remained in the ground was on the verge of breaking out of apathy into dormancy, so there was little point in trying to get something going in the ground. Instead, I announced to anyone who was around me and listening that I was going to the Directors Car Park to, er, well I didn't know what I was going to do. But I thought I'd see what happened.

By the time I got there, about 20 people had followed and we just started shouting 'We want Petchey out'. Stewards came waddling down Occupation Road, then the police showed up with a degree of interest and before long there were more of them then there was of us.

Other people came out of the ground – we hoped they had come to see what was going on, but more than likely they were just off home! It was obvious we were harmless. The fact was that if we wanted to have done something to Petchey's big white Rolls Royce, which sat like a bloated representation of the haves and have nots, we could easily have done so in the first few minutes without anyone knowing who had done it. But this was not about anger; it was just frustration.

The final whistle blew and we stayed on, joined by more and more people without it ever being a 'mass movement' of people. Applauded by the Plymouth fans who were celebrating their victory as they left through the same car park we were being kept outside of (by both the stewards, police and ourselves), I remember a few people coming up and saying that they would join in, but they had work the next day and had to get home. It was that kind of demo. The one people would have joined in if only they could have been more arsed!

REBELLION

Someone from the local radio was broadcasting live from inside the ground that Petchey was being kept in the ground for his own safety. He could not confirm the numbers in the demonstration, nor what was actually going on, but Chinese Whispers certainly took on the role of fact that night. All the chap had to do was walk outside the press box and go to the end of his row to see everything (and nothing) that was going on!

We stayed about an hour, by which time the only people who remained were two token coppers who smiled throughout at the dwindling gaggle of pissed off, knackered fans. Petchey was apparently 'still in the ground', unless he had been smuggled out of a side entrance to avoid the baying mob and jumped in a cab. His car didn't leave while we were still there.

I got a few calls over the next few days, mainly asking what I had hoped to achieve. The real answer was that I didn't know. We were not going to force a multi-millionaire out of the club by just yelling a bit. The crowds had dropped to as low as 1,700 in one first team game and less than 5,000 for a league game, so if the harsh realities of Division Three football weren't going to force him out, what hope had we? And if he did go, who would take over and do anything different? The local paper ran the headline 'Crowd revolts over Petchey' in that week's edition, but while the headline said what we had hoped it would, a more realistic headline might have been, 'Pete and a few other blokes yelled at Petchey's car for an hour'.

As it turned out, the season ended with change, with things improving off the field, temporarily. Ironically, some of the people who managed to provide Petchey with a reason to leave, helped oversee a far greater crisis in

2001/02; starting with Vialli and ending with the sale of our ground to pay wages and meet liabilities! The following year's losses dwarfed anything the Petchey era had brought to the club. The club had been knocked to its knees in a way not even Petchey had managed to do. And from the fan base, not even a whimper of protest. If Petchey had caused the financial ruin of the club in the same way that season of madness did, that nice white Rolls certainly would not have been sitting proudly in the car park as it did that night in August 1996.

Peter Fincham has supported Watford since he was 5-years-old. He is a co-founder of the Watford Supporters Trust, which was set up in 2002 in the wake of the Vialli–ITV Digital crisis which nearly bankrupted Watford Football Club.

A passionate supporter of his team, he attends matches with his wife Michelle and one-year-old daughter, Grace, who attended her first match at just 5 weeks old.

CHAPTER SIX

WIMBLEDON FC – NO TO MERTON! AND OFF TO MILTON KEYNES!

BY MICHAEL JOYCE

SO THERE WE are, a group of maybe twenty odd Wimbledon fans, standing in a cordoned off section of Soho Square outside the headquarters of the FA, that gleaming palace where some groping baldies and silver-haired smoothies that run the game spend their days slobbering over non-photogenic ex-models and throwing money at swarthy foreigners. We're in to day, twenty-something-or-other of a vigil, to remind them of our concerns over their decision-making process over the whole Milton Keynes thing, when a local resident decides to come over and make a complaint. He has been following our case and explains that he is sympathetic to our aims but is concerned about one thing – he doesn't think we're making enough noise.

Well as you know, there is now a football team in Milton Keynes, so perhaps he was right. It was a very 'Wimbledon' protest – we wrote considered letters to the papers, formed committees, submitted considered evidence to the adjudicating committees and thought up larky stunts to try and get some attention. At the time it felt like we won every round, had all the best arguments, but ended up losing on a technicality. Looking back, I still feel we did the best possible job of opposing the move, yet there's always that little voice at the back of your head that insists, 'They'd never have dared to try this on at Millwall.'

Of course by the time the move to Milton Keynes became a firm proposal, protesting had become almost second-nature to a Wimbledon fan. As a mid nineties Donny-come-lately, one of my first memories of being a Dons fan was staying behind after a Southampton game to protest against the proposed Dublin move. The Wimbledon Independent Supporters Association (WISA) were already grizzled old hands at this kind of thing. Ever since Sam Hamman had hiked the club 10 miles across South London from Plough Lane to a 'temporary ground-share' with Palace at Selhurst Park in the close season of 1991 they been carefully preparing, getting their constitution in order in readiness for the final conflict.

Looking back now it seems ridiculous that we could've allowed the club to exist in limbo at Selhurst for more than a decade, but such was The Dons preposterous over-achieving in the Premiership that somehow it was never quite the moment to force the issue. In 1997 it seemed like things were coming to a head. In the summer the club had been bought by a pair of Norwegian billionaires, Rokke and Gjelsten. They may have been among Europe's richest men but were played like a pair of simple rubes by Hamman who got them to part with £22 million for not very much at all. He induced them into paying so much for a club with no real assets by promising them that the move to Dublin was a done deal. Instead, the whole thing fell through almost immediately when the various football authorities from UEFA downwards made it clear that it would never be sanctioned. Our post-match protest was largely irrelevant, though Hamman did explain later that the sight of a thousand of us hanging from the rafters of the Holmesdale Lane End had persuaded him that the move would never happen.

So what would the Norwegians do next? They allowed things to drift along for a few seasons with success on the field once again keeping a lid on things and preventing any need for them to dip their hands into their considerable pockets. Their attitude changed considerably when towards the end of the 1998/99 season Joe Kinnear had a heart attack and left, perhaps not entirely of his own choosing, in the summer. Norwegian national legend, Egil Olsen, was installed as manager and suddenly the frugal billionaires expressed an interest in spending a bit of money, building us up into a European force like they had their Norwegian team Molde, and even building a new stadium in Merton. All that talk stopped when we got relegated at the end of the season and Olsen was sacked.

Shortly before the end of that last Premiership season Sam Hamman finally left the club after falling out with Rokke and Gjelsten. Apparently they weren't too impressed with the decision to break the club's record transfer fee to buy John Hartson from West Ham, which is understandable – who would pleased to see more than seven million of their hard-earned pounds handed over to 'Appy 'Arry Redknapp?

There had always been talk of Milton Keynes. As early as 1977 Ron Noades had supposedly been looking into options and the name would keep coming up, like some dark unseen beast that lurked in the wood, something to frighten naughty children. So in November 2000, when renewed rumours that a deal to move to Milton Keynes had been done started up, there was a resigned feeling that we had heard it all before. We gave it little more credence than the previous tales of us moving to (drumroll please) Basingstoke, Cardiff, Glasgow and Wigan.

The difference this time was the arrival of a Mr Charles Koppel, a goatee-bearded lawyer, to become chairman on WFC soon after. His dad had enjoyed considerable success as a businessman and he was a power-boating friend of Rokke and Gjelsten, which was enough to get him the job. The MK rumours became a Five Live news story quoting Gjelsten as saying, 'Buckinghamshire was the best option.' But Koppel quickly appeared to poo-poo the story, though not rule it out, and it was swiftly dropped from their bulletins.

That was enough to start the ball rolling and WISA quickly organised a demo for after the FA Cup clash with Notts County on the Saturday. About 500 of us stayed behind in the Holmesdale Lane End after a 2-2 draw and it was like the Anti-Dublin protest all over again. After an initial burst of chanting 'You can stuff your Milton Keynes up your arse,' or variations on that theme, and after a bit of seat-stamping, the portly frame of Reg Davis, club PR man and contributor to the match day programme, popped his head out from the tunnel to find out what was going on but he was sent back with the message that we wanted to be recognised by someone important from the club. Predictably, neither Gjelsten or Rokke were in attendance and Koppel was on holiday in Florida, so that left Chief Executive David Barnard as the next in the chain in command and it was him we wanted to see.

After about 45 minutes a sheepish looking Barnard appeared with a megaphone. He attempted to address the whole crowd but, in truth, he got rather bogged down with answering questions from nearby fans.

Asked about his feelings on Milton Keynes he said, 'I don't believe anyone connected with Wimbledon football club wants to move to Milton Keynes,' and he accepted a Save Our Dons badge, which he stuck to his club tracksuit. After about an hour we dispersed.

In the days that followed it became clear that the story had caught the club, or at least the English element of it, completely on the hop. Club secretary Steve Rooke offers 'cast-iron guarantee that everything is being done to find a new site preferably in London and we are also perhaps looking at sharing with another club or maybe building a new stadium in conjunction with someone else.' But MK rumours dogged the rest of the season with the club denying a deal had been done, but refusing to rule out the possibility. In truth more alarm bells should've sounded when David Barnard quietly left a few weeks later. (Being a man of some competence and lots of experience he soon got a position high up at Chelsea FC. He would later be seen attending AFC games in windswept muddy fields while fielding calls from Ken Bates on his mobile.)

For a while, the threat seemed to retreat and our local MP Roger Casale was even confident enough to announce that 'I'm glad that we have been able to scotch the rumour that the club was about to move to Milton Keynes.' But the club had another surprise to pull before the end of the season. The *Sun* revealed that we were in negotiations to merge with QPR. That was hastily denied, but not before demos were called for the last game of the season, Norwich at home. During the match itself, a painful 0-0 in freezing conditions, we were more concerned about the chances of Palace getting relegated to Division Two. As each goal around the country seemed to be banging a nail in Palace's coffin, the mood in the Holmesdale lifted noticeably. We were up to 'Six men went to laugh at Palace' when the news of Dougie Freedman's lifeline winner for Palace came through.

If Palace had been relegated it's possible that Chairman Koppel might've received a better reception when he came on at the end to address us. Possible, but unlikely. He appeared behind a wall of nightclub bouncers and stood near the halfway line speaking through a megaphone to the fans who had waited behind the goal. I'd gone down the front to get a better listen but the booing and barracking was so loud it was impossible to make out what he was saying. All in all a fairly pointless exercise, though it did neatly set the tone for our relationship with our new chairman. The QPR story disappeared as hastily as it appeared, though it appeared that negotiations had gotten a lot further than Koppel's 'merger was never an option,' denials gave credit to and who knows what might have happened had the *Sun* not broken the story.

The only up side was that the story gave hope that perhaps MK had been put to rest. That hope was strengthened when representatives of the QPR First Supporters Group were treated to a Bank Holiday Monday presentation by Peter Winkelman of the MK Stadium Consortium. He outlined his plans to 'save' QPR to a sceptical audience of around 50 fans in the Queen Adelaide pub (nice PR move that, show the fans you're on our level) in a Norman Collier-style with the microphone constantly cutting out. Looking on from afar we reassured ourselves that these MK types were just a bunch of hopeless chancers, but went into the summer feeling uncertain about the future. We had now been ten years without a home and even Moses and the crew of the *Battlestar Galactica* hadn't spent this long in the wilderness. As our departure from Plough Lane had showed us, bad news always comes in the close season.

In July, Koppel and WISA representatives were taken round various possible sites in Merton. He didn't seem too keen to announce that redeveloping Plough Lane would cost £60 million and found all kinds of reasons why sharing the greyhound stadium wouldn't work. He arranged a Sunday afternoon meet-the-fans session at Wimbledon Theatre, but then didn't show, leaving us to talk amongst ourselves and with MP Casale, who did turn up.

The bombshell arrived in a letter from Koppel dropped onto the doormats of selected season ticket holders. (I wasn't deemed worthy and neither was WISA chair Kris Stewart.) We all knew it was coming, but it still hurt like hell, especially as most of us had only just renewed our season tickets. The letter saw the launching of Koppel's 'unique position' mantra, a line he would repeat ceaselessly for the next year until he got his way.

In the following days a gleeful Winkelman would talk about 'the red carpet welcome' we would receive at MK if we could just leave 'an hour earlier' and 'make a day of it.' Ah, Pete Winkelman. How to describe the former pop promoter? Think Pete Waterman without the hit records. Many a successful recording artist has recorded at his Great Linford Manor studios. If Koppel and the Norwegians with their champagne sipping, powerboat-racing existence live their life like a 1970s Cinzano Bianco advert, then the relentlessly upbeat and enthusiastic Winkelman lives his like it's a 1980s Radio One roadshow. He looks like Bruno Brookes, his straggles of hair blown back into a mullet, but his boundless energy and enthusiasm allows him to triumph over his physical disadvantages. Everybody always wonders where he gets his limitless energy from – it's clear that if somebody could bottle it and sell it they'd make a fortune.

In his role as frontman for the mysterious MK stadium consortium he'd appear before ailing football teams such as Luton and QPR and offer them an 'afterlife' (his word) in Milton Keynes. During that summer he'd take calls from irate fans at his Great Linford Manor which would end up as long monologues about how great MK was and how we'd really love it up there if we just gave it a chance. I seem to remember something about an indoor snowdome that was supposed to clinch the deal. Most fans got the impression that he didn't really understand what he was getting into or why we were so upset.

So now the lines were drawn. On one side Koppel and Winkelman, on the other the guys and girls of WISA. Too many to single out really, though some who pop up in this story are Kris Stewart, the chair of WISA, who would discover in himself quite a gift for public speaking; Marc Jones the webmaster whose *Weirdandwonderfulworld* guestbook became the fans' focus point and the imposing figure of Lee Willets.

A total boycott of all WFC games was mooted, but quickly dropped. We'd already paid for our season tickets and more empty seats would only hurt our argument. Instead, it was decided to starve the club of match-day revenue, not to buy any merchandise or programmes. A series of protests were orchestrated for the opening day fixture with Birmingham City. The best of these was the release of hundreds of black balloons at the start of the game. Doesn't sound like much, but it was a fantastic spectacle, really memorable and startling.

Also, WISA are the protest that keeps on giving. They were a constant presence swirling back into view at inopportune times during the match, like gangs of naughty children annoying the photographers and playing chicken with the Wimbledon bench. More than two hours later there were still a few straggler balloons swirling around, making their protest felt during the post match stayback.

The pre-match activities had centred around the Thomas Farley, the only pub in the Thornton Heath area that was sympathetic to Dons fans. The two hours before the match were spent acting up for the benefit of Sky Sports, petition signing and getting passing cars hooting their support. The two fans dressed as the Grim Reapers got lots of attention and a bit of horsing around provoked the memorable chant 'Death fell over, Death fell over.' The Birmingham coach passed by, the ashen face of forever-forlorn Trevor Francis clearly visible sitting up front all on his own, but they didn't hoot their support. Around 2.20 pm there was a march to the stadium and during the match the crowd maintained a fine balance between protest songs and supporting the team. Chris Philips, the Kiss FM DJ had resigned as match-day announcer, so instead of cool stuff like the theme to 'Enter the Dragon' the team now ran out to Robbie Williams's 'Let Me Entertain You'.

There were the occasional mishaps and disappointments. Ten minutes before half-time the word went around to boycott the bar during the break. Wondering how that would work, I went back out at half-time to see how it was being observed and saw the boycott advisers tucking into a beer, the discovery having been made that the bar money went, not to Koppel and the club, but the stadium itself and Ron Noades.

The important bit was to stay behind at the end of the match. It seemed to me that more people stayed behind than ever before, at least three-quarters of the Holmesdale Lane end, plus a large number from the main stand and the Whitehorse Lane Four at the other end of the ground who refused to move, despite being harassed by the stewards.

After half an hour a man was wheeled out to speak to us, Graham Thorley the new PR man. He was greeted by a chorus of 'Who?' and when he spoke he was drowned out by booing and chanting. Normally I'd say what was the point of demanding someone come and speak to us if we're not going to listen, but Thorley's little speech was full of such empty platitudes like 'We empathise with your feelings,' and 'We respect your right to protest peacefully', that it really didn't deserve our attention.

This was slightly tough on Thorley as he'd only been on the job for three weeks but presumably his duties in 'facing down the angry mob' were fully explained to him at the job interview. Now I'm no expert on the ways of PR but does a man reading out a short vacuous statement haltingly off a little card really count as a PR triumph? After that, Lee Willets came out and took his moment beautifully, giving the assembled protesters the 'I'm-not-worthy', and thanking Wimbledon FC for spouting 'their usual bollocks'. He called on him to resign and find someone 'with the balls to get us back to Merton' and then wound up by saying that we would be doing this at every home game until the move was stopped.

It was a rousing climax to a great day (and we won 3-1) but it was all a bit disquieting. 'The Thorley Show' had demonstrated that the club weren't about to budge an inch. Previously at these demos we'd get placated in some way.

This time the organ grinder sent out their monkey to effectively give us the finger.

It worked though. Within days the eight-man Football League board had provided a swift rebuke, unanimously refusing to sanction the move. Football League chief executive David Burns announced, 'Following a long and detailed discussion the board has concluded that the proposed move by Wimbledon Football Club to Milton Keynes cannot be sanctioned. League rules clearly state that, clubs should play in the conurbation from which they derive their name or are traditionally associated unless given the approval to do otherwise by the board. To allow this move would have created a precedent at odds with the heritage of football in this country.'

'8-0 to the Football League,' became a popular match-day chant, but this was not to be the decisive blow we all hoped it would be. The 'long and detailed discussions' turned out to be just 45 minutes and their brevity would be the basis for various legal challenges from the club under the guise that they didn't get a fair hearing. Also Football League rules about conurbations turned out to be not so firm as that statement had led us to believe.

For the time being, though, the club kept their council and the next game saw WISA up the ante with the launch of an alternative fan-written match-day magazine called *Yellow and Blue*. One of the disappointments of the Birmingham game was that a number of fans had ignored calls to boycott the official match-day programme. I remember being knocked out by the quality of *Yellow and Blue* when I first picked it up and remained so for the next three years until the AFC board finally decided, wrongly I think, that it should be replaced by a more standard programme. I don't think the importance of *Yellow and Blue* can be overstated. Most immediately, it sucked away a major source of revenue for Koppel as well as providing a really effective way for WISA to disseminate information to home and visiting fans alike. More than that though was the way that it showed us that fans really know more about football than the clubs they support. It was just very, very good, it was everything you want from a football programme and showed us that a 'why-don't-you-stop-just-following-football-clubs-and-start-running-them-yourself' attitude might work.

The main event of that day, though, was the Walk For Wimbledon, an epic march from Plough Lane to the Thomas Farley (where else to end a ten-mile hike than a pub?). Around a thousand people were involved in the walk at various stages and nearly 400 did the whole damn thing on one of the hottest days of that summer. Tough on the fan in the Womble suit or the one who carried the coffin all the way. I managed about six miles and after about an hour-and-half I staggered up to the Thomas Farley in what Big Ron might've called 'a Beau Geste situation,' a red-faced ball of perspiration gasping for a drink. By 2.30 pm, all the stragglers had arrived and two thousand people did the short march to the stadium. The Coffin lead the way, though it had to be pulled back a couple of times as it was setting too fast a pace and was in danger of creating a breakaway march.

I last saw the coffin bearer trying to buy a ticket for the coffin, saying, 'My granddad's in it'. The confused look on the face of the Selhurst functionary in the ticket office when confronted with this request was priceless. I don't think he got it in but five minutes before kick off, head stewards and coppers were in consultations as to the implications of the matter.

In the ground a group of Brentford supporters, then threatened by Noades' proposed move to Woking and similarly grateful to the Football League for their swift rejection of same, were recognised and saluted with a chant of 'We'll never go to Woking.'

There was a sit-in after the match and it was sad to see so many fans streaming home past WISA members asking them to stay. The number that stayed behind was less than half that managed at the Birmingham game, though still enough to look respectable. Those that stayed were soon rewarded by the bing-bong sound of the tannoy and the announcement that the club would not be issuing a statement today.

Things got farcical when the Mayor of Merton, Mr Pickover, attempted to address us with a non-functioning megaphone. The club refused to provide either a megaphone or access to the tannoy because 'the man with the keys had gone home.'

Finally, the mayor, a rotund chap, was hoisted on to a wall by a number of people and had to address us unplugged, a feat achieved through the time-honoured tradition of mass 'ssshh-ing' at anyone who tried to interrupt. (The now ex-Mayor can usually be found in the John Smith's stand of Kingsmeadow on AFC match days.)

Koppel responded by calling for an Emergency General Meeting of the Football League to go over the issue and by being divisive in an interview with the *Guardian*, suggesting we didn't have the stomach for non-league football. 'They'll end up buying a season ticket at Fulham. People will stay for a year, but it will drop off and drop off, and in five years' time we'll be playing Southern Conference football against Kingstonian in front of 400 fans.'

He also formed an Official Wimbledon Fans Forum as a

way to communicate with the fans, but he soon lost interest in it when the elections returned a committee totally opposed to the move. The only pro-MK candidate got 30 votes.

Saturday afternoon staybacks are now a regular part of every home game, but WISA tried to concentrate efforts on the televised matches, the first of which was a big day at Watford. The fans gathered at a Firkin pub just outside the train station for a long liquid afternoon. Everybody was clad in the all new 'Wanted: Charles Club Killer Koppel' black T-shirts, the latest snazzy number from the House of WISA designer label, and as we march towards Vicarage Road it's great to see the puzzled looks of the locals, 'who's this Koppel geezer anyway and why do they want him?'

At the ground, people were just too pumped up to stick to the original plan of only demonstrating at half-time. So with the pre-match anti-Koppel chanting continuing well into the first half the WISA organisers seemed to decide to go with the flow and a big group of supporters massed at the front of the stand to get things going.

The noise during the first half was loud and constant – including a nice 'we'll never go to Fulham' chant – and at the stroke of half-time the unleashing of the Black Balloons. Looked impressive (even though Tony Cottee on Five Live dismissed it as 'lame') but as the players exited at the other end it's doubtful if any of the cameras caught it. (Still it was only ITV digital; we'd get more viewers on CCTV.)

At half time we all held up our 'MK Noway' posters – it was nice to see lots of Watford fans joining in – but attempts to sing up were drowned out by loud music and the inane prattle of their ground announcer who had a seemingly unending list of trivial messages to read out. At one stage a light plane flew over the ground trailing a poster saying 'Dons Fans Say Koppel Out.'

On the pitch things weren't going so well. After reserve keeper, Paul Heald, got sent off for handling outside the area, our ten men quickly shipped three goals. The third of these came shortly after half-time from former Don, Marcus Gayle, and with the game thus lost, one brave Womble fan saw his chance and took it upon himself to take the protest a bit further.

Leaping over the barrier, he raced for the centre spot, coppers and stewards flailing and tumbling in his wake. Weaving past the returning, jubilant Watford players he reached his objective and held his MK Noway poster high, before then being carted off by assorted plod.

The demo got good coverage right across the media and ITV Digital apparently had lots of shots of protesters down the front in their black 'Wanted' shirts. It was featured in all the reports I read, though it was noticeable that in the *Guardian* the sit-in by just 200 Coventry fans got a bigger picture and a larger feature than our protest.

It wasn't all pats on the back though. During the match some of the people who were sitting at the front had a go at the ones standing and protesting at the barrier because they couldn't see, while some of the stuff that was posted on the message boards afterwards was none too pretty: supporters moaning about the anti-Koppel chanting during the match, supporters criticising WISA for not controlling the demo properly. 3-0 defeats don't bring out the best in people, but it is the case that unless the loaded gun is actually cocked and placed on the temple, fans are very reluctant to rock the boat. Over the years, WISA mainstays had become hardened to the sight of fans streaming past them at full time while they man the exits and ask them to stay behind for a demo.

The game also featured an early, and perhaps most striking example, of the schism between fans and players, when WISA mainstay Marc Jones was lambasted at the match by Neal Ardley's dad who blasted him and WISA for not getting behind the team. The point here is that Ardley, a right midfielder whose occasional forays down the wing would culminate in a deadly cross (or aimless hoof to the left corner flag) was the longest serving player at the club. He'd come through the ranks from the youth set-up and had shed tears at the Dell when we were relegated. The fans saw him as 'one of their own' and yet here we were on the edge of extinction and he just couldn't see beyond his own immediate concerns. I shouldn't pick on Ardley because he does genuinely care, he's been down to Kingsmeadow a few times to watch AFC games, but it would've meant so much more if he or one of the other players had gotten off the fence and supported us, rather than making quotes about how poor the atmosphere was at Selhurst Park.

To be fair, I think we could all imagine the pressure the players were put under to toe the party line, but it got a bit much. In the season after the decision was reached, when the team was playing to a near empty house at Selhurst Park, players would secretly tell WISA types how much they hated it and wanted out but to the media it was always 'can't wait to get to Milton Keynes'. When the chips are down they follow the money and will do anything to avoid having to trade down that Page 3 girlfriend for something more in the *Daily Sport* range or moving out of a mansion of the mock Tudor variety.

I think we are all now a lot more wary of hero-worshipping players. FA Cup hero Dave Beasant has turned up a number of times at Kingsmeadow, and seemed proud as punch when his young son Nick made his debut at the heart of our defence. Yet when Winkelman was floating the idea of putting up a statue of his save in the FA Cup final outside the new stadium in Milton Keynes he told the papers he thought it would be 'a great idea... it would be a great honour.'

In the weeks after the Watford game the campaign went into its shell a little. WISA at the time were calling this phase two of the operation, which would be less public though perhaps it was no more than an expected cooling-off period after the campaign had been launched at such a ferocious pace. This scaling down was inevitable and desirable. Early in the season it was getting so that the football was just a distraction from the demonstrating. It became almost institutionalised: the march from the Farley, the protesting outside the entrance to executive lounge. Every week we'd see that same smiling copper leading us to the ground, overjoyed at getting the easiest, most trouble-free football detail going.

You'll remember that September 2001 was quite a momentous month, beginning with England's 5-1 defeat of Germany and ending with Beckham's goal against Greece. Between those games, the Dons managed to give away a 3-0 lead to end up drawing at home to Pompey. That game was played on the 12th September, the day after the terrorist attacks in New York. I still don't know why Nationwide fixtures were made to go on while every other sporting event was called off, but events in New York brought a bit of perspective to the campaign. Nobody would be dressing up as the Grim Reaper or bringing a coffin to a match in the foreseeable future. After the events of 9/11, manager Terry Burton (Kinnear's old assistant who'd been called back to the club shortly before Olsen was sacked at the end of the season) had a good old whinge to the press, threatening to quit and complaining, saying that, 'There's a bad vibe now and the place is not pleasant. When things are not going well you need something to hang onto and there's nothing. We've always had spirit, a joint thing with the supporters and the players, and that's not portrayed at the moment.' The inference was that the fans weren't getting behind the team and thats why they hadn't won since the opening day of the season. Whether by accident or design, Burton post- Pompey outburst went a long way to dampen down anti-Koppel chanting at matches.

And for a while the results picked up. The end of the month saw a deliriously entertaining trip to Maine Road and a 4-0 away win. After that game I spoke to a supporter who said he was glad that there hadn't been any 'Koppel out' chanting at the match. (In fact there had been plenty but the fact that he hadn't heard it suggests that the numbers joining in had been much diminished.) He said that though he was anti-Milton Keynes, he felt that Koppel was a good man in a difficult position. At that stage we didn't really know if there was any kind of pro-MK sentiment building. You'd never meet anyone who was pro-MK but that didn't mean they didn't exist. The occasional pro-MK sentiments posted on a message board would be quickly dismissed as the work of a Koppel stooge, Thorley or someone from Brunswick, the pricey PR firm the cash strapped and on-the-verge-of-bankruptcy club had employed to put their side of the story across.

We had blithely assumed that we had the support of all the fans, but always at Selhurst Park there are rows and rows of Quiet Ones, Shrinking Violets and Wilting Wallflowers, the fans who turn up pretty much week in week out, but whose opinions and feelings remain as opaque and inscrutable as those of the Queen.

In October Merton Council took Koppel on a bus tour of possible sites in Merton. Despite excited speculation, the Magical Mystery Tour didn't visit a Railtrack site a mile away from Plough Lane, just the Greyhound stadium, Plough Lane and the Prince George's Playing Field. The Tour was supposed to be top secret but reports of it appeared in the media on Monday afternoon and the inference then was that perhaps Koppel had leaked news to the press in order to awaken local opposition. However, according to Kris Stewart and Marc Jones (the WISA representatives on the trip) it was Merton Council who had informed the press, unbeknownst to the rest of those present.

Either way, Koppel was markedly unenthused by the whole experience. At the time he claimed to have exhausted all options but it would become clear that his exhaustive search involved writing letters to all the local councils, the gist of which was 'Got any spare land? fancy building us a stadium? Nah, well don't worry about it.'

Wimbledon fans were now busy doing their own bit of letter writing to the FA, where the club were now heading in the hope that their arbitration committee would overturn the Football League decision. Still it wasn't all protesting. At the end of a meeting at the Wimbledon Community Centre the supporters voted unanimously to start up a Trust. As the hands shot up the two representatives from Supporters Direct, Brian Lomax and David Boyle, must've wondered why they'd bothered spending the last two hours carefully explaining what a Trust does and how it could help us. After so much energy expended on explaining what we didn't want, the urge to actually do something, to stand for something, was overwhelming. At the time we told ourselves that the Trust would be there to help us to organise and communicate better with the club, that it was something that fans who were a bit wary of WISA could feel more comfortable being involved with. In fact, as Marc Jones pointed out on the night (though I didn't want to hear it at the time), what we were doing was creating the body that would oversee the reformation of the club when the time came.

The next memorable match protest came in the middle of November. The mad demands of the select ITV Digital audience saw us playing Sheffield Utd at home on a Friday night. It was televised, so some kind of protest was demanded, though as the teams walked out to the release of some yellow and blue balloons, it was looking like we were running out of steam. But then a few of the empty seats began to fill up and small white pieces of paper with instructions on were passed along the rows. About ten minutes into the game a whistle was sounded and everyone leapt up and started making a mighty noise while releasing the remaining balloons.

It was a magnificently dramatic, this cacophony of whistling and chanting leaping unexpectedly out of the Selhurst gloom: the chanting carefully alternating between 'Koppel out' and 'MK stuff' and 'get behind the team' messages. A smallish group were standing at the front and trying to get something going but it didn't look like really taking hold until two coppers appeared to be trying to arrest Lee Willets. At this point masses of fans started to vacate their seats at the back and went to stand at the front, before a long line of policemen.

The demonstration certainly caught the attention of one of

On 29 May 1985, Liverpool played Juventus in the European Cup final. Rioting led to the collapse of a retaining wall in the Heysel stadium, and 39 football fans were killed, mostly Juventus fans. Out of the disaster came new laws to improve the safety and security of football grounds, leading to fundamental changes in the English domestic game – among them, the end of terracing.

On 21 September 1985, Charlton played their last game at the old Valley, versus Stoke City, and some of the fans took away mementoes of the now defunct stadium. While the old stadium terraces and pitch rotted, fans endured seven years of uncertainty and groundshares before watching their team play return to the newly refurbished Valley, seen here below in December 1992.

MESSAGE TO OUR SUPPORTERS

It is with regret that we must announce that we will be obliged to leave The Valley the home of Charlton Athletic Football Club for 66 years.

Recent events have forced this unhappy decision upon us. On 1st July the owners of the land behind the West Stand gave notice terminating our right to use or occupy the land. Court proceedings were commenced to evict and we have been obliged to agree to go by the end of September.

On 6th August 1984, the Greenwich Magistrates ordered that the East Terrace be closed as work was required to the concrete steps and crush barriers. We were not informed of defects to the crush barriers when we were given an opportunity to take a lease of The Valley literally two hours before we appeared before the High Court Judge in March 1984 to obtain consent for the arrangements to save the Club.

The facilities at The Valley for the safe and orderly entrance and segregation of fans and accommodation for spectators and car parking have been so drastically curtailed by the effect of the two sets of court proceedings that we have had no alternative but to make other arrangements.

With effect from 5th October, the home matches of Charlton Athletic Football Club will be held at Selhurst Park which will be in future home for both Charlton and Crystal Palace who will keep their separate identities. We are delighted with this arrangement and the big welcome Crystal Palace Directors are giving us.

HOW TO GET THERE

BY BUS

No. 75. From Charlton Village to Selhurst/Norwood Junction (every fifteen minutes) — journey 50 minutes.

BY TRAIN

Charlton to Norwood Junction.
Change at London Bridge.
Charlton to London Bridge 2 trains every hour journey time 14 minutes.
London Bridge to Norwood Junction 3 trains every hour journey time 20 minutes.

The shaded part of the drawing below shows the land we cannot use as from 30th September 1985.

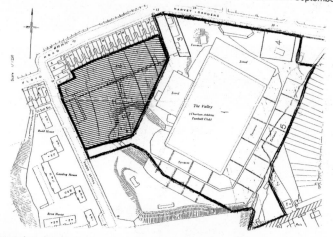

In the crisis we endeavoured to find a home in the London Borough of Greenwich, but although the Council was most helpful, to find even merely adequate facilities was impossible. Our players will continue to train locally at Charlton Park and our South Eastern Counties League matches will continue to be played at Meridan Sports Ground. It is still uncertain where we will play our home Football Combination Matches. It is our firm intention to make Charlton Athletic a First Division Club and we are delighted with such a good start to the season. Our big worry is the inconvenience which will affect you, our supporters, practically and emotionally. Like most of you I have been a supporter of Charlton Athletic for many, many years and feel very sad indeed at the prospect of football no longer being played at The "Valley", but delighted with our prospects at Selhurst Park.

We wanted you, our supporters to be the first to know. To help supporters who find it impossible to get to Selhurst Park we are prepared in the interim to provide a number of coaches. Please contact the Secretary if you wish to travel this way.

Season Ticket Holders will be offered the best seats in the house, with enormous regret, a refund, if they do not wish or cannot carry on supporting Charlton Athletic. We expect to be able to make special discount arrangements for people who wish to watch both Charlton and Crystal Palace first team games. A letter will be sent out soon to all season ticket holders.

Some compensation is that facilities at Selhurst Park are superior to those at "The Valley" and the playing field is in first class condition too.

Lets give the lads a bigger cheer this afternoon and encourage them to provide a result to take us nearer Division One.

JOHN FRYER

Above: Peter Noonan, target of AFC Bournemouth fans' ire, posing in front of the new stadium.

Below: Cherries fans express themselves in unequivocal terms.

Once the saviour of AFC Bournemouth, chairman Peter Phillips – The Man in the Hat – became known as 'The Man Who Sold the Ground' when he oversaw the sale of Dean Court on a leaseback arrangement.

In November 1996, Brighton fans boycotted games in protest at the club's directors. Against Mansfield Town, they watched from outside the ground, then climbed the gates at half time to join the home fans.

Brighton & Hove Albion's last game at the Goldstone Football Club, versus
Doncaster Rovers, on 26 April 1997. BAHA then moved to a makeshift ground at
Withdean.

Above: Wimbledon v Southampton in the Premiership, 7 December 1997 – and Wimbledon fans make clear their opinion of a proposed move to Dublin!

Below: Black Balloon Day, 11 August 2001, organised to defy another move, this time away from their groundshare at Selhurst Park.

Above: 21 April 2002, and frustrated Dons turn their backs to the game.

Below: Newspaper tycoon Robert Maxwell, then-chairman of Oxford United, with managing director Brian Dalton. Maxwell proved an unpopular man at Oxford and Reading when he proposed their merger into the 'Thames Valley Royals'.

One of the popular unofficial West Ham fanzines sums up the fans' reaction to the idea of a fund-raising bond to pay for club improvements.

The job of promoting the bond scheme fell to West Ham director Peter Storrie.
The job of opposing it fell to many an outraged Hammers fan. Here Julian Dicks
and Martin Allen negotiate with a sit-down protester.

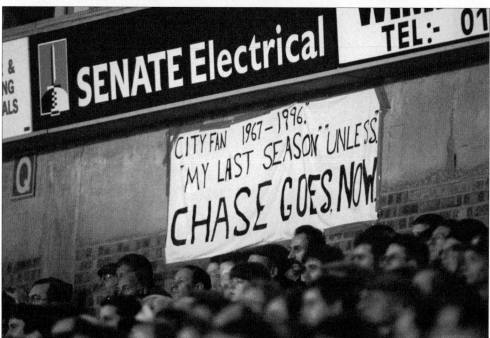

Norwich City fans make their feelings known against club chairman Robert Chase, above in 1993 and below still seen demanding his departure in 1996.

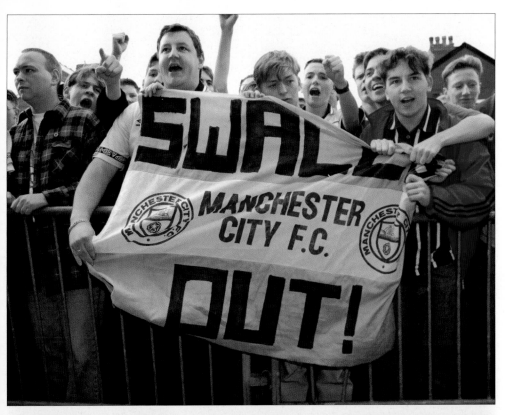

Peter Swales, chairman of Manchester City during one of its worst slides in recent
memory, was eventually ousted and replaced by the 'Forward with Franny' campaign.
Former player Francis Lee soon ran into his own difficulties after an encouraging start.

Malcolm Glazer, owner of Tampa Bay Buccaners American football team – and now owner of the controlling stake in Manchester United FC – was the target of particularly vitriolic and well-publicised protests at his takeover.

October 2004, and just one of dozens of 'Not For Sale' banners is unfurled inside Old Trafford and on the streets outside, while an even more forceful 'health' message is displayed to the acquisitive Glazer faction.

Above: April 2002, and ITV Digital finally goes off-air, owing the Football League millions of pounds in broadcast rights and threatening the survival of several clubs including QPR, Bury and Swindon Town.

Below: The Football Supporters' Federation continues to provide a united platform for a wide variety of campaigns aimed at keeping football's most valuable asset – its support – as involved in their clubs as possible.

the cameramen who turned around to film us for a while. The second half was a bit calmer, but still noisy. Willets had charmed his way back into the ground but one poor unfortunate was hauled off after celebrating our goal.

At full time it was round to the director's entrance with a few hundred other fans for a bit of anti-Koppel chanting as planned. But after that the protest just seemed to take off, spiralling away in strange directions, following its own herd instinct. First there was an attempt to get into the players' lounge that was repulsed, just, by the police. Then a group of people tried to block the car park entrance and, for no particular reason, it was decided that we'd prevent the Sheffield Utd team coach from leaving. Why? Well it was there wasn't it? Somebody said jokingly 'You're not going home,' and the two things kind of clicked. Seconds later, rows of Wombles were sitting down on the tarmac, preventing exit. (Though I believe Neil Warnock's car managed to get through after he made a few 'solidarity brothers' type comments.)

Realising the coach was planning to turn around and go the other way, a number of fans had to jog around the back streets to block the other exit. The coach was now trapped and it was something to see the confused faces of the United players on the coach. Around 11 o'clock the police decided enough was enough and they were able to move us back and free the coach with comparative ease. This is a good example of how peaceable the protest was. Considering we were basically an angry mob, everybody behaved immaculately. Asked by WISA chair Kris Stewart to explain why we'd let the coach out all we could say was 'Well, they asked us to.'

Afterwards people wondered what the point of it all was (some Blades fans were a bit riled by our actions) but after sitting through a miserable 1-1 draw it was just all bloody good fun. In fact, so much of that 2001/02 season was about making our own entertainment.

WISA still had one more big set piece protest planned for the year – a Fans United game called for the last home game before Christmas, a televised Sunday afternoon clash with Forest. Since Brighton and Hove Albion came up with the idea as part of their struggle to get a home ground, the Fans United concept – getting fans from as many different clubs as you can to come to one game and show solidarity – has become something of a franchise. You're not a club in crisis until you've had you're Fans United day.

Months in the planning, the club had expended much energy on trying to ruin it, mainly by opposing a rule that no non-Wimbledon fan would be allowed to stand in the Holmesdale Lane End. All supporters of any team other than Wimbledon or Forest turning up for Fans United Day would be housed in the far end of the Arthur Wait Stand. And, by extension any Wimbledon fan who felt that they wanted to stand with the visiting fans would be obliged to swap their season ticket for a place in the Arthur Wait. And why was this significant? Because the Arthur Wait is the only stand that is not visible on TV.

The club claimed that this decision was taken on police advice, though quite why the police advised this was never really made explicit. It seemed to be the old principle of no away fans in the Holmesdale Lane End, though nobody seemed too bothered about that when Man Utd came to play. The move placed WISA in a dilemma. They decided to go along with it and tell fans to make the switch, although the club made that as difficult as possible right up to the day itself, when reports that tickets could be bought on the gate of the Arthur Wait proved false and meant a trek back to the ticket office.

The Fans United day was a great success, a memorable occasion and a happy memory.

Any last lingering fears that the thing was going to be a limp flop were dispelled inside the ground as the Fans United contingent flooded into the Arthur Wait stand, quickly spreading out into the overspill section. It was great to be surrounded by fans from across the country all singing 'Koppel out'. I think the final count included representatives from over ninety other clubs in attendance.

The epic scarf, made up from the tied-together scarves of all the different teams supporting Fans United, was a moving testament to supporters' unity in the face of a shared adversity, as was Lee Willets who thanked all the non-Dons for their support, escorted from a distance by his own personal policeman. The scarf of all scarves was last seen in the second half being used for a tug of war between two fans.

It was a great, fun day but did it really get us anywhere? On the way home, listening to Five Live, it was depressing to hear that it was being completely ignored. *606* featured Scousers complaining that their team lacked world-class players – the day before Owen was voted European Footballer of the Year. Even a fatuous protest by Villa fans on the Monday night about Doug Ellis not spending enough money on players probably got more national media coverage than Fans United.

Most national newspapers led their match report with the Fans United demo and only mentioned the game in the closing paragraphs. The *Sun*'s report in Monday's Supergoals supplement was particularly favourable to the cause, headlining the attendance of Ajax and Barcelona fans; this from the paper that once called Koppel a brave man of vision.

On the TV though there were just enough fans scattered across the Holmesdale for the casual TV viewer to dismiss it as another poor Wimbledon attendance. The fact that many of them held up anti-MK banners may even have been counterproductive, suggesting that that was the sum total of the protest. True, Koppel was given enough rope to hang himself. In his mind he comes across as a suave mastermind, able to outmanoeuvre the WISA with a single command. Then David Pleat was brought on to reassure everyone that big business knows best.

It felt like the plight of WFC was like that of some kind of Third World country stuck in a murderous dirty war, where people can act with impunity because the western press simply isn't reporting it, save a one-off visit from John Pilger to ease everyone's conscience.

The club continued to be run in an inept fashion. On FU day they couldn't find a parking space for Allen Batsford, the manager who steered Wimbledon into the Football League. It then put out a statement to visiting supporters warning them not to be 'duped' into buying *Yellow and Blue*. Koppel loaned out striker David Neilson to rivals Norwich weeks before we were due to play them and forgot to put in any clause to prevent him facing us. He promptly scored and was awarded a debatable penalty in their 2-1 victory. Keeper Kelvin Davis then threw the ball at him and got sent off. Next, the Boxing Day fixture was lost to a bit of light frost, with rumours abounding that nobody had bothered to cover up the pitch over Christmas.

But 2002 was to show us that we hadn't seen anything yet. In January, Koppel was to pull a stunt that took the breath away. He was taped addressing the Haydon's Bridge Residents' Association, a small NIMBY group for people who live near the old Plough Lane site. He would've got away with it if local Dons fans hadn't found out and secretly recorded Koppel telling them, 'Football supporters are not the kind of people you want on your doorstep'. He also offered them the use of PR company, Brunswick, to help draft their press release opposing any stadium development on Plough Lane. All these years fans had held on, trudged over to Selhurst Park, south London's Abattoir of Dreams, hoping that maybe, perhaps one day we could effect a return to Merton, to Plough Lane, and here was the chairman of our football club organising opposition to our return, deriding us for being 'obsessed with it, they won't get out of their thick…' At which point his lawyer, Dan Tench, stepped in to stop him finishing his thought.

Things got nastier after that. Koppel claimed his garden had been vandalised. He didn't trouble the police with this incident but it found its way into the Sunday papers. The club then chose to snub a meeting of the Fans Forum they set up, but sent along a group of coppers instead.

The three-man arbitration panel reported back but their decision was no decision except to recommend that the Football League look again. The move was debated in Parliament with 105 MPs signing an early-day motion opposing the club's refusal to accept the League's decision not to allow the MK move. (Of 250 previous early-day motions, the only one to raise more support was one concerning the India/Pakistan border tension.)

With the struggling ITV Digital shunning us for matches, the focus of our activities moved away from the ground. After Koppel's talk to the residents association, there really didn't seem to be much point talking with the club. February saw the launch of the Dons Trust at the Wimbledon theatre. The best moment was the sight of former striker Carl Leaburn joining the queue of people paying £10 to have their photo taken with the very same FA Cup lifted by Beasant. He looked so happy you'd have thought he'd just won it and I'm not even sure there was a Leaburn junior there to use as an excuse!

Koppel tried and failed to get himself elected to the Football League board. It was revealed that Koppel's various legal challenges had cost each Football League club over £10,000 in fees. WFC, that's the cash-strapped WFC that have to move or go bankrupt, ended up spending over a £1 million on lawyers' fees. Finally, in April, tiring of the expense of fighting Koppel's legal challenges, especially as the financial disaster of the collapse of the ITV Digital deal was looming, David Burns announced that the issue of the Milton Keynes move would be referred to an FA Commission. Their decision would be final with no right of appeal.

At the same time WISA called on fans to boycott season tickets for next season. The club was so rattled by this that Koppel was moved to turn up for the next meeting of the Fans Forum, right before the last game of the season. He attempted a 'I feel your pain' manner for this gathering, though he ended up mostly bleating on about his own problems. Asked about whether a season ticket purchased now would definitely be for Selhurst Park he gave an unequivocal 'yes', before adding, 'unless it isn't'. So it was a 'yes', but he refused to rule out the possibility of it being a 'no'.

In the event, this 'we-meet-at-last-Mr Koppel' moment was a bit underwhelming as Wimbledon fans are used to dealing with heavyweight figures like Noades and Hamman. Still, you have to give him credit for one thing – he managed to totally unite the Wimbledon support. WISA had organised a greatest hits package of protests for the final game of season with black balloons, black confetti, a magic bus ride from Wimbledon to Selhurst and everybody clad in the new yellow 'Back To Merton' T-shirts. There was a nice party atmosphere with a giant conga going, about sixty strong at its peak and even a small group of supporters in the main stand got in on the conga action. The critical and most daring idea, though, was a plan for everyone to stand up and turn their backs to the pitch for the last five minutes of the first half. Even at this desperate juncture I thought this was bound to fall flat, but when the time came the entire Holmesdale Lane stand and much of the main stand rose up and turned their backs on the pitch. It had taken a whole season, but now even the Quiet Ones, Shrinking Violets and Wilting Wallflowers stood opposed to Koppel.

Events after the final whistle were instructive. While the Wimbledon players trudged quickly off, the relegated Barnsley players went over to their fans, applauded them and threw shirts into the crowd. Then, as they marched off, their players applauded us as well. The Barnsley fans, who'd been among the more supportive we met that season, applauded the thousands of Wimbledon fans who had stayed behind to protest at the end. Burton applauded us from the main stand, and told the media that, 'They have organised themselves really well and it is clear that they are doing it with their hearts,' and was sacked by the club a few days later. We stayed for about an hour after the match and got a statement over the public address about how things are 'tough all over', '...doing the best for the club', '...respect your right to express your opinion', 'we're almost certain to be playing at Selhurst next season, now sod off'. I'm sure I wasn't the only one who had one last look back at Selhurst, probably knowing that this would be the last time.

For most of us it was just a matter of going off to await our fate and putting in an occasional appearance at the vigil fans set up outside FA headquarters to mark the secretive and lengthy deliberations of the three-man FA Commission panel. We waited and we waited as they dragged things out ever nearer the 2002 World Cup. Then on the morning of May 28, the news dribbled out, first on the *Evening Standard* website and then was quickly picked by the BBC. At the time of the announcement it was a big story for a couple of hours, briefly squeezing out Roy Keane walking his dog after leaving the Ireland camp and David Beckham's metatarsal. On the Five Live the introduction of 'Franchising in English Football' is the fourth headline in their sports bulletin behind Keane and Beck's. Even Canigga's exit from the Argentina squad is higher up the running order. The most astute comment came from Simon Mayo while interviewing Winkelman on Five Live: 'Wimbledon. In Milton Keynes. It's a nonsense isn't it?'

The FA Commission report, passed on a 2-1 majority vote, can I think fairly be described as unacceptable. Any evidence put forward by WISA, the Dons Trust or any of the other organisations opposed to the move, is subjected to intense scrutiny, while any promises put forward by Koppel and Winkelman are waved through without investigation.

Winkelman is called 'a passionate and frank witness, who is genuinely concerned to promote the interests of Milton Keynes and WFC'. Totally unsubstantiated statements are accepted as fact just on his say-so. When

Winkelman claims he 'believes the majority of WFC fans will travel and feel at home at the National Bowl', not only do his assertions go unchallenged, you feel that the Commission wants to award a gold star to their best pupil for his good work. The Commission report also contains a number of recommendations on how the club can retain links with its home borough. They will all be brushed aside in a matter of weeks.

The basic argument was that Wimbledon FC would have gone into liquidation if the move hadn't been granted. This was the stance Koppel had been using all along. It should be noted that as WFC failed to file their accounts in time the financial statement presented to the Commission was out of date, and failed to include the income from such big money transfers as Carl Cort to Newcastle (£7 million) or Jason Euell to Charlton (£4 million).

The final little dig was their assertion that, 'furthermore, resurrecting the club from its ashes as, say, "Wimbledon Town" is, with respect to those supporters who would rather that happened so that they could go back to the position the club started in 113 years ago, would not be in the wider interests of football.'

Back in Soho Square, fans gathered and there was a brief flurry of excitement when some tried to storm the FA and threw some paint around. Fans then retreated back to the Fox and Grape pub on Wimbledon Common, the pub the team stayed in (and stayed up to get drunk in) before the FA Cup Final. There were tears and long faces, but a few fans tried to lift the spirits, telling fans that this was not the end. Two nights later the queue ran down St George's Road as over 600 Dons fans crammed into the Community Hall for an AGM that would be the most momentous night in WISAs history. Three proposals were to be debated and the first two, to boycott Wimbledon games next season and to continue fighting Koppel's plans, were swiftly passed. Debate over a third, that we should act to create a Wimbledon team to start at the appropriate level next season was initially a bit more fractious. A lot of us were finding it hard to let go, but I think the argument had already been won when WISA President Kris Stewart, excused himself from his duties chairing the meeting, made his way down to the floor and made his now famous 'I just want to go and watch football again in Wimbledon,' speech.

In the end, the motion was passed with a large majority. The meeting ended with a rousing burst of 'Wombles are back', but I left with mixed feelings. I didn't really hold out much hope for a continued protest against the move. Anyone who was there could tell you that the AFC Wimbledon proposals were the only thing really galvanising people. And why not? After years of battling, the fans want to fight for something. But for me, as a fan of a team with no link to the place, I couldn't see myself making 60-mile trips to London to watch Ryman league football.

At the local Wetherspoon's afterwards I contemplated the end of my association with the Dons while all around me my fellow fans celebrated. Everybody looked happy, overjoyed, indulging themselves with wild talk that Carl Leaburn was going to lead the line for the new team. As one Don said to me, 'it's like waking from a nightmare.'

The summer of 2002 will be one of the best anyone can remember. AFC Wimbledon play their first game in front of more than 5,000 people at Sutton. They lost 4-0 and the final whistle produced a euphoric pitch invasion. Meanwhile Koppel and Winkelman were busy trying, and failing, to get their franchise up to Milton Keynes. Prior to the start of the season, *Newsnight* did a piece on the two Wimbledons. Filming at one of the franchise's new youth Football schemes in MK, one of the local urchins let the cat out of the bag, telling the interviewer that they'd been told by the trainers that the club would be renamed MK Dons soon.

With the AFC season not due to start until the following week, the Football League WISA organised a farewell Party in the Park. There were more fans outside Selhurst than inside when the franchise took on Gillingham in the opening game of the season. Asked to boycott, the travelling Gills support was way down on the previous season but they still outnumbered the 'home' support many times over.

We won't quickly forget the thrill of peeking through the railings to see the rows and rows of empty seats. Outside, rumours flashed through the crowd of protesters about how many people were inside. At 3.15 someone announced that the BBC had called the attendance as 600, a figure so preposterously low even the copper standing next to me mouthed a silent, shocked expletive. Sadly, it was a bit too good to be true. The next hour felt a bit like 1992 election night as the initial exit poll predictions of a hung Parliament with Labour as the largest party slowly began to shift slowly but inexorably Toryward until six hours later when John Major secured a small majority. By 3.30 word was getting round the car park that the figure was larger than 600, and the hope was that the figure would stay under a thousand, but by about half-time even that figure was being surpassed. The figure for the home support was 197, given to me by a Gills fan who'd been ejected from the Arthur Wait stand midway through the second half.

Koppel managed to concoct an attendance of around 2,400 based on a figure of 668 Wimbledon supporters, which itself was based on having supposedly sold over 500 season tickets. In fact, that figure included many fans who'd renewed prior to May 28th but had since cancelled and received refunds but had been allowed to keep their tickets. Even that official, but clearly bogus, attendance represents a post-war low. The Sunday papers had a field day with the story but it was too little too late. Where was this righteous anger when we needed it? For most fans that Party in the Park provided the closure we needed to say our goodbyes to Selhurst and, with more enthusiasm, the Farley, and to gloat at the franchise's struggles. Most of all though, we could leave Selhurst Park with a season of football in Merton (well, very near) to look forward to safe in the knowledge that Koppel, Winkelman and their franchise football team were someone else's problem now.

Where are they now?
The mysterious Milton Keynes stadium consortium: it turned out that 100-plus years of Wimbledon Football Club were snuffed out so that Wal-Mart could get some market penetration in Milton Keynes. Planning rules made it difficult to open up an Asda out-of-town superstore so it became the 'enabling development' that would help to fund the new stadium. At the time of writing the new superstore is up and open for business while progress on the stadium has been a bit slower.

Franchise FC: So far they have managed two relegations in their four-year existence, Danny Wilson finally managing to take them down to Division Two (that's four in old money) at the second attempt. The season before, only Wrexham being deducted ten points for going into administration saved them from the drop. This was particularly cruel as the rule under which they were penalised only came in shortly after Franchise took their own dip into administration. They eventually made it to the national hockey stadium at Milton Keynes after another season at a deserted Selhurst which including two stupendously low gates for midweek games with Rotherham: 849 in the league and 664 in the League Cup.

Winkelman has steadily broken all links with Wimbledon. The club logo was changed to a parrot in a feather boa which, if you look closely, spells out the letters MK. As they never got round to paying for the design and it would eventually be dropped for a new logo incorporating the Roman numerals for 2004, the year 'new club', in Winkelman's own words, was born.

The day after the England-France opening game in the European championships the club announced that the name was changing to MK Dons. It had been a long time coming – on 23 June 2000 Winkelman registered the Internet domain name www.mkdons.co.uk. The transformation was completed a few days later when the club colours were changed from yellow and blue to white – just like Real Madrid.

Before the move, Winkelman promised us that there was a 'football frenzy waiting to happen' in MK. This may still be true, but it seems to be biding its time. The first game at MK against Burnley brought a frenzy of 5,639 spectators. That's more than 2,000 down on the last Wimbledon home game with Burnley.

Charles Koppel: Having fulfilled his role, he fell from favour almost immediately after the move to MK was completed. Presumably he was handsomely paid for his work, though, as his Norwegian friends seem to have lost their entire investment maybe this was not the case. Still, he remains a man with connections, and will always fall into work. Of course we knew all along that he wasn't the real villain, but he was such a convenient hate figure we couldn't help getting suckered into it.

WISA: Still calling on other fans to boycott games at Milton Keynes and some fans respond at every game. In the first few seasons it was common to see the fans of the team that were playing turn up at Kingsmeadow to see the Dons and a few still come. Franchise still find it difficult to organise pre-season friendlies – the fans of Charlton, Spurs and Luton had proposed games called off within days. The main thrust has been trying to deny Franchise and their fans legitimacy, blocking attempts for them to join the Football Supporters Federation or set up a Trust with Supporters Direct. WISA recently negotiated with the Franchise Supporters Association to have all the honours returned to Merton Council.

The Football League: is undergoing a revival with crowds and business looking healthy. Four years ago with the collapse of ITV digital the financial climate looked bleak and people were talking gloomily about clubs going under. Then Koppel's move or die threat had some credibility and was just one more problem to deal with. Given the situation, the temptation to clutch at a quick and easy solution and give themselves one less thing to worry about is understandable (though not forgivable). Thankfully, since the demise of ITV Digital, precisely no clubs have gone under.

AFC Wimbledon: Two promotions in four seasons and up to the Ryman Premier just below the Conference South. Kris Stewart has proved to be an excellent Football club chairman. What a stroke of luck it was him losing his job on the exact same day that the three-man Commission lost us our place in Football League – he became available at the exact time the position needed filling. Marc Jones and Chris Phillips have gone on to form two-thirds of the incomparable Radio Wdon team, who broadcast rambling pop culture infused with commentaries across the Net every match day at the Meadow.

In many ways it's all worked out perfectly. By starting again we skipped that whole dreary slide down the table and have gone pretty much straight from the glory days of the Premiership to the glory days of climbing back up the pyramid. It was probably inevitable that we'd have to start again at the bottom, not because Wimbledon FC is inherently under-supported, but because after having frittered away all the Premiership year at Selhurst and allowing a whole generation of fans to be sucked away by United or Liverpool or even the pre-Abramovich Chelsea, we had nothing to fall back on. If we'd just had one chairman who'd just wanted to watch some football in Wimbledon, instead of constantly looking for an over-ambitious scheme, we'd have been alright and no football fan would ever have had to go to Milton Keynes.

Michael Joyce inhabits the jewel of the south coast that is Hastings from where he regularly travels up for AFC Wimbledon games via the hazards of the local train network. He has always had strong feelings about Wimbledon FC, regularly denouncing them as 'Long ball bollocks' and 'talentless hoofers', until he was taken to see them play at Selhurst Park in the mid-nineties. Somewhere in that 3-3 draw he saw something that won him over though it wasn't until the opening day of the next season and the sight of Beckham scoring from the halfway line that he made a commitment to the Dons.

Other than swearing at Ryman League-level referees from the corners of Surrey football fields he contributes to the Big Tissue *website, provides music reviews for the* Hampstead and Highgate Gazette *and attempts to teach English to foreigners, a profession that sees him live abroad once every decade or so. He is currently working on an epic prose poem about the empty bars of Shanghai.*

CHAPTER 7

THAMES VALLEY ROYALS – MAXWELL'S NIGHTMARE PLAN

BY STEVE GUSCOTT

THE 2006/07 FOOTBALL season will see Reading in the Premiership while Oxford United languish in the Conference. How different it all could have been if a gentleman called Robert Maxwell had had his way back in 1983.

Maxwell was born Jan Ludvic Hoch in 1923 in Slovakia, then part of Hungary. Although he fled to Britain in 1940 and joined the British Army, most of his Jewish family were killed by the Nazis there. He started out as a humble Private, and rose through the ranks to become a Captain, even winning the Military Cross. However, he was alleged to have shot dead the mayor of the German town his regiment was invading, and the subsequent controversy was instrumental in him changing his name to Robert Maxwell.

In 1964 he was elected to the House of Commons as a Labour Party MP but he was not a popular figure and lost his seat six years later for his 'arrogant and domineering manner'. As the '60s turned to the '70s, Maxwell became involved in a bitter dispute with media tycoon Rupert Murdoch after the latter blocked his bid to buy the *News of the World* newspaper. Thus began a rivalry that would dominate the publishing industry over the next few years.

In 1982 Maxwell bought Third Division Oxford United football club, who, after entering the league in 1962, replacing the bankrupt Accrington Stanley, found themselves up in the third division. Promotion in 1965 saw them play in the third tier of English football until they won the third division title in 1968. Eight years in the second division ended in 1975/76 following relegation, meaning their first season under Maxwell's 'guidance' was their sixth season back in Division Three, but they were regarded as one of the better teams in the division.

Meanwhile, across the Thames Valley, Reading Football Club were in worrying financial trouble, forcing costs to be cut, including the sale of the talented Steve Hetzke and local lad Neil Webb who made a surprise move to fellow third division club Portsmouth. It wasn't the fact that Webb had moved that was came as a surprise, it was that he didn't move to a higher level, although that would, of course, come later in his career. Players who departed were not replaced, forcing manager Maurice Evans to rely on local youngsters and loan players.

It was a worrying time at Elm Park, both on and off the pitch, and less than a quarter of the way through the season the club found themselves bottom of the division on the day fans unfurled a banner demanding the resignation of chairman Frank Waller.

The pressure had become too much for Waller and just three days later he and the board announced that they were open to offers from parties interested in buying the club.

Literally days later Bill Dore, the owner of Reading speedway, former Royals player Roger Smee and one time Deep Purple singer Ian Gillan all made their interests known. Gillan was the man most wanted by the increasingly worried and frustrated Reading faithful, who were becoming more and more annoyed at the lack of regard shown for them, when major decisions were made at the club.

Gillan was eventually left as the only real bidder, but after many longwinded attempts to arrange a meeting with the board of directors, a breakthrough appeared to have been reached when one was finally arranged. The former Deep Purple man was late though, fittingly by 90 minutes, and the directors had given up waiting. Gillan eventually drifted off the scene and finally in December 1982 he withdrew from the running. Things were looking up on the pitch though, as the club moved out of the relegation zone – mainly due to the goals of Kerry Dixon – although non-league Bishop Stortford later caused a massive FA Cup upset when they beat Reading at home.

But if this cup performance was bad, then it was the complete opposite just three weeks later when a group cup quarter-final saw Watford beaten 5-3 at Elm Park, despite the visitors leading 3-1 with just four minutes to go in normal time, thanks largely to two goals from England's John Barnes.

After a decent league run things were beginning to look up until star striker Dixon suffered a pelvic injury. After some poor performances and a group cup defeat, remarkably Maurice Evans lifted his troops and somehow sent them on a run of only one defeat in 11 games. Dixon then returned, and despite an unlucky defeat against Bristol Rovers, the problems appeared to have eased with the club sitting just above the dreaded drop zone. This was still the case when Gillingham arrived at Elm Park for a league game in March 1983. This was when the problems really began.

This was not your typical 0-0 draw, it was much worse. In fact, it was so bad that the only action of note was the Gill's goalkeeper, Ron Hillyard, saving a bird from being trampled on the pitch. However, the quality of play paled into insignificance thanks to the bombshell that was dropped by the Reading board and Robert Maxwell even as the second half was still going on.

Reporters who had the misfortune to sit through the game in the so-called press box, listened to a statement from Maxwell and were absolutely stunned. He announced his clear intention to buy Reading Football Club and merge it with his current club, its local rivals Oxford United. The new club would then become known as the Thames Valley Royals and would alternate the venue of home fixtures between Elm Park and the Manor Ground, thus giving each community a home fixture a month, until a new ground was built in Didcot, a small town approximately halfway between the two clubs. His idea included the sale of both current grounds to fund this project.

The announcement was greeted with first shock and then pure anger. Not only by Reading fans but also fans of Oxford United, with many of the club's directors also voicing their concerns. On 18 April 1983, the *Reading Evening Post*, and other local papers, began a Save Our Soccer campaign, producing stickers and leaflets and offering their newspapers as a way for the fans to voice their opinions, printing hundreds of letters each day from the thousands sent in. Local politicians were also fiercely against the merger and backing for the campaign was received from all major parties.

There were those closer to the club who were also strongly against the plan and two of the club's newest directors, Richard Cox and Roy Tranter, along with Jim Brooks began legal action against Waller by obtaining a court injunction stopping him from selling the shares he owned. The dispute was taken to the Football Association headquarters and an angry meeting that led to Maxwell demanding that any director who did not back his plan should resign with immediate effect and that the 'Thames would flow backwards before the merger failed'. This led to a famous comment from Brooks, branding Maxwell a 'dictator' – he couldn't have been more right. A further injunction prevented Maxwell from dealing with the disputed shares and delayed matters, at least in the short term.

Meanwhile, Roger Smee was back on the scene, expressing an interest in buying the club, but the problem was that Maxwell's price of £3 per share could not be met by the former Royals player who had since become a property developer. Most shareholders wanted the club to survive far more than they cared about making money off the back of their shares, so the vast majority were staunchly against the proposed merger. The supporters club threw its weight behind the bid from Smee whilst more local polls saw a 782 to 15 vote against the merger.

In a week dominated by goings on regarding the merger bid, it was rather overlooked that the club had a massive relegation six pointer at home to Millwall. Maurice Evans had the task of preparing a group of players who were lacking any real confidence and concerned for their futures. With Oxford near the top end of the table it appeared that if the bid was a success then most of the new Thames Valley Royals team would be made up of United players, leaving over half of the first team squad at Reading looking for new clubs.

Significantly, at this point, a key member of Manchester United's squad threw his support firmly against the merger – Steve Coppell, the man who would have such a huge impact with the Royals over twenty years later. At that point he was Chairman of the Professional Footballers' Association (PFA), and expressed an interest in representing any players who were worried for their futures, assuring them that they would not find themselves without a job.

Before the game could take place, thanks mainly to the Save Our Soccer campaign, a protest march was planned against the merger in the build up to the game, with thousands of fans marching from the town centre to the ground led by a coffin which symbolised the death of Reading Football Club and supporters carrying banners with witty slogans such as 'We Don't Want This Brand Of Maxwell House'.

Whilst the march went off peacefully and was as dignified and as orderly as it could possibly be, the police had a lot to contend with in a busy afternoon watched by almost double the season's average. Millwall fans had already caused trouble in the town centre before launching a pitch invasion after their team went two goals down before the Royals added a third goal and were dominant. The afternoon got even better when Lion's player Ian Stewart was sent off for kicking Steve Richardson and was restrained by two police officers as he tried to attack the referee! Tensions were boiling over but surely now this was three points gained in the fight against relegation, if the club was still in existence of course. Not so, Millwall hit back before half time and in the second half two more goals gave them a share of the spoils even after they had had another man sent off.

A massive coincidence in the fixture list saw Reading travel to Oxford in the very next league game, dubbed as the last between the sides as individual clubs by many national reporters whilst the local papers continued with the Save Our Soccer campaign.

With both sets of fans united against the merger, the game saw more protests and banners fiercely protesting against Maxwell and Waller were out in force.

The game itself produced an upset, of sorts, with the Royals winning 2-1 thanks to an own goal and a penalty. Both goals arrived in the last six minutes and the prolific Kerry Dixon converted a nerve-wracking penalty after an Oxford fan had run onto the playing area and kicked the ball away just as he'd stepped up to take it the first time. That goal was with just two minutes to play but it lifted a little of the gloom surrounding the club and gave fans the belief the team could stay up. A defeat in the next game at Preston though, left the club needing a win in the final game of the season at home to Wrexham whilst hoping that others lost.

It didn't take long for the attention to turn back to matters off the pitch though. The hearing of the High Court injunction took place resulting in a further suspension of the clubs shares until 13 June 1983 casting doubt over the merger and giving the community of Reading real hope that they would still have a team in the town. Then, the late Frank Orton – grandson of Sir Edwin Jesse, the original owner of the land Elm Park was built on – revealed that the covenant gave him the ability to block any proposed sale of the ground if the club were ever to move out of the town itself.

Finally, on the eve of the massive final game of the season, the merger was called off after Waller and the only two directors were in favour. Les Davies and John Briggs resigned leaving the way clear for Smee to resurrect his bid to buy the club and relocate it to a new stadium in Smallmead in the south of Reading.

Smee had funded the High Court injunction and was seen by the fans as the saviour of Reading Football Club. He took a place in the directors' box for the Wrexham game.

It needed a Royals win and an Exeter defeat at Newport for Third Division football to be preserved and Reading did all they could. A Kerry Dixon goal in the twenty-seventh minute was good enough for a 1-0 win and Newport were a goal up against Exeter but there was still over quarter of an hour to play at Somerton Park, after the kick off there had been delayed. Fans gathered on the pitch and were half celebrating survival when a late goal saw the Exeter game end 1-1, meaning relegation back to Division Four for the 1983/84 season.

When you assess the whole season, the obvious reason for Reading's relegation was the ongoing problems at board level and on the pitch the failure to replace properly the players who had departed the summer before, which left the squad appearing to lack any real passion or fight in many matches including those high-profile 'six pointers' like the Millwall game. No matter how badly you're playing or how low on confidence you are, it's simply criminal to let a three goal lead slip against ten men, let alone nine. A sure sign of the desperation the players had shown was summed up by the statistics: five players sent off, thirty two bookings and a whopping eighteen spot kicks conceded. Another major factor in the failed survival battle was the new points system. Under the old one in which two points meant a win and one a draw, survival would have been guaranteed long before that fateful final game of the season. But with three points on offer for a win, the Royals record of drawing a lot of games made it hard to gather enough points to overhaul those above. It was the third time in thirteen seasons that the club had been relegated and preparations for life back in the bottom tier of English League football began.

In the summer of 1983 the club had to defeat yet another attempt by Maxwell to take over at Elm Park. He offered all shareholders 50 pence per share as he launched a bid to buy a controlling interest in the club, but Maxwell's interest was finally killed off on 21 June. It was on a Tuesday evening and a shareholders' meeting was held at the Post House chaired by a former Reading director, Ronald Palfreyman, and with both Maxwell and Smee vying for the support of all those shareholders in attendance.

The first vote was to decide whether or not the whole meeting should be adjourned after revelations that not all shareholders had been contacted. A close vote saw 19,448 vote against the adjournment whilst 18,653 were for it, so the meeting continued. Shareholders then listened to the two contenders giving their ideas on how they would run and organise Reading FC. It came down to the all-important final vote which saw 19,462 in favour of Smee, Brooks and Tranter with Maxwell's nomination of Bill Blake, Malcolm Davies and Cyril Townsend receiving 16,420 votes. Maxwell was finally defeated, and the new board was able to plan the club's future. They soon announced proposals for a new club strip, a restyled programme, a sponsors' box in the stand and a general improvement in attitude from top to bottom at the club. Fans were promised that they would be consulted on all major decisions that the club had to make and the coaching and scouting staff were greatly improved by the appointment of a new assistant manager – Ian Branfoot, who would later go on to become the club's manager – and former player Stewart Henderson to the role of Youth Development Officer.

As for Maxwell, on 5 November 1991, at the age of 68, his body was found floating in the Atlantic Ocean after he had vanished whilst cruising off the Canary Islands on his luxury yacht, *Lady Ghislaine*. The official verdict was accidental drowning but his daughter, Ghislaine Maxwell, publicly rubbished the notion of an accidental death on television.

In 2005 a television programme, *Conspiracies on Trial*, claimed that even if Maxwell had suffered a heart attack, it is unlikely that he would have fallen overboard without help. The broadcast concluded that the most likely cause of death was the injection of air into his bloodstream to cause a heart attack, after which he was allegedly dropped into the sea. In short, like many others they believed he was murdered.

Regardless of the controversy surrounding his death, on 10 November 1991 Robert Maxwell was buried on the Mount of Olives in Jerusalem, the resting place for the nation's most revered heroes.

The funeral had all the trappings of a state occasion and was attended by the country's government and opposition leaders. No fewer than six serving and former heads of the Israeli intelligence community listened as Prime Minister Shamir announced: 'He has done more for Israel than can today be said.'

To Steve Guscott, football is not just about the game, it is about the whole day out. You can't beat standing on a cold terrace somewhere far out in the north of England on a

Tuesday night with a hundred or so people just as mad as you, and Steve has certainly done that a few times!

His love for Reading FC is as strong now as it was when his dad took him to his first game and hopefully in a year or so when he takes his own son to watch his team it will be a well-established Premiership club. Something that over 20 years ago was certainly no more than a distant dream.

CHAPTER 8

WEST HAM UNITED FC – BREAKING THE BOND

BY JIM DRURY

MANY SUSPICIOUS WEST Ham fans believe the club's ill-fated Bond Scheme was thought up by our board of directors in direct response to the astonishing display of loyalty we showed during our FA Cup semi-final thrashing at Villa Park. On that infamous day in April 1991 the Irons were battered 4-0 by Nottingham Forest in a match ended as a contest in the opening minutes by referee Keith Hackett. His debatable decision to send off Hammers defender Tony Gale rendered the match unwinnable for the Second Division side. Yet there was no sense of doom in the stands and those of us who had travelled to the Midlands weren't content to have our day ruined by the man in black.

What followed was an unprecedented demonstration of devotion by a set of supporters to their team. For the entire second half the 20,000 strong Hammers contingent sang 'Billy Bonds's claret and blue army' at full pelt, despite the team being torn asunder on the pitch. Even as Forest's fourth goal hit the back of the net the East End

173

throng continued with the mantra, like the attendees of a Muslim Fundamentalist rally. The match itself had long ceased to matter.

At the final whistle hundreds of spectators streamed on to the pitch to celebrate. Oddly most of them weren't wearing the red and white of Nottingham Forest, but the claret and blue of West Ham. The sight of a nonplussed Hammers skipper, Ian Bishop, being hoisted on to a fan's shoulders and carried 'chariot-like' off the pitch past a teeming mass of claret and blue was extraordinary.

Those involved in the subsequent fight against the Bond Scheme point to that sunny afternoon in Birmingham as the day the board rubbed their hands together and decided we were a herd of cash cows to be milked mercilessly. If that really was the case, and our board of directors saw pound signs in front of their eyes as we danced on the Villa Park turf, they were making a calamitous mistake.

Any West Ham fan present that day will tell you that this loyalty was to our gutsy team, our manager Billy Bonds, and to ourselves as supporters. It was never a display of blind loyalty to the club.

The theory of an out-of-touch board of directors mistaking their ultra-loyal fanbase for unquestioning mugs is certainly plausible. Four weeks after the semi-final, West Ham meekly surrendered the Second Division championship to Oldham Athletic by losing 2-1 at home to Notts County. The celebrations accompanying the final whistle were almost as fervent as those at Villa Park. The club's incompetent announcer had falsely proclaimed us as champions, resulting in ten minutes of riotous celebration on the pitch by 10,000 partying fans. When the embarrassed man with the mike informed us that Oldham had in fact scored a last-minute winner to steal our trophy, the party, bizarrely, continued. The Upton Park faithful preferred to concentrate on our imminent return to the First Division rather than another lacklustre collapse by our hapless heroes which had deprived us of silverware.

The West Ham Board were an odd collection of individuals, none of whom seemed to have brought much money to the pot in recent times. At the helm were the Cearns family, who had been running the show for decades. Martin Cearns, a bank manager with Barclays, had recently taken over as club chairman from his father Len. Martin's uncle, Will, was also on the board, alongside a small number of businessmen and the Hills family, whose ancestors had founded the club almost a century earlier.

Mr Len, as he was known at West Ham, looked like Monty Burns from *The Simpsons*, and shared the Springfield nuclear power station owner's parsimony. At this stage, though, Mr Len and the Cearns clan were not viewed with hostility by the club's fanbase. They were a patrician family, eager to do things the 'West Ham way', which pleased the club's supporters, who were proud of the club's tradition. The West Ham way involved appointing managers committed to playing attractive football (with the disastrous exception of Lou Macari) and being the only London side before the Hillsborough disaster to refuse to pen their supporters into cages on the terraces.

In the pre-Bond days it really did feel like a family club; as Ron Greenwood said, West Ham was 'a little bit different from everybody else'. Despite decades of under-investment, Irons fans had continued to flock to the Boleyn Ground to watch a series of wonderfully attacking sides fluctuate in fortunes. For every FA Cup success there was an ignominious relegation or a pathetic cup defeat to a lower league side. That was all part of the joy of being a West Ham fan. In the pre-Premiership days, before English supporters' expectations rose almost in line with the obscene ticket price hikes, being a West Ham fan wasn't about winning. Although frustrated at the club's lack of ambition, there was no real desire to unseat the Cearns.

It was only when the board made the catastrophic decision to launch the Bond Scheme that this unwritten pact between the fans and the Cearns family was destroyed. The board sorely underestimated its fanbase and their misjudgement permanently altered the relationship that the supporters had with their club. After the events of 1991–92, West Ham would never be the same again.

After the Hillsborough disaster of 15 April 1989 in which 95 Liverpool supporters were crushed to death in the Leppings Lane cages, football needed to act. The majority of grounds were dilapidated and in some cases dangerous, although the simple removal of all fences around the country in the wake of the events at Sheffield meant that such a disaster could probably never occur again. Predictably, the authorities decided that a knee-jerk response was beneficial to the long-term future of the game and Prime Minister Margaret Thatcher launched an inquiry into the whole future of the sport, to be chaired by a High Court judge who'd never been to a football match in his life.

Lord Justice Taylor was given the onerous task of providing a blueprint for the game, a task that for the most part he performed pretty well. Taylor genuinely wanted to save the game from itself. In the Sky-fuelled era of today where English football is a worldwide marketing miracle and the top division is awash with cash it's hard to remember that football was in serious decline at the end of the 1980s. Gates were at an all-time low, fans were regarded as little better than vermin, and the product itself was almost entirely devoid of entertainment. Attacking football was something that foreigners did.

Taylor understood that the fans had endured a raw deal from the clubs for too long. He was strongly in favour of 'fan power' and recommended that fans clubs consulted their supporters in its decision making. He also told Thatcher that her compulsory football ID card scheme was unworkable. The ID card was Thatcher's pet project, spawned in the messy aftermath of Heysel, English football's previous dark day, which led to the country's clubs being banned from European competition for five years.

Unfortunately, the Taylor Report is remembered for just one thing: his insistence that terracing be scrapped and all-seater stadia made compulsory for clubs in the top two divisions. Taylor naively believed that seats would be safer than standing, failing to realise that clubs would maximise their profit by squeezing in as many seats as they could, regardless of legroom.

With promotion to the top flight secured, West Ham announced that they were working on a scheme to redevelop the ground, making them the first major club to address the issue of funding all-seater stadia. The fans were a little wary that the scheme would inevitably cost them all some money but relieved to hear that, contrary to rumour, the scheme would not involve moving to another stadium. The idea of the club becoming a PLC was rumoured to be on the table and some felt that the potential opportunity to buy shares in their football club was an exciting one.

By November 1991 nothing had been heard from the

board on their plans to renovate Upton Park and the West Ham faithful were more concerned about the club's dismal start to life back in Division One. Manager, Billy Bonds, had wasted almost the entire summer budget on journeymen Mitchell Thomas and Mike Small, and results had been poor. As autumn turned into winter, West Ham revealed in the newspapers that a debenture scheme was being considered by the club. Many fans were suspicious and awaited the news with baited breath.

A brief turnaround in fortunes saw the Hammers beat hated rivals Arsenal and Tottenham in the space of a week, and it was on the back of this mini-revival that the board launched their scheme via an announcement in the *Evening Standard*. The club's new mouthpiece, a chap by the name of Peter Storrie who had recently joined the board as managing director with a 1 per cent stake, was put up to explain the scheme.

West Ham would build a state-of-the-art, 25,000-seater stadium at the cost of a staggering £15 million. There would be no share issue. Instead, each of us would be asked to buy a Bond (or debenture) to finance the stadium rebuilding. Bonds would be available at three prices, £500, £750, and £950, depending on where we wanted to sit in the ground. The board hoped to sell 20,000 of these bonds, allowing it to finance the redevelopment without paying a penny itself.

Details were sketchy but most fans still believed that when the plan was unveiled officially we would see substantial benefits in return for investing in a Bond. The fans waited to read the full facts in the Liverpool match-day programme a few days later.

What we read that Sunday afternoon was enough to make us question our sanity. Making full use of the club's history, the club had roped in heroes Trevor Brooking and Billy Bonds, now the manager, to back the scheme. The programme, *Hammer*, was full of photos of the pair grinning like schoolboys over a model of the proposed new stadium. Hammers' editorial lackeys wrote page after page of guff that would have put the Soviet newspaper *Pravda* to shame, explaining what an exciting opportunity the scheme was for fans.

So, what exactly were we getting in return for our hefty investment?

1. The right to buy a season ticket for a named seat.
2. The right to buy tickets for other games at Upton Park not covered by the season ticket.
3. Priority tickets for away games.
4. The opportunity to buy Bond merchandise.
5. A certificate and the opportunity to have our photograph taken with a player or the manager.
6. The possibility of selling the Bond in the future when it became valuable.

Fans in the stadium turned to each other and laughed. This was clearly some sort of a joke, wasn't it? For a start, the first three benefits were available already for no cost at all. The fourth was irrelevant. The fifth and sixth were merely laughable. The laughter quickly turned to anger. The Bond Scheme was blackmail, pure and simple. For £500 or more we would have the 'right' to buy a season ticket. The price of this ticket would be additional to that cost. If we didn't buy a Bond we wouldn't be allowed to buy a season ticket in two years' time. It was a cold, elitist approach that threatened to disenfranchise its large working-class supporter base. The inference was clear: 'If you're not rich enough to buy a Bond you can't come in.'

The club's justification for the scheme, made by its mouthpiece, Storrie, was sheer effrontery. 'We felt the debenture route offered everything we are looking for in our fundraising. We raise the money, we do not take on huge debt, the club remains under internal control, and monies for the team are not affected.' This was blatant highway robbery. The club would take £20 million from its supporters without losing any power and giving nothing in return. Did they really expect us to fall for it? Yes, they did. And without the quick thinking of a group of dedicated fans and fanzine editors they might have pulled it off.

Although anger had quickly taken hold among the supporters, there was also a feeling of panic. Football fans are irrational creatures and the idea that every other bastard might buy a Bond and leave us locked out of our fortnightly place of worship made many of us wonder whether we ought to cough up, especially when the posh prospectus thudded on the doorstep warning us that we could all miss out. A few hundred of the club's middle class contingent immediately opened their wallets and signed up for a debenture, anxious not to get left behind.

Until the weeks leading up to the Bond's launch there was no single organisation of West Ham fans, outside of the ultra-loyal official supporters' club, and it appeared that the faithful might sleepwalk into backing this scheme. Even if 10,000 of the 20,000 debentures were sold the club could still pull off their heist and leave its non-Bond holding fans as second-class fans. It needed to be stopped.

When the three West Ham fanzines first got wind of the Bond Scheme some weeks earlier, they got together and decided to lead a joint fight against it. The editors of *Over land and Sea*, *Fortunes Always Hiding*, and *On The Terraces* all realised that unity was imperative. Three campaigns would be contradictory and result in a weakened message, so it was important that the supporters were represented by one voice. They decided to form the Hammers Independent Supporters' Association (HISA). The editors themselves wisely decided to distance themselves from the running of the campaign, realising that this would be virtually a full-time occupation. What they would give was their unqualified support for the dedicated band of HISA volunteers and the oxygen of publicity that their pages brought.

Before the official announcement of the scheme, the three fanzine editors, Gary Firmager of *OLAS*, Steve Rapport of *Fortunes*, and Marc Williams of *OTT*, had been invited to a meeting at the club to give their opinions on the proposed debenture. Having raised a myriad of objections to such a scheme the trio outlined their alternative proposal, which involved a combination of a private, limited share issue, a small debenture scheme, and extended season tickets. The two representatives of the club, Storrie and club secretary Tom Finn, assured them that their opinions were valued and that the meeting marked 'the beginning of a new and historic phase in club/supporter relationships'.

A further meeting was arranged and HISA agreed to suspend its initial Red Card protest planned for the Liverpool game, which was being televised live on ITV. When HISA's inaugural members read of the scheme's details in that afternoon's *Hammer* they knew they had been hoodwinked by the club, so that the scheme couldn't be undermined live on terrestrial television. The gloves were off.

Membership of the HISA committee was immediately

opened to all supporters and anyone who wanted a role was invited to put themselves forward for election at a public meeting in a function room at the Boleyn pub, close to the ground. In a recruitment advertisement in the fanzines HISA stated its desire to resist the Bond Scheme and asked fans for a donation of £5 to help fund the campaign. Their first full-page ad entreated: 'In short (it's) a club happy to call its fans the best in the land, but continually refuses to treat us as such. We want all West Ham supporters to join HISA so that we can have one united voice and ultimately have a bigger say in what happens at the club, both on and off the field.'

By getting HISA up and running, and leafleting fans outside the ground to inform them of their intention to fight the board, HISA bought some much-needed time for our supporters. If thousands of us had decided that buying a bond was inevitable and sent our money then the Bond might have become unstoppable.

At HISA's first public meeting, organisers were unsure how many would turn up. In the event, the Boleyn was packed to the rafters with disaffected fans willing to pledge their money and allegiance to the anti-Bond effort. HISA was buoyed by the success of the evening and set about organising the first of many skilful protests that would help kill the Bond Scheme stone dead.

Before the meeting HISA's founders held several brainstorming sessions and devised a clear strategy. HISA would be run like a military organisation rather than a genuinely democratic group. Although it wanted to recruit as many fans as possible, our role would be that of the organisation's infantry while the HISA committee would be the generals. HISA believed that it had to offer fans strong leadership and keep decision making within a small committee. Holding a vote on every single suggestion risked consensus and inertia. HISA was also wary of revealing its hand. Guessing that the club would probably send spies to their meetings, HISA was determined to keep its cards close to its chest.

The first HISA protest was the highly visible and relatively inexpensive Red Card protests. Large A4 red cards emblazoned with the slogan 'Resign' were handed out to supporters before home matches to be held up at half-time. On the reverse of the card was HISA's manifesto, denouncing the scheme as 'attempted blackmail'.

On the field, West Ham's fortunes went from bad to worse. The Bond had been launched in the middle of November. Two months later the team had failed to win another league match and had plunged into the relegation zone. Matters came to a head when we failed to beat non-league Farnborough Town at home in the FA Cup Third Round. After the final whistle 300 fans invaded the pitch and chanted 'Sack the board'. This act of rebellion would soon become a regular event at Upton Park. A week later, the Hammers drew a dreary match 1-1 with Wimbledon, one that would have been entirely forgettable but for the post-match protest.

At the final whistle one lad ran out to the centre circle and sat down. He wasn't alone for long. Another fan sat and joined him in the mud. Within a matter of seconds fans were clambering from the Chicken Run terrace on the east side of the ground and running past the hapless stewards. The dam had burst and fans from the North Bank and South Bank ends of the ground soon joined in the stampede. Thousands more, particularly in the upper stands, stayed in their seats for more than an hour to make their protest. In all there were

3,000 supporters on the pitch, joined by three times that number in the stands, singing 'We won't take this shit no more' and 'Cearns Out' for more than an hour, even after the club had switched the floodlights off.

With revolution in the air, one group of fans were reported to have tried to storm the directors' lounge and poor old Billy Bonds was sent out with a microphone to the directors' box to calm the masses. One might have expected Martin Cearns to have stood up and spoken, but he and his fellow members on the board lost their bottle. It was left to Bonzo, the man who had lifted two FA Cups as our captain in the days when West Ham was a family club, to carry the can. In typical West Ham fashion Billy was given a mike that didn't work and the beleaguered manager was forced to make placatory gestures to the Upton Park faithful to calm down as small bonfires were lit on the grass below.

The protest had spread so quickly that the members of the press hadn't managed to escape for their post-match cup of weak tea. As a result, the event received widespread coverage in the following day's papers. A photograph of the angry mob on the pitch beneath one fan's magnificent banner which read 'Lying Thieving Cheats' made many of the Sunday rags. The die was cast. The Bond Scheme was going to be resisted by the fans and, by God, everyone in the country was going to know it.

Although the demo was exciting, the smell of decay hung in the air that day. One memorable account in *Fortunes Always Hiding* written under the pseudonym, Mister Essex, illustrated vividly this air of melancholy. He wrote: 'One bloke, keen to prove that you can play on six pints of lager, had a scrunched up *Hammers News/Pravda* which he'd salvaged from a bonfire. As the cross came in from the right he chested it down, rounded the bewildered steward and struck a wicked volley into the roof of the net. The boy done brilliant. I laughed my bollocks off, even though inside I was sad.' After performing an enormous Hokey Cokey in the middle of the pitch the crowd dispersed, knowing that it had started, quite spontaneously, a lasting rebellion.

Although the pitch invasion had not been sanctioned by HISA, they had fuelled the protest against the Bond and were quick to maintain their campaign's momentum over the coming weeks. They were eager to capitalise on the Wimbledon demonstration, but knew that there was a risk of fans turning to violence, as the attempted storming of the boardroom had proved, and that peaceful protests were the way to get the media on side.

HISA committee members cultivated contacts in the press and tipped off various reporters and photographers of impending stunts including the Stand Up, Sit Down demo at the FA Cup tie against Wrexham. As the Wrexham game kicked off the majority of fans on the terraces, almost without exception, sat on the floor and stayed there for five minutes. At the same time thousands in the stands stood up. It was good-humoured, highly visual, and importantly it was also peaceful. Peter Cullen and the rest of the committee were at pains not to be blamed by the club for West Ham's poor form on the field. Cullen told reporters in the build-up to the Wrexham game that the protest was aimed not at the players, but at the board. The team would be supported whatever happened.

By the time of HISA's second public meeting on 10 February, the club had gone into denial mode and foolishly tried to sow the seeds of panic among supporters. Stating that the Bond Scheme was here to stay, they announced that sales were in four figures. This information was contradicted by other reports in the newspapers, apparently garnered from within the club, that the entire first team was up for sale to raise funds.

Although Peter Storrie denied the story, which ran in several newspapers, there was a sense that the board was in disarray. Rather than face up to the fact that their scheme was a dud, they appeared to prefer the idea of flogging the family silver. And with the team marooned at the bottom of the First Division the silver was looking more like scrap metal.

The Denmark Arms in East Ham was the venue for HISA's second public meeting. Storrie did his reputation the world of good with the fans by agreeing not only to attend the meeting, but to stand on a wobbly chair and address us. Accompanied only by West Ham's Stadium Manager John Ball, it took some balls to address 200 or so fans baying for his blood. Storrie clearly had some guts, although his chairman never spoke to HISA.

As angry fans shouted a series of accusations at him, the call of 'One meeting, one meeting' came from the committee and Storrie was allowed to speak uninterrupted. After speaking without notes, he then took questions from the floor, staying for an hour and a half. Although not giving any new concessions, Storrie was applauded vigorously when he finally stood down gingerly from the rickety chair. Storrie at least was one member of the board who had the respect of the fans.

Before that night Storrie, as the public face of the board, was definitely regarded as 'the enemy'. One infamous chant around the ground on match-days was sung to the tune of 'Knees Up Mother Brown': 'Who's up Cearnsy's arse?

Who's up Cearnsy's arse? Peter, Peter Storrie is! Peter, Peter Storrie is!'

After Storrie left the meeting, HISA's committee revealed that it had large-scale demonstrations planned for each of the next two home matches. It refused to reveal details to its membership and asked those assembled to trust them to deliver the goods. The meeting broke up in customary fashion with those assembled singing 'I'm Forever Blowing Bubbles'. The stage was set for the biggest two days of the entire protest.

By now, HISA's protest had built up a head of steam in the national press, and members of the committee, such as Peter Cullen and Shane Barber, had appeared on regional news bulletins on BBC and ITV, as well as Sky. The highlight of the TV campaign was undoubtedly the interview on ITV's *London Tonight* with Chicken Ron, a 6ft-tall HISA committee member, dressed as a chicken.

In the build-up to the home match against Everton on 29 February, HISA used their media profile to advertise a day of nationwide protests against all-seater stadia, the largest of which would take place at Upton Park. The *Daily Mirror*, which saw itself as the game's authentic working class flag-bearer, jumped on the bandwagon, writing a two-page editorial on the morning of the match encouraging fans to 'Stand up and be Counted'. Fans at Old Trafford, Maine Road, and Highfield Road brandished red cards while at Anfield Koppites sang 'We all hate seat' and 'You'll never seat the Kop'.

Upton Park was, of course, the central focus of the campaign. After all we had a specific battle that needed to be won. In addition to the obligatory waving of red cards at half time, HISA volunteers stood outside every turnstile entrance and handed out 11,000 red balloons. It was an inspired move, creating a good-natured, peaceful protest that was also highly visual. When the balloons were released by the crowd at kick-off it sent a powerful message to the board that couldn't easily be ignored. It also provided rich pickings for Sunday sports photographers with 'The Balloon Goes Up' one of the following day's tabloid headlines. HISA's planning left nothing to chance. Snappers were informed in advance which areas in the ground would have most balloons and an off-duty Sky cameraman was smuggled into the West Stand with a camcorder in his bag.

The game itself saw yet another inept performance by West Ham. Everton goalkeeper, Neville Southall, spent much of the first ten minutes stamping on the balloons that were unsighting him in his goalmouth. Big Nev really needn't have bothered. He might just as well have taken the party atmosphere at face value, brought out a cake, and played pass the parcel with the Everton back-four, such was West Ham's attacking impotence.

Shortly after Everton took a 2-0 lead one plucky Hammers fan, wearing a putrid orange sweatshirt, decided he'd had enough. Rather than wait until the end of the game to make his protest the guy seized a corner flag and ran to the centre circle where he embedded it into the turf and sat down, arms folded. Captain Julian Dicks strolled over, but instead of kicking the bloke into the Chicken Run, as might have been expected, The Terminator put a consoling arm around him before removing the flag and returning it to its rightful place. Midfielder Martin Allen then tried gamely to persuade the intruder to leave. Within seconds scores of others from the terraces had made their way on to the pitch. Many were surely emboldened by the fact that the team's two hardest players had been so obliging to that first invader!

Police belatedly moved in, but with so many people on the pitch referee Arthur Smith had little option but to ask both teams to leave the field for ten minutes.

The coverage in the Sunday newspapers was sensational, although HISA spokesperson Peter Cullen feared that the pitch invasion would backfire. He told the *People*: 'We organised the balloons as a proper protest. Invasions (during the game) destroy everything we're doing.' His caution was understandable, particularly in the light of the on-pitch battle between fans of Birmingham and Stoke which took place on the same day. Although the fight at St Andrews was old-fashioned hooliganism whereas the Upton Park invasion had been political, some newspapers lumped the two incidents together.

Perhaps surprisingly, the pitch invasion was not condemned outright by the media. Many sports writers were West Ham fans themselves and objected to the way the club was being treated by its own board. Respected journalist, Jack Steggles, wrote an open letter to the directors in the following Monday's *Daily Star*, 'Dear Sirs, I have a simple question to ask you, the people running – or should I say ruining – West Ham: What the hell are you doing to the club I love?'

Former West Ham striking legend Tony Cottee, playing for Everton that fateful day, also stuck up for the fans. He told reporters, 'What has happened to all the money they had from transfers, like the £2 million they got from me? Of course I feel sympathy for the fans. If you've got a family of four, how the hell are they meant to pay out for those bonds? What this club needs is for the directors to dip their hands in their pockets.'

Worse followed for the club when terrace hero Julian

Dicks joined in the condemnation. He told reporters: 'I agree with what they [the fans] are doing, even if I don't agree with the way they are doing it. Their actions could cost us points but it's their way of showing the club they are unhappy. I think they are totally justified in doing that. They pay our wages and pay to keep this club alive. The Bond Scheme is wrong, you can't ask an ordinary bloke to pay £975 just to watch his favourite football team. Something has to be done, and quickly.' It was an astonishing public rebuke for the directors. Dicks even suggested that it was only his position as an employee of the club that prevented him from joining the fans on the barricades. 'The unrest has been there for a long time. I'd like to help, but there's nothing I can do.'

The following week it was reported that Storrie had driven to the training ground to 'tell off' Julian. Trying to get Julian to step into line was of course a waste of time. In a fanzine interview weeks later, Dicksy repeated his statements and added that other players agreed with him. 'I wouldn't buy one (a Bond) because they are a lot of money and are morally wrong. There is a lot said by quite a few of the lads, but they won't say anything in public. I was the only one that spoke up, so it was obvious that I was the only one that would get spoken to.'

In retrospect, it would seem that the demonstration at the Everton match effectively killed off the Bond Scheme. But it didn't feel like it at the time. There was a sense that the board had dug their heels in and wouldn't budge an inch. If it had been public knowledge that a mere 500 bonds had been sold the board would have been sunk. Despite these figures being secret, the scheme was clearly in serious trouble and HISA, scenting blood, went in for the kill.

Instead of negotiating their surrender, the board

pigheadedly refused to back down, even relaunching the Bond with minor modifications. Those that couldn't afford to buy a Bond over five years were offered a 'preferential loan', enabling them to spread the cost over two years. This was a rather strange business decision. What made West Ham think that those supporters who couldn't afford to pay the Bond over five years would be able be pay for it over two years? It was another example of muddled thinking at the top.

The club also announced big increases in season ticket prices for the following year, regardless of which division the club found itself in. If we caved in and bought a Bond they'd give us £100 off for 10 years. Despite the recent on-pitch demonstrations the club still believed they could resort to this kind of blackmail. Realising the futility of making the Bond compulsory, they had announced that instead Bond-holders would be able to buy season tickets for the following season at this season's prices while the rest of us would be forced to pay more. Hardly a sensible move considering the club were hurtling towards the Second Division. Season tickets were not going to be a hot property.

The next home match against Arsenal saw 24,000 balloons handed out by both HISA and a group of Arsenal fans (The Independent Arsenal Supporters' Association). IASA, run by Arsenal fans Dyll Davies and Tony Willis, were protesting against the North Londoners' own Bond Scheme. Although similarly punitive financially, the Arsenal scheme was not compulsory and the Highbury Board were actually putting in some money themselves – £8 million – unlike their West Ham counterparts who were contributing nothing.

Both HISA and IASA met in various City pubs in the build-up to the match and decided that a public show of unity would play well in the press. HISA's increasingly media-savvy organisers suggested giving red balloons to the West Ham fans and claret ones to the Arsenal contingent. A banner saying 'Ban the West Ham Bond' was also displayed in the Arsenal end. This was a masterstroke, indicating that football fans were not mindless hooligans, as many lazy tabloid hacks had suggested, but thoughtful people genuinely concerned about the future of their beloved game.

Despite another tepid 2-0 defeat the fans remained in the stands during and after the match. One large banner in the stands, aimed at the board, read 'Wanted for the murder of West Ham'. There was no real desire for the fans to muddy their trainers on the pitch for a fourth time.

The Arsenal match protest was well covered in the press, and by this stage barely a day went by without a newspaper report on the anti-Bond campaign. The mood at the club was further darkened by HISA's boycott which was beginning to hit the club in the pocket. Sales of official merchandise were down, as were matchday programmes. The fanzines, by contrast, had never seen such good trade. HISA had even introduced their own coach service to away matches undercutting the club's official transport by 25 per cent. Vindictive attempts to undermine HISA by sending bailiffs to the group's merchandise stall only increased the group's determination. HISA's 'crime' was to use crossed hammers in the design of some T-shirts. Tellingly, the host of other unlicensed vendor stalls around the ground were left untouched. This was an act of war, and not a clever one considering the heavy beating that HISA were inflicting upon the board.

Behind the scenes, HISA still held occasional meetings with Storrie, but the MD, despite his best efforts, was unable to make much progress with such a stubborn regime behind him. He had been put up to soothe the fans without giving anything away. HISA regarded Storrie as well-meaning but they knew that at this stage he had little say in the club, and that until the final battle was won their protests had to continue.

The committee now believed that the red cards and balloon protests, although unquestionably effective, had been done to death. The campaign needed to be stepped up to a different level. One member suggested using the ultimate weapon against the club – the boycotting of matches. This would be a much harder protest to sell to the fans, particularly those who religiously attended every home match.

Instead of imposing the idea and risking a complete loss of face if it failed, HISA decided to change policy and ballot its members at the group's third and final public meeting. This took place at the Broadway Theatre in Barking during the final week of March. The meeting vindicated HISA's initial reluctance to democratise the protest. As a microphone was passed around the audience confusion reigned as a series of half-baked compromises were suggested from those assembled. As tempers frayed one man grabbed the mike, pointed at his fellow West Ham fans and bellowed, 'If you don't stand in the Chicken Run you're nuffink'. If the first two meetings had been allowed to proceed in this manner the campaign would have been an unmitigated disaster.

As the committee struggled to maintain order one HISA leader proposed that the entire crowd stand outside the ground for the duration of the Norwich City game the following weekend. It was a bold gesture, one that offered the board a glimpse into an apocalyptic future in which games would be played in front of empty stands. Most fans were reluctant to miss their football fix, though, and the motion was heavily defeated.

In a messy compromise, members agreed to stage a walkout at half-time of the following Tuesday's home match against Southampton. This was a total flop, the first and only HISA demonstration to fail. The West Ham team had thrown an unexpected spanner in the works by putting on their best display of the season against Norwich, winning 4-0 and offering fans a tantalising glimpse of a revival. After a decent first-half performance against Southampton the Hammers went into the break at 0-0. Faced with the prospect of missing another crucial victory the vast majority of fans lost their nerve and abandoned the protest to watch the second half. Predictably, Southampton scored the only goal of the game in the final minute.

HISA's final protest of the season came after West Ham's last match at home to Nottingham Forest when fans were asked to tear up their season tickets on the pitch. A week earlier West Ham's relegation had been confirmed and dark rumours of violence surrounded the match as the fans prepared for the wilderness of the Second Division or, as it was renamed that summer, the First Division. West Ham were about to miss out on the inauguration of the Premier league and many fans wondered whether Upton Park would ever witness top flight football again. Thousands of season tickets remained unsold for the following campaign and many fans, including *Fortunes* editor Steve Rapport, had decided this would be their last match at the Boleyn. There was a feeling that all hell could break loose.

An *OLAS* editorial called for calm, urging supporters to behave themselves. It read: 'I've heard a lot of talk about violent action at the last match. Violence towards members of the West Ham board, stewards, and the Old Bill. I have also heard reports that the ground is going to be smashed up. Come on gang, do us a favour. What the hell do you think that will achieve? I'll tell you. Nothing. All that will achieve is more than likely the end of West Ham United.'

In the event, there was no mutiny, partly because of the general air of apathy now that West Ham had been relegated and also because of a rare home win. After Frank McAvennie had signed off his West Ham career with a second-half hat-trick many of us invaded the pitch and tore up our season tickets as HISA had requested. I still chuckle now when I think of my brother and I taking a carrier bag full of 11-years' worth of season tickets (33 in all, including our Dad's) and tearing them joyously on the pitch... having carefully removed our renewal voucher for next season. Solidarity, Brother!

A few days after the season ended, and with the Bond Scheme in ruins, the board wrote to some season ticket holders to inform them they had given away their seats. The letter, written by Ann Rush of the ticket office, stated, 'we regret to inform you that a Bond holder has requested and been allocated your seat. Therefore it will not be available to you for renewal in the future'. With sales of the Bond barely nudging 500 it's safe to say that not many of these insulting letters were sent out. It was just as well. Five months later the club would be sending out letters very different in both tone and content.

By the end of May, Martin Cearns had resigned as Chairman, demoting himself to vice-chairman, while the mysterious Terence Brown became 'numero uno'. Rumours circulated that the final straw for Cearns came when a group of angry fans surrounded his car in the club car park after a match and began rocking it and threatening to overturn it.

Little was known about Brown except that he had recently bought a third of the club's shares to become the largest shareholder. Although he had been on the board at the time the Bond Scheme was announced, he was largely untainted by the fiasco, which had focused almost entirely on the Cearns family. Brown's appointment meant that when the club eventually backed down it could so without looking quite so ridiculous. With a new man at the helm it appeared as if the Club was under new stewardship, although in reality the Cearns were still very much on the board and would remain so for some time.

It was two months into the 1992/93 campaign that the club finally conceded defeat. The club was in a parlous financial state. The club's sponsorship deal with BAC Windows had expired and it was barely a week before the new season started that a replacement, in Dagenham Motors, was found. Even then the figure paid by the Ford dealership was believed to be worth a mere £100,000 a year. It was nowhere near enough to get the club out of its hole. In addition, West Ham had squandered an estimated £1.3 million advertising the Bond, money which arguably might have been better spent on buying a new defence, and a striker who knew where the goal was.

The club had all but acknowledged the failure of the Bond Scheme when it had announced the punitive season ticket price rises for non-bondholders. They hoped that this would help them raise the money to at least develop the South Bank and Chicken Run. Yet the club's demotion to Division One meant few fans were prepared to stump up even more cash to watch the team than they had in the top tier. Predictably, sales of season tickets halved and the club's attendances crashed to an all-time low. Attendances of 11,921 against

Watford, 11,493 against Derby County, and 10,326 against Sunderland terrified the board. Crowds at Upton Park had halved in just six months and there were genuine fears that attendances could fall even lower.

The club had dug itself into a corner. It had threatened the fans with being barred from watching their team but found itself wrong-footed at every turn by HISA's well-organised campaign. The club needed to step back from what seemed to be a kamikaze mission. They had threatened to make outsiders of those who resisted their scheme, but the simple fact was that there were now more outsiders than insiders. West Ham was haemorrhaging support. By this stage HISA had done its job. There was simply no need for more public meetings or demonstrations. The campaign had been won. All that was left was for the board to hoist the white flag.

Finally, in October 1992 the club's nerve cracked. Spurred on by the one voice of reason in the boardroom, Peter Storrie, chairman Brown made the club's first sensible move in the whole Bond Scheme debacle. He wrote personally to former season ticket holders who had stayed away, offering a guarded apology. Brown didn't apologise for the Bond Scheme. That would clearly have been too much to ask. But he did confess to the 'stayaways' that the season ticket price rises had been misguided and, accordingly, he had slashed the prices for anyone who decided to come back. Those who had renewed their season tickets were also given a £50 refund. In addition, the club cut admission fees for the home match against Swindon Town.

This single act of penance drained the poison from the festering situation, allowing HISA and the West Ham fanzines to encourage exiled fans to return to Upton Park. The most memorable plea came from a leading member of

HISA, who wishes to remain anonymous, in an impassioned piece entitled 'The War Is Over'. He argued that West Ham fans had forced the club to back down, but the club was now on its knees financially and there was no need to kick them when they were down.

Speaking 15 years later, the writer recalls the soul-searching discussion with *OLAS* editor, Gary Firmager, which inspired his article. 'Gates had fallen to ludicrous levels and I said to Gary, "They've met us halfway with this major cut in prices. If we don't say fair enough and give them a chance we are in deep doo-doos because when people start doing other things on Saturdays it's difficult to get them back.' So Gary agreed to run an *OLAS* editorial over several pages saying the war was over and it was time to go back to Upton Park. The local papers picked it up and the following week we had our highest gate of the season.

'Personally I think Storrie had a major part in turning it around and getting Brown to see sense in putting a decent offer on the table. I said to Gary, "If we don't do something soon it'll be a fight to the death and our club will have gone so far down the Swanee it won't come back". Gary agreed with me and ran the article. It could have backfired on him and indeed he did get stick from some fans. Gary really put his head on the chopping block by running the piece and he deserves a lot of credit for that.'

HISA vice-chairman Shane Barber had recently launched his own fanzine, *On a Mission From God*, and in an eloquent editorial implored fans to accept the club's offer of a truce. Barber wrote: 'What HISA have done is unrivalled in British football. You've forced your club to the position where they have to consult with you. Now that, my friends, is progress. Under all the bravado on both sides, no-one wants to see Upton Park with only 10,000 in it… We have to face reality and concede that we may never control the boardroom, but by our actions on the terraces we have shown them who's really in charge. We have the power to bring them all down – the good, the bad, and the ugly.'

A crowd of almost 18,000 attended the Swindon match, although it would take West Ham's presence in the promotion race before the crowds began regularly topping the 15,000 mark, a figure well down on previous years' attendances. But the rot had been stopped.

Although the Bond itself was clearly a dead duck, the club could not publicly declare it so, in case the banks who had underwritten the scheme pulled the plug on their investment. In fact, it was the underwriting of the Bond Scheme which allowed the club to rebuild the ground the following season. Peter Storrie admitted as much in an interview with *On The Terraces* in November 1992. 'Clearly if we could put the clock back we wouldn't have done the Bond Scheme. However, some pluses have come out of it, notably the underwriting. That is a very important aspect of the Bond.'

One fact mentioned rarely, if at all, is that the bank's underwriting secured Upton Park as West Ham's home for at least a decade, if not many more to come. The underwriting agreement that the board had somehow managed to wangle was specifically for the redevelopment of Upton Park. In previous years local newspapers had on more than one occasion reported that the club was considering moving to nearby Stratford. Yet if the club moved, the banks would have been within their rights to demand back their entire £15 million input. The underwriting scheme gave the club virtual carte blanche to develop the ground into an all-seater stadium for no outlay themselves. Maybe the club had known what

199

they were doing from the start. More likely they just got lucky.

In the final reckoning, all sides came out smelling of roses. West Ham got their new ground and the fans retained their self-respect and the money in their wallets. After the board's about-face HISA disbanded, having successfully orchestrated the defeat of the debenture. The committee kept in touch but with the Bond Scheme dead there was no reason to keep the organisation going. The campaign had taken over the lives of its committee members for the best part of a year. They deserved a rest.

It was left to the fanzines, increasingly empowered by the events of 1992, to occasionally remind the board of what it faced dare it make the same mistake twice. As one fanzine editorial declared: 'A message to the board. We are watching every move you make. This is your last chance, your very last chance, and you really don't deserve this one.'

Our victory over the West Ham board has left a lasting legacy on the club. The relationship between the board and fans was permanently shattered. The board would permanently be regarded with suspicion. If the directors were in any doubt about the level of antipathy that remains among the Upton Park faithful, they were reminded on the night West Ham played Manchester City in November 1993. Will Cearns had died a few days beforehand and the club announced a minute's silence to honour him before kick-off. With the Bond Scheme a fading memory and the club mid-table in the Premiership one might have expected the supporters to let bygones be bygones and pay their respects to a dead man. Instead a loud cry of 'Cearns Out' rang around the ground, forcing the referee to blow his whistle early and start the match.

The club treads more carefully around its supporters these

days, although the club's renaissance under Harry Redknapp in the Premiership did allow them to impose inflation-busting year-on-year ticket price rises. No doubt the success of last season will encourage the further taking of liberties, yet the board does seem far more aware of the potential power of West Ham fans.

In January 1997, the fans' weapon of on-pitch protests was dusted down after a dismal 1-0 home FA Cup defeat to lower division Wrexham. The Irons faced the likelihood of relegation and the supporters were angry at what we saw as the under-investment in the team. Five years after the Bond Scheme debacle it only took a few chants of 'Sack the Board' and 'Brown Out' to make the board see sense. If relegation from the old First Division was bad, demotion from the money factory of the Premiership was potentially disastrous, and Brown and co. put their hands in their pockets, giving Redknapp an unprecedented war chest of £7 million. Redknapp's subsequent signings of John Hartson, Paul Kitson and Steve Lomas ultimately enabled West Ham to stay up. There's no way the board would have acted the same way were they not still bearing the scars of the Bond Scheme.

When West Ham finally lost the battle to stay in the top tier in 2003 the board acted skilfully before the club's relegation to nip any protest in the bud. Towards the end of the season, they announced that season ticket prices would be cut in the event of relegation. They would only rise if we defied the odds and stayed up. Admittedly, tickets were still more expensive than any other First Division club, but the announcement of a price cut, any price cut, would have been unthinkable a decade earlier.

When Brown and Roeder conducted the necessary fire-sale

to keep the club afloat the situation was in many ways worse than our relegation in 1992. Yet protests by the fans largely boiled down to a few dozen demonstrators staying in the club car park after a pre-season friendly and the regular chants of 'Brown Out' from the stands. Some argue that the West Ham faithful no longer had the stomach for a scrap and that apathy ruled the day. My view is that the vast majority of fans realised that relegation was primarily the fault of an unsuitable manager, Glenn Roeder, and an uncommitted, yet incredibly talented team. We knew that the board had paid our star players obscene salaries and although they should have sacked Roeder months earlier, they had at least splashed the cash in living the dream over recent years.

A handful of businessmen launched 'Whistle', a half-hearted attempt to force out the board and persuade a new consortium to buy them out, but their efforts quickly petered out when Brown took them to the High Court. There were of course justifiable grumbles among the fans that Brown had misled us by first announcing that no player sales were necessary and then after the season ticket money had been counted overseeing the sale of £29 million worth of players and the loss of 21 first team squad players. Yet Brown argued successfully that to announce that the club was in enormous financial difficulty would have merely encouraged other clubs to make derisory bids for players, which the club would have been forced to accept. He just about kept the fans on board, although had we failed to secure promotion in 2005 one wonders how quickly protests of the magnitude of the Bond Scheme dispute would have returned.

During our two-year sabbatical in the Championship there was a general sense of gloom among fans and people appeared to be waiting for the board to make one final mistake before we pounced. In the event there was no need for a return to the dark days of the previous decade. With the aid of some canny management from manager Alan Pardew and a huge slice of luck in scraping into the play-offs the club managed to conjour success from two years of adversity. We are now in pretty decent shape on and off the field.

Meanwhile, the positive legacy of the Bond Scheme remains. After promotion, rather than service the club's debt as many of us feared, Brown allowed Pardew to spend around £12 million on players to secure our Premiership status. I'm convinced that this decision can be traced back to our protests from 13 years earlier. The board knew it had escaped by the seat of its collective pants and that ignoring the mistakes of 1991/92 would put them on the fast track to oblivion. For that reason alone all of us who protested against the Bond should give ourselves a pat on the back.

However, last season did see a brief return to the old boardroom complacency in the shape of May's FA Cup Final ticket debacle. West Ham had enough tickets for each season ticket holder to be satisfied and the club rightly promised that these people would get priority. Yet their lazy, cack-handed decision to hand over responsibility to Ticketmaster resulted in more than 1,000 season ticket holders missing out on the club's first major cup final in 25 years. Despite the club's promises to remove tickets from those who had used out-of-date season ticket reference numbers, nothing was done. Quite disgraceful. These are the people, lest the board forget, who stuck with the club after we were relegated and gave the club the money to plot its escape from the Coca Cola Championship. When the next relegation comes, as it inevitably will (this is West Ham after all), the club will look to these loyal fans to bail them out. I'm sure many will tell them where to stick it.

The FA Cup Final of 2006 seems a fitting place to end this tale. At the Millennium Stadium we staged an extraordinary show of loyalty to the team, the equal of that fateful day at Villa Park 15 years earlier. We out-sang Liverpool throughout the 90 minutes, through all of extra-time, and during the agony of the penalty shoot-out. When poor Anton Ferdinand missed our last kick there was a split-second of silence in the West Ham half of the ground as 25 years of disappointment flashed before our eyes. This was followed by an ear-bursting rendition of 'Alan Pardew's claret and blue army'. We continued to out-sing the Scousers throughout the presentations, even as Liverpool picked up the trophy that was so nearly ours, and showed the world what a resolute and proud bunch of supporters we are.

In case the board didn't get the message at Villa Park I shall repeat it. What you saw on 13 May 2006 was a display of loyalty to our gutsy team, our manager, and ourselves as supporters. Don't even think about using it for your own advantage again. We brought the club to its knees once, guys. We can certainly do it again. Some of us still have our red cards, Mr Brown, and we'll never be afraid to use them!

Jim Drury was a wide-eyed 6 year old when he first visited Upton Park in 1979. Standing on the South Bank terraces on a wooden stall made by his father he was instantly hooked by the stench of cigarettes, the surge of the crowd, and the foul-mouthed banter.

In Jim's first two years following the Hammers he watched them at two Wembley cup finals and saw them win the

Second Division championship by a record margin. Perhaps understandably, he was fooled into thinking that life as a West Ham fan was a bed of roses.

Jim's teenage years saw the growing realisation that he was supporting one of the most frustrating teams in the country, capable of producing thrilling and embarrassing football in equal measure.

Despite the many frustrations it entailed, being a West Ham supporter always felt special. But when the board used the pretext of the Taylor Report to blackmail their fans the innocent, unquestioning support of Jim – and thousands like him – was destroyed forever.

CHAPTER 9

NORWICH CITY FC – CHASE OUT!

BY RICKY BILVERSTONE

ROBERT CHASE, JUST where do you begin with this man? He oversaw some of the greatest times the club has ever had, including two FA Cup semi-finals, entrance into the inaugural season of the Premier League – which Norwich led for much of the season before finally finishing third – and finally, a place in Europe. Something we'd missed out on twice before because of the post-Heysel ban on English clubs.

It was during this 1993/94 European campaign that Norwich City first demolished the powerful Dutch side Vitesse Arnheim and then became the only British side to beat the mighty Bayern Munich – possibly the greatest European club side at the time – at home. A feat that will never be bettered now that Bayern ground-share with their near neighbours 1860 Munich.

Sadly, defeat came in the next round with a 2-0 aggregate loss to Inter Milan. Hardly something to be ashamed of.

Before all this, City became one of the first grounds to

remove the fencing around the terracing and with it, one of the first all seated stadiums. Carrow Road is also being credited as the first ground in England to have under-soil heating. All of which occurred because of the man at the top – Robert Chase.

Now, after reading that you may be wondering how this man has made his way into a book about football protests after overseeing so much success and change for a club as 'small' as Norwich City? Well the answer is quite simple, money!

Chase made his fortune through a property and land development business – don't get me wrong, he was no 'Red Rom' but he wasn't short of a few quid either – and after realising that the formation of the Premier League provided an opportunity to make some more he went about doing what he does best, making money.

The whole 'saga' seemed to start in 1993 after we went out of the UEFA Cup and ended the season in a mid-table placing. The then-manager, Mike Walker, went to Chase and the board suggested that the club could do with bringing in a new player or two in order to bolster the squad and ensure that they would have the best chance possible of staying up there with the rest of the best in English football. Given the relative success of the previous season, he believed that there would be no problem with this request but he was to find he was very much mistaken.

Chase refused this request, and instead suggested that rather than bringing in new faces, the club may actually have to start losing some of its stars to improve their financial footing.

With this at the back of his mind and just three months after going out of Europe, Walker resigned as Norwich manager on the eve of their FA Cup third round tie away to Wycombe in January 1994 and left to sign a two-and-a-half-year contract with Premiership rivals Everton.

When asked why he left a club he so clearly loved and whose fans adored him, he said that an 'exchange of views' with chairman Robert Chase was behind his move. (The club's fans were to later to discover the truth behind that statement.)

At this time, the club included players such as Ruel Fox, an up-and-coming Darren Eadie, Mark Robins, and of course the man that was to be the accelerant for what can only be described as some of the biggest protests and riots this club is ever likely to see again, Chris Sutton.

Despite starting his playing career as a centre back, Sutton's conversion to striker saw him explode on to the footballing scene. During the club's European season he netted 28 goals and became the club's top scorer for any season spent in the top flight.

Following Walker's resignation, assistant manager John Deehan was moved up the ranks from assistant to manager and led City to a safe, if unexciting, final placing of twelfth – nine places lower than the previous season.

During the close-season speculation was rife that some of the club's top stars would be on the move, with Chris Sutton being linked with a summer move to either Man Utd or Jack Walker's big-spending Blackburn Rovers.

For all City fans, the feeling was that selling Sutton would be like committing Hari Kari. After all, we still had the nucleus of the side, which had battled away in Europe just months ago, and, with a couple of new signings Norwich could once again become a fighting force. Were the rumours that Walker left because Chase told him the club would have to sell finally coming true? Not according to Robert Chase, as he came out to deny Sutton would be on the move by telling a press conference, 'If Chris Sutton is not here next season, then neither will I be.' So that was that. Sutton was staying and the club was setting up for another push for the title, or at least a season that would end with European qualification.

However, just as pre-season was about to begin, Chase announced an impromptu press conference and produced one of the biggest U-turns the English game has ever seen. Just weeks after categorically denying that Sutton would be leaving the club and backing it up with the notion that he would walk should such a catastrophe happen, he said: 'Chris Sutton will now be leaving the club, but only when our £5 million valuation has been met.'

At the time, £5 million would have broken the transfer record for a player in the English game. So, many outside the club suggested that rather than admitting defeat Chase was raising the bar as the likelihood of someone from a club such at Norwich going for such a mammoth fee was highly unlikely. But those of us in the inner circle knew that it was just a matter of time before the bids came in as we knew what the player could do, and that Jack Walker of Blackburn had a bigger bank balance than the FA.

Sure enough, that offer soon came in and Sutton was allowed to talk to Rovers. It didn't take long for him to make up his mind, and who could blame him? He was leaving a club that in just a year had gone from title contenders and one of the biggest clubs in the country, to a selling club that now only had a relegation battle to look forward to.

It was not necessarily the sale of the club's star asset that had now enraged the fans but the way that Chase had handled things, not only by what he said about a possible move, but also for employing a manager than seemed content to be compliant and see his star assets leave.

Why didn't he say that the bidding was to start at £5 million and see where it went? After all, the club would have been in a no-lose situation (unless you suggest Sutton had to go). No one comes in, he stays, more clubs come in and his transfer fee would rocket. However, now, with the most attractive transfer fund any manager at the club had ever seen, it was expected that new and better players would be coming in, and our first transfer was defiantly bigger. Our new signing was announced weeks later with its fee coming in at the not-so-small sum of £1 million, so there was still a chance that Sutton had been replaced with a half decent player.

The signing was strong, big and superb in the air and had a lot of say in what would happen in the area surrounding him. No, we hadn't bought Duncan Ferguson, we had bought the flour mill and land at the back of the South Stand.

Some of the money was made available for new players and a striker was finally brought in, but not until two months had passed since Sutton's departure. Mike Sheron came in in an attempt to bolster the goals for section. While any new signing is normally welcomed, Sutton's replacement, at £800,000, cost less than 20 per cent of the fee we received, with the fans being told the cut-price striker was brought in due to the 'poor' financial situation at the club. This started off one of the most unanswered questions ever, where had all the money the gone?

Not happy with what was happening, fans started descending on the roads outside Carrow Road and opposite the boardroom with chants of 'Chase Out' and 'Sack The

Board' echoing from the hundred or so that had finally decided enough was enough. The Chase Out era had now well and truly begun.

Had they known what was to happen I am sure there would have been thousands more joining in with those who could already see what was coming. This was a trend set to continue not only till the end of that season, but for many more months as well. Following this, yet another striker left in a cut-price deal with Efan Ekoku flying the nest.

The following season saw Norwich go from seventh place at Christmas to relegation in May, after taking just 13 points from 23 games. Deehan resigned with just five games left.

Fans could at last see what was happening with more and more starting to stay behind after games to vent their anger against Chase, leaving the main man no choice but to bring in extra police to supervise the fans who were now starting to descend en masse, with some of the group more intent on causing trouble than protesting legally. Another home and away double defeat brought more fans out on to the streets and this time they meant business. The local TV companies had seen this coming, and the next day the angry scenes were shown all over the region.

Many fans had tried to barge their way into the boardroom but could only get as far as the club's main reception before being hit by a screen of security, while others hurled stones at windows and chanted for the main man's head.

The club soon found itself at the wrong end of the table and was staring relegation in the face. This, added to the publicity of the previous protest, acted as a catalyst, and worst was yet to come. The club must have seen what was going to happen and ordered many more local police to be outside at the end of the next game, with Chase digging into his own pocket to bring in horses from London and a close protection team, such was the hatred that was starting to build against him.

Yet again, City lost at home, and once again more fans waited outside for blood. Two thousand angry fans marched on Carrow Road, but this time were faced by around a hundred uniformed officers, half of who were kitted in full riot gear, half a dozen police horses, a handful of dogs and a large number of journalists and TV cameras.

It all started peacefully with the usual 'Chase Out' chants, but among the protesters was a handful of fans that wanted nothing more than to get their hands on Chase himself and, once again, a push for the boardroom was made. More and more protesters followed, but they were being pushed back by the police until what seemed around half of the fans joined in and the police could not hold out anymore.

Around ten fans did finally make it into the building and headed for the boardroom and for Chase. By that time, the chairman had seen what was happening and had already fled. The unlucky few that had made it were quickly arrested and were to never to be seen again at the protests, following cautions from the police.

Meanwhile, outside, the melee had developed into a mass brawl. The protesters seemed to have the upper hand over the police until the dogs and horses moved in. At that point, people rushed to get out of the way and, while most managed it, one unlucky soul was about to have his five minutes of fame. Seeing what was about to happen, an eagle-eyed photographer from the local press started snapping frantically as one of the protesters got trampled by a horse –

his picture ended up on the front page of the *Eastern Daily Press* the next day.

Over the next couple of weeks the violent side of the protesting started to die down after it was thought that it could be doing the fans and their aim more harm than good, and that while there was still a chance of staying up, maybe the fans' passion should be aimed at trying to gee the players on. This, however, didn't continue for long. In fact, the protests soon began to be taken into the ground with most of the anger and noise coming from The Barclay end behind one of the goals. Carrow Road was now no longer a place for families to take their kids at the weekend, it was a war zone.

At this point, a group of local lads began to realise that both the protests inside the ground and the bad press the club and fans were getting was starting to affect the players during home games, so they set about attempting to bring the protests back to outside the ground, while also trying to produce some good press for the supporters. After all, all they wanted was the removal of Robert Chase and for the club they loved to once again have a chance of competing at the top.

They came up with the idea of 'Chase Out' mugs, cups and pin badges. All the money raised was to go into producing more items and promoting the campaign. The campaign was such a success that they moved on to bigger and better ideas while also trying to get more organised. In doing this, they were turning the bad press the fans had received in previous months into good and sympathetic reviews, both locally and nationally. The next idea was a 'red card day'. Every fan was to be passed a 'red card' as they approached the ground with instructions on what to do with it on the back.

The idea was to try and get the fans to unite and remove the negative atmosphere around the ground by asking all those who wanted Chase out to hold the cards up at a given time (during the half time interval if I remember correctly). While the cards did indeed go up, it didn't exactly work out as planned, as they were held up at more than one point during the game and accompanied with 'Chase Out' chants.

The club now found itself at the wrong end of the table with less than a month of the season left. Seeing that the chances of survival were slim, to say the least, manager John Deehan decided that it was time to jump ship. He resigned on 8 April, following a 3-0 hammering away to Newcastle.

Deehan blamed Chase for the club's freefall into the relegation zone and said that he was given an almost impossible job to do by selling players and not being able to reinvest the money in the right places.

He was later quoted as saying: 'I think I was probably a bit ill myself in the end. I was going home and not sleeping because I was trying to come up with the answer to an equation that was unanswerable – how to help a young side stay in the Premiership with no money. I felt like I'd been in a car crash and I could either sit there and look at the wreckage of what had happened and dither around or get up and start walking. I got up and started walking.'

The impossible task of saving the Canaries from the drop was handed to a former player and Deehan's assistant, Gary Megson, who was given the caretaker job. Following a home loss against Forest, fans once again gathered outside and demanded that Chase and his board leave. As a result, Chase tried, unsuccessfully, to quell the protests by saying that the money for the police was coming from the club's finances and that it was the fans, not him, who were killing the club.

This claim did not go down too well amongst the supporters. This carried on until the inevitable happened – we were relegated. Defeat away to Leeds meant it was impossible for the Canaries to keep their place in the England elite. The fans now had to face the prospect of playing, what was then, First Division football. The protests outside the ground became even fiercer.

Club shareholder and director Jimmy Jones came out and said that he was heading the 'Chase Out' campaign within the club and that he was attempting to buy Chase's shares. As a result, every time he was seen anywhere near a protest his name was chanted and people rushed to shake the hand of the man that was said to be the only one that could save the club. The final game of the season saw us take on Villa, who themselves wanted their own chairman, Doug Ellis, out. This meant that for the first time ever, even the away end would be protesting. It produced one of the most hostile atmospheres that I and many others have ever experienced at Carrow Road. Banners such as 'Chase Ellis Out' and 'The Two Fat Controllers Must Go' could be seen dangling from the Villa support.

At the final whistle, a number of fans ran onto the pitch with 'Chase Out' placards and declared they would not move from the centre circle till he was removed from the club. Outside, the three or so Villa fans joined around two thousand angry City fans for the final protest of the season, which thankfully went off without any trouble and included families with small children, which not only showed how deep the rage for this man went, but that the good publicity that had been built up had also worked.

In June that year (1995) the club appointed Martin

O'Neill to take over full management duties at City. At the press conference, Chase declared that O'Neill would get all the help he needed to get City bouncing straight back up and that there was a war chest available for him, although he did not go into details of how much was actually in there.

Things started brightly with a 3-1 away victory over 'local rivals' Luton Town on the first day of the season, bringing many fans to believe that maybe things were about change for the better and, with that, the Chase Out protests died an almost instant death, but they were soon to resurrect themselves.

Norwich enjoyed a solid first half to the season and were sitting pretty in fifth place by Christmas. All seemed well at Carrow Road for the first time in two years, but that was all set to change.

O'Neill went to Chase and asked if he could open up the club's war chest for the powerful and potent Bradford striker Dean Windass, a player whom O'Neill felt would be the missing piece of the jigsaw and who would be the man to fire the club to promotion. Now, while he may have scored fifty-odd goals in two seasons, Dean was not going to break the bank and could have been acquired for around £500,000, just 10 per cent of the Sutton fee, and for such a prolific striker it seemed to be a snip.

But Chase went back on his word and said that the club would have to sell before they could bring in any new faces, which again begged the question – just what had happened to all our millions? If Chase thought that that would be the end of it and that O'Neill would go running with his tail between his legs he had another think coming.

The former City hero once more asked for the money

to bring in Windass but was once again refused. So, on Sunday 17th December 1995, just 6 months after taking the job, City lost yet another manager when Martin O'Neill decided enough was enough and resigned from his position.

To make things even worse, he did so just three hours before he was set to take charge of a vital away clash with promotion rivals Leicester City, which we went on to lose 3-2. Four days later, O'Neill was announced as the Fox's new manager.

Yet again, money and the decision of Chase had helped the club to lose one of its key members. Former caretaker manager, Gary Megson, was quickly appointed as his successor. Not necessarily because of his previous connections with the club but more to do with the fact that Chase felt he wouldn't ask for too much money to spend. It was also felt that he was the sort of manager who would accept what the board said as gospel and wouldn't question their word.

But if he thought that the club could progress on the cheap or that the appointment of a former player and crowd favourite would keep the fans happy, then he had just made his biggest and, as we now know, last mistake as chairman of Norwich City Football Club.

Having only been a manager for five games the previous season – none of which had been won – Megson's reign started in defeat, and it soon became apparent that it could become a pattern.

A Boxing Day home defeat to lowly Southend United followed by ejection from the FA Cup at the hands of Division Two strugglers Brentford saw the protests make a welcome return. Chants of 'Chase Out' echoed around the ground and following the final whistle hundreds of angry fans once again decided enough was enough and gathered outside the boardroom window.

From being a top six side with ambitions of reaching the playoffs a distinct possibility, we had once again turned into relegation battlers with Megson winning just five games out of the 27 he was in charge for. Every home game ended with a protest outside the ground, with away matches being dominated by 'Chase Out' and 'Sack The Board' chants rather than the club's powerful and inspirational anthem 'On The Ball City'.

Finally, in April 1996, Chase decided that he had taken enough from the fans and could no longer handle the pressure that was being put on him. He resigned from his position as Chairman with immediate effect. Norwich ended the season safe from relegation but miles from sixth place which, at the start of the season, was the very least they had expected. On the 21st June, Megson was sacked and replaced by Mike Walker, whom it was hoped would be able to recreate the bond and togetherness the club had so dearly been missing.

To be fair, at first it looked like it was going to work. The next season saw Carrow Road returned to how most fans would like to remember it. An intimidating, but friendly ground, which takes something special to happen for the away side to leave with something, but unfortunately the passion and belief was to be short-lived as, once again, the club ended the season outside the top six.

Finally, in 2005, Norwich City Football Club gained promotion back to the Premiership two seasons after being beaten in the playoff final by Birmingham City as Champions of the new League Championship. Again, the dream was short-lived, however, and we once again find ourselves battling it out in the country's second tier.

Whilst I remain critical of Chase, his acquisition of the flour mill behind the south stand did, in the long run, pay off, with the club receiving millions more than what they had paid for it and its surrounding land, which is, at the time of writing, currently being turned into riverside flats and a hotel.

In April 2006, Robert Chase spoke openly to a local TV station for the first time since resigning from the board and said that he still believed that he did the right thing and that the fans should not forget that he oversaw the best times the club had ever had. Furthermore, as far as he was concerned he'd saved the club by investing in the land.

It is not a sentiment shared by many at the club, the vast majority of whom would rather have seen that money reinvested in the club. But equally, they and I still firmly believe that had we not sold Sutton, but had instead brought in a new face or two, Norwich City could and would still now be battling it out with the big boys.

That's the real tragedy and it also explains why the fans will never welcome Robert Chase back at Carrow Road until his dying day.

Ricky Bilverstone's first encounter with our national game was during Norwich's first ever trot into the world of European football following their third place finish in the Premiership's first ever season and he has been hooked ever since.

A season ticket holder from that time, he has undoubtedly seen the best and the worst of the club over the last decade, but that has not deterred him from following the club he so dearly loves, even if it did nearly cost him his job a couple of years ago, after attending two away matches, despite being warned he had no holiday left.

He now runs his own website in conjunction with an international network, which can be found at www.norwichcity.rivals.net.

CHAPTER 10

MANCHESTER CITY FC – THE ONE THAT WENT WRONG

BY EAMONN MONKS

IT'S HARD TO compete with your local neighbours in a city with two major football clubs. Then, when your city rivals are Manchester United, the task becomes utterly thankless. When your chairman dedicates himself to this solitary aim it's easy to regard the other clubs you have to face along the way as less of a priority, and the results of this thinking can be disastrous. Peter Swales learned this lesson the hard way at Manchester City...

Swales was an Ardwick-born City fan who realised a dream when the winning faction of a boardroom coup installed him as the club's chairman in the early 1970s. He once said that he was sick and tired of hearing the word 'United' every time he told anyone he was from Manchester, and was therefore determined that in future Manchester City would become as synonymous with the city as the Reds.

With former assistant to Joe Mercer, the legendary coach Malcolm Allison, in charge when Swales took over, the Blues looked forward to continuing the success the club had enjoyed in the second half of the 1960s. However, Big Mal on his own could never recapture the magic of his partnership with Mercer and left the club in 1973. His replacement, Johnny Hart, had to relinquish the post due to ill health shortly afterward, and although Ron Saunders led City to a League Cup final in 1974, he fell out with the senior players after Swales had publicly backed him and was dismissed. Tony Book, who had captained the Blues to all their triumphs during the Mercer-Allison era, took over and took City back to Wembley in 1976 to win the League Cup. Three seasons of European football followed, during which City missed a League Championship by a point but reached the UEFA Cup quarter-finals in 1979.

This was not good enough for Swales, who in January 1979 brought Allison back to City, initially to assist Book, but after a narrow brush with relegation in 1980, Big Mal was once again in charge. Clearly, nothing had been learned from his earlier tenure at Maine Road since millions of pounds were arguably squandered in the transfer market, clearing out established internationals and replacing them with lower league wannabes. As a result, City were converted from being a major force in English and European football to relegation certainties by the autumn of 1980, lying bottom of the First Division in mid-October without a League win to their name. Allison and Book were dismissed, as Swales brought John Bond in to restore the Blues to mid-table, reaching the FA Cup final and League Cup semi-final in the process. Instead of building on such relative success, Bond led City into difficulties before resigning in 1983, as the club became a debt-ridden outfit yo-yoing between the top two divisions within twenty years, with two relegations to their name by 1987.

Most people would think that the City supporters' campaign to oust Swales from the boardroom began in 1993, but in fact the first real opposition to his regime was with a 'Swales out' petition on the train down to Southend in September 1986 for a league cup tie after McNeill had jumped ship to Villa, followed by a protest during a 4-0 defeat at Leicester City in the spring of 1987, when a 'Swales Out' banner was unfurled in the away end and the chant repeated during the second half. With no money to improve the squad after the spending of Allison and his predecessor John Bond, City had been reduced to a poor side merely supplying fixture congestion to the likes of Liverpool, Arsenal, Everton and Manchester United. Worse still, with average gates dipping below the 20,000 mark for most of the season, the fans started to voice their disapproval of the club's parlous state. However, when the Blues returned to the top flight again in 1989 under Mel Machin there was a certain air of optimism that at least the team was strong enough to survive, especially with the recruitment of former England striker Clive Allen. But by early December, City were marooned at the bottom of the table once more and Swales had fired Machin.

Machin's replacement Howard Kendall had steadied the ship by wheeling and dealing in the transfer market, moving out most of the promotion squad and replacing them with cut-price recruitments from his successful era at Everton in the mid-1980s. In the summer of 1990, Kendall ruled himself out of the running to replace Bobby Robson as England manager and Swales thought he had at last secured the services of the man who would finally restore the Blues to their position as one of the country's foremost clubs. Kendall, however, defected to Everton in the November when the Merseysiders sacked their boss Colin Harvey, leaving City in the lurch. It transpired that when Kendall had arrived at Maine Road he had insisted that a release clause must be inserted into his contract, allowing him to apply for whatever managerial post he fancied at any time during his time at City. Swales had reluctantly agreed to the inclusion of the clause and Kendall now exercised the condition. On his departure he suggested that his coach Peter Reid be chosen to replace him and Reid was eventually given the job on a permanent basis, becoming the club's first-ever player-manager.

Under Reid, City maintained a steady improvement, twice finishing fifth in the table in his first 18 months in charge. However, the qualified success came at a price as Reid dismantled Kendall's squad and spent heavily in replacing them with the likes of Keith Curle and Terry Phelan from Wimbledon at £2.5 million each, Steve McMahon from Liverpool at £900,000 and Fitzroy Simpson from Portsmouth at £750,000. The Blues looked forward to the first season of the new FA Premier League in August 1992, but their optimism soon faded as a poor start to the campaign left them well out of contention for the championship or European qualification. Hope lay in an FA Cup run and City reached the quarter-finals.

Their home tie with Tottenham Hotspur was chosen by the BBC for a live Sunday afternoon broadcast, and the club chose the fixture for the opening of their new Platt Lane Stand, which unambitiously cut City's capacity even further. It all seemed to be going to plan as City scored early on, but their abject performance saw them go 4-1 down as the clock ticked away. A wonderful solo goal from Phelan served as little more than a consolation, but it triggered a pitch invasion which resulted in the referee taking both teams off and the iconic sight of a row of mounted police horses lining up across the north stand penalty area.

Once more, the Blues had snatched embarrassing defeat from the jaws of beckoning success and it signalled a dismal end to yet another season of failure. Gates suffered and there was mounting disquiet as the season petered out to an anonymous end, made even less bearable by United's first league Championship win for over a quarter of a century.

As luck would have it, the final game of the season was a home match with Everton, managed by Howard Kendall, who most of the Blues' support still viewed as a traitor for his defection in 1990. City turned in another dire showing, losing 5-2 to a run-of-the-mill Everton side who exposed the inexperienced goalkeeper Martyn Margetson to the extent that the young Welshman was substituted at half-time on his home debut with the team 3-1 down. The rest of the game was played out to a series of abusive chants demanding that Swales and his board should leave the club immediately, much to the amusement of the Liverpudlians who taunted their hosts about United's success and City's continued failure. Even the normally placid main stand was the scene of discontent as burgers, pies and eggs were launched into the directors' box with Swales as the intended target. The game finished to a cacophony of boos and chants of 'Swales Out!' and 'Sack the board' and the team's traditional lap of honour was cancelled. After the game the police had to disperse a gathering of Blues outside the main entrance who waited to subject Swales to further abuse.

The knives were by now well and truly out. Swales was by far the largest shareholder at the club and still had the backing of most of the board. Better still, more financial support for his position was provided by the shareholding of Stephen Boler, a low-profile investor who had propped up the Swales regime for many years. It now dawned on the chairman that his latest managerial appointment had failed and needed replacing.

The close season was marked by a definite breakdown in Swales' relationship with Reid, to the extent that they were hardly speaking. The manager had to upgrade the squad yet again and supplied several lists of transfer targets for the chairman's consideration. Each name was summarily dismissed as being too expensive, and City's only new signing was the little-known Dutch midfielder Alfons Groenendijk for £30,000 from Sparta Rotterdam. Things got even worse for Reid when a story was run in the media that several first-team players had failed to board a plane returning them home from a pre-season tour due to a drinking session at an airport bar. Although the incident had been wildly exaggerated – three players and two of the coaching staff failed to hear the last call to board the plane while they were in a coffee bar and the departure was delayed while they were found – it was seen as evidence that Reid was now incapable of maintaining discipline within his squad and his position was therefore even more hopeless.

Swales decided he needed to act, but his problem was that after having vociferously backed Reid for the previous two years he could not now afford to be openly seen to oppose the manager, or to visibly wield the axe yet again. How then could he sack Reid without being seen to have failed in his choice of manager yet again?

The answer came when Swales remembered a meeting with a former *Sunday People* sportswriter John Maddock, who had been running the sports department of a number of national newspapers. Maddock was appointed as City's general manager with full administrative responsibilities including the power to hire and fire as he saw fit, basically allowing Swales to step back and avoid responsibility for any future failure. More importantly he was used as the last remaining means of official communication between Swales and Reid.

At the press conference to announce his appointment, Maddock made it clear that he was now effectively running the club and he would not hesitate to remove anyone who failed to shape up, a statement which was taken as the first indication that Reid's days at City were numbered in single figures.

The new season began with City producing more abject performances, drawing the first match 1-1 with Leeds but losing the next three. Their showing in the fourth match, a Tuesday night home game against Blackburn, suggested that yet another relegation loomed as the players gave the impression that they were by now incapable of even passing the ball to one another. City lost 2-0 and once more the match ended in abuse aimed at the team, Reid and especially Swales, who was still viewed as being ultimately responsible. Once more, the supporters gathered outside the main entrance and Swales had to wait for a couple of hours before it was deemed safe enough for him to leave the ground. Maddock duly sacked Reid and his assistant Sam Ellis within 48 hours and during the press conference to announce the dismissals, Maddock informed the attendant media that a new and exciting top-class manager would be unveiled within a matter of days. Amid all the resultant speculation, Maddock was seen at Piccadilly station boarding a train for London early the next day, the morning of another home match, this time on Sky TV against Coventry.

City at least produced a better performance under caretaker boss Tony Book and were unlucky to concede a late equaliser in the 1-1 draw. Swales' absence from the boardroom and directors' box was conspicuous, however, as the chairman watched the game with Maddock and former Luton and Brighton skipper Brian Horton. As the fans returned to their cars following the end of the game, the local radio station reported that Horton had been recruited from Oxford United as City's new boss. Word spread and yes, yet another angry demonstration on the Maine Road forecourt ensued, lasting well over an hour before the police dispersed the crowd. Horton, with a reputation for relegating lower league clubs, was seen as an anonymous no-hoper who had no chance of success at City. The fans braced themselves for more failure and the inevitable drop, with 37 league games still to go.

Horton got lucky in that – due to international fixtures – he had almost a fortnight before his first game in charge, a midweek visit to newly-promoted Swindon Town. In interviews he made all the right noises about the opportunity he had been given at City and also about what needed to be done to improve the team's morale and form, but for all the supporters cared he need not have bothered. City fell a goal behind at the County Ground but won 3-1 to give the new boss the start he needed. But the biggest development in the story was still to take place. On the following Monday Alec Johnson of the *Daily Mirror* ran an exclusive report that former City and England legend Francis Lee was launching an £8 million bid to oust Swales and take the club over. The fans could hardly believe it; for the previous few years there had been mutterings in various fanzines that it would need someone like Lee to step up and help the club out financially but nothing ever seemed to come of it. Now at last their hero was standing up to be counted, promising that 'if it is the wish of the supporters and the shareholders, I am prepared to invest substantial funds to assist the club at this moment'.

Lee duly held a press conference at a hotel near his Wilmslow home later that day and the story made the national TV news bulletins. Even a swift rebuttal from Swales and Maddock later that afternoon couldn't dampen the spirits of the supporters, for at long last help was at hand to remove Swales and Maddock and the opportunity was not to be wasted. To all intents and purposes a boardroom war was now under way, there could only be one winner and the supporters decided that the winner must only be Francis Lee. If Swales and his supporters wanted a battle, they would get a rout; it was merely a matter of time.

The fans mobilised through the *Blueprint* and *King Of The Kippax* fanzines, and a sit-down demonstration was arranged for the home match with QPR the following Saturday. Intense media coverage was guaranteed and a huge crowd gathered on the Maine Road forecourt once more, only this time the mood was one of celebration as the fans awaited the arrival of Francis Lee in the warm September sun. Lee was duly mobbed as he struggled to reach the main entrance as a guest of shareholder and former City winger Colin Barlow, and after he disappeared into the foyer the crowd still remained, singing pro-Lee songs and waving double-page photos of Lee provided by the tabloid papers. Swales and Maddock had prepared for such events, however, and put in place their own countermeasures. Prior to kick-off the club had installed large blue advertising hoardings just inside the touchlines, facing the stands and portraying a message from Brian Horton asking for the fans' total support to aid the team. As the ground filled, the diehards on the Kippax terrace amended local band James' recent hit 'Oh sit down, oh sit down, oh sit down, sit down next to me, sit down, down, down, down, dow-ow-own with Franny Lee!' and cheered to the rooftops when the man himself took the acclaim as he made his way to his seat. As far as they were concerned the war had already been won and surely Swales and his regime would crumble.

City comfortably beat QPR 3-0 to the beat of more pro-Lee and anti-Swales chanting throughout the game. Another sit-in was staged on the Kippax terrace for about an hour after the match and I can remember my brother and I taking part and then making our way to the Maine Road forecourt to join in with any further show of support, but finding it surprisingly rather quiet on the western front. No matter, the point had been well and truly made, the team hadn't suffered as a result and we were on the right lines as a great start to the campaign to replace Swales with Lee had been made. Leaflets had been passed around announcing a meeting to inaugurate the 'Forward With Franny' campaign at Sacha's hotel the following Tuesday night. I attended and was surprised to be one of a few fans briefly interviewed in the foyer by Sky Sports News, who seemed more interested in asking me about how I felt about comparing City's misfortunes with United's championship success. Since I was not a satellite TV subscriber at the time, I doubt my response that I wasn't interested in United at all and that Swales' decades of trying to solely outdo the Reds had put the club in this sorry mess in the first place, would have been used. I went on to drinks at the bar and then into the room where the purpose of the campaign, its strategy and plans were to be discussed.

Over the next hour or so I learned quite a bit about the origins of the Lee takeover bid, that he had been interested in offering to lend a financial hand for a few years previously but had been ignored or refused on each occasion, and that the campaign was not funded or run by anyone involved either at Manchester City FC or connected to Francis Lee, his businesses or his family. It transpired that Lee already had a large shareholding in the club which had previously not been widely publicised, but after Swales and Stephen Boler, the next biggest holding belonged to Greenalls Brewery (aha, so that's why they always seemed to get the supplier's contract renewed every few years) and the rest was more or less split between thousands of smaller investors. Swales and Boler's combined share was estimated at being between 60 and 70 per cent, with Greenalls owning a further 25 per cent.

Since Boler had an arrangement that the block vote his holding earned would always be used to support Swales the chairman effectively more than qualified for the 51 per cent majority sharing that the rules stated he must provide to take overall control. Put this way, it seemed that financially ousting Swales was an impossible dream if he or Boler refused to sell up, so the plan was to try and chip away at Boler's holding and convince the other investors, including Greenalls, to back Lee. By now the 'Forward with Franny' campaign was well under way with regular newspaper articles, discussions on local radio, boycotts, bans, protests, public meetings, and visits to supporters clubs with a breakaway independent supporters club being formed.

Support for the fanzines was encouraged and the fanzines themselves were viewed as invaluable publicists for the campaign. Furthermore, if any fans wished to buy voting shares in the club they were encouraged to do so, and to attend the AGM. More fixtures would be used for peaceful demonstrations, with an upcoming home game on Sky against Oldham seen as a prime opportunity. Finally, the supporters' campaign needed funding and any donations at this meeting or in the future would be greatly welcomed. I can vividly recall fanzine editor – and now published writer – Dante Friend summing up the mood by standing up in open forum and declaring 'after almost 20 years of failure, it's time for a change'. The meeting was adjourned and further meetings were arranged.

The club's Annual General Meeting in November was targeted for a concerted attempt to gain financial support and a motion would be proposed that in view of the club's perilous financial position the shareholders no longer wanted Swales to remain as chairman. Non-shareholding fans were also seen as vital in publicising the campaign, but only by peaceful means.

We carried on demonstrating, as the games were played out to a sonic background of 'We want Swales Out!' but the team continued to struggle. November was an especially difficult month, with the derby visit of United and the AGM looming. Predictably, Sky chose the United game for a Sunday live broadcast and extra spice was added by their capitulation in a European home game with Galatasaray the previous Wednesday, as the Reds conceded two late goals to draw a home leg 3-3. At least we had some terrace ammo ready to counter their inevitable taunts about our contrasting fortunes, and to get over the expected annihilation! City famously squandered a two-goal lead to lose in the dying minutes and of the course the 'There's only One Peter Swales' chanting punctuated the course of events.

We just decided that although a relatively small battle had been lost, the war would still be won.

Two weeks later we were stuffed 3-1 by Sheffield Wednesday at home. During the second half a City fan got onto the pitch and tore up his season ticket, dumping it on the ground with his scarf and heading for the exit to the tumultuous applause of the Kippax terrace. 'Swales Out!' was by now running neck-and-neck with 'What The F*ck Is Going On?' as the terrace song of choice and the *Manchester Evening News* highlighted various alleged attempts to physically attack Swales in the directors' box during the match on its front page the following Monday. The paper also reported that a ground closure was inevitable after the club was warned about failing to control its supporters during the FA Cup debacle the previous March. So much for the success of the 'Forward With Franny' campaign. The *Manchester Evening News* City correspondent Paul Hince, a former reserve team player at Maine Road in the 1960s whose pro-Alex Ferguson bias had already planted him in the minds of *most* Blues as an enemy, was therefore deemed persona non grata and a legitimate target for abuse. The paper received many letters of condemnation, not just of Hince and its failure to back the Lee campaign, but also of its anti-City and pro-United editorial policy, with various match reports and biased accounts of campaign activities provided as evidence. The paper responded within a few days by running a front page story claiming that City fans had subjected Swales' mother to abuse and threats of violence at the old people's home she resided at in north Cheshire. Predictably, the national tabloid press picked up and amplified the story, but a report on the BBC's local radio station featured an interview with the matron denying that anyone had in fact turned up at the home, much less threatened any of the residents either inside or outside the premises. The *Manchester Evening News* was, therefore, added to the list of Swales sympathisers to be boycotted, including his TV and audio business Yeoman and Russell. Lee's group continued to publicly demand that they be shown the books in order to assess the true financial state of the club, but the board refused each time, insisting the books would only be opened after completion of any deal to buy the club outright.

The fanzines continued to play their part in the campaign. *BluePrint* ran various updates on its progress and added a 'Forward With Franny'/'Backwards With Swales' strap across each front cover. *King of the Kippax* did likewise and Noel Bayley's excellent *Bert Trautmann's Helmet* continued to print various anti-Swales articles, pointing out that it has consistently called for Swales to go since its birth in 1989. All three however ran articles stating that the anti-Swales singing had created for a poor atmosphere at matches and that henceforth such chants when the team was actually on the pitch should be avoided, in an effort to improve morale and results.

King of the Kippax's financial expert, the accountant Paul Stanley, was present to report on the AGM, but for once his efforts were superfluous as even brief reference to the events in the City Social Club made the national TV news accompanied by footage of a decidedly frail-looking Swales shuffling into the venue on his customary Cuban heels.

The most eagerly-awaited AGM in the club's recent history was a fairly explosive affair (though the *King Of The Kippax* editor was banned by the club from attending) with Swales, Maddock and the board holding court and trying to avoid eye contact with Lee, who remained silent throughout, electing for the fans to do his talking and questioning for him. A motion to be decided by a show of hands vote proposed that Swales was no longer capable of continuing as chairman and that he should step down and sell up immediately (no-one was proposed as a replacement).

Swales was almost unanimously defeated, but responded by proposing a similar motion to be decided by a block vote proportional to the number of shares held. Of course he won hands down, but announced that he would step down as chairman due to ill health whilst still retaining his shareholding in the club. The outraged supporters viewed this as nothing more than a two-fingered salute, determining that the away League Cup tie at Nottingham Forest would be the next event at which anti-Swales campaigning would be stepped up.

For City fans any game in Nottingham is almost a guaranteed great day out, with plenty of watering holes available in north Derbyshire for stops along the way and many fan-friendly pubs in the city happy to take our cash. Even though the Cup-tie was held on a freezing Wednesday night it was well attended with the new away end virtually sold out. My brother hired a minibus for about a dozen of us to go to the game in, and after parking up near to the ground we were allowed to hunt down a suitable bar in which to refuel in readiness for the game. We passed pub after pub with the 'full' signs up as we headed away, finally finding a noisy one on the main road which still seemed to be admitting visitors. Once inside, we found it packed to the rafters with City fans dancing on the tables, blasting the air with anti-Swales and pro-Lee singing. A few beers and back up the road for the game. Plenty more of the same, until the teams came out to kick off, then as directed in the fanzines and elsewhere, 101 per cent support for a poor City facing a Forest side a division below them. Goalless and tedious, but a replay and a quick night drive home. Having stopped off at one of our familiar watering holes on the outskirts of Nottingham for last orders, a Forest fan tells me we've been the best support he's seen in years because we kept it up all game long and turned the protests off when the game was on.

It was still a stalemate on the takeover as we went into December, and then suddenly the board announced that talks were at an advanced stage with a consortium not involving anyone from Francis Lee's group and an announcement would be made shortly. On the face of it, the board were keeping up the appearance of making sure the fans and shareholders were the first to know about any possible takeover, but in truth it was yet another thumbing of the nose to the Lee consortium and the fans; basically the message was 'anyone but Franny Lee'. It transpired that Mike McDonald, a Manchester scrap metal millionaire, had approached the board and his bid was given careful consideration to the extent that several meetings had taken place.

City continued to struggle in the League and lost the League Cup replay against Forest. There was still no news as the new year approached, and a home League game against Ipswich was abandoned while Lee took his customary family holiday in Barbados. Then, just when it seemed the campaign had stalled, local radio station BBC GMR reported on the first Friday in February that Swales and the board were in final negotiations with Francis Lee's consortium about buying a controlling interest in the club.

As things turned out, the meeting was adjourned and re-opened at several venues throughout the day and into the night, finally being concluded in the early hours of Saturday morning at a hotel near Wilmslow. Having jetted back to England less than 24 hours before, Francis Lee was the new chairman of Manchester City, with a controlling interest in the club. John Maddock was immediately dismissed and replaced by Colin Barlow as Chief Executive.

City fans woke up on Saturday morning, the day of the rearranged home match with Ipswich, to learn the news. The war was over, and we had won. Thanks for twenty years Mr Swales, now close the door on the way out.

It was party time at Maine Road, with a big red bag of balloons in the centre circle and a ball boys' parade holding a 'Welcome Francis' banner. Shortly before the teams came out for the game, Lee took the acclaim in the directors' box, wearing a sky blue and white pinstriped shirt, blue tie and light blue jacket. Let the good times roll. Funny how no-one had informed Ipswich or Garry Flitcroft of the script though, as the young City midfielder put through his own goal to dampen proceedings. No matter, as a piece of incredible skill on the right wing from David Rocastle released Carl Griffiths to score the first goal of the new era. Flitcroft added another in the second half and the Blues were up and running with their first win for two months, having been dumped out of the FA Cup at Cardiff the week before. The air reverberated to the old City battle hymns of the Mercer-Allison years a quarter of a century before as renewed optimism that we could somehow escape the drop surfaced once more.

Results soon went on the slide again, with only one more win – over doomed Swindon – until Easter. Lee had promised substantial investment, hadn't he? So where were the new players to keep us up and move us forward? The answer lay in three signings which proved to be crucial. Paul Walsh was signed from Portsmouth for a nominal fee, to be quickly followed by East German striker Uwe Rösler, who went straight into the first team after scoring twice in the first twenty minutes of his reserve team debut. Both were willing workers, but neither could find the net.

A supply line was needed and on transfer deadline day at the end of March speculation was rife that Anders Limpar was on his way from Arsenal to provide the ammo for the new strike force.

In fact, the Swede joined Everton but this freed up the Toffees' Peter Beagrie to move to Maine Road for £1 million. He provided both goals for Walsh and Rösler in a 2-2 draw at Ipswich, and the Blues then won their next three games against Villa, Southampton and Newcastle to climb out of the relegation zone. What had seemed impossible jut a couple of weeks before now looked to be well and truly on as the Blues secured three points from the last four games to save themselves, the penultimate game being an emotional affair against Chelsea as it was the last match in front of the Kippax terrace, to be replaced under the requirements of the Taylor Report.

On a day of celebration at Maine Road, Lee and Barlow took their places amongst a parade of City legends and the Blues stormed back from being two down to earn a point. The job had been well and truly done, and with less than half of the season to achieve it in. As over 15,000 City fans streamed away from Hillsborough on the last day there was genuine hope for the next season in the air. City were safe, Swales was gone and the team now had a few new exciting players playing attacking football. The long months of campaigning and crossing fingers had finally paid off. Surely it was now only a matter of time before the glory days were back for good?

History, of course, tells us a different story. Immediately after taking over, Lee and Barlow realised that the true financial meltdown the club was facing had been hidden away from them. The chairman later remarked that had he known when launching his bid what he found out in the first month of his leadership he would never have become involved in the first place. He said there were still certain people doing the same jobs they'd done when he'd left the club as a player two decades before, and some of them were on more or less the same wages as well. The facilities were dreadful and in dire need of an upgrade, but the most pressing matter was the replacement of the 17,000-capacity Kippax terrace. The longest terraced stand in the country, its covered section ran the full length of the touchline and included triangular corners where it met the North and Platt Lane Stands.

The previous regime had published plans for a new two-tiered stand in the programmes from half of the home matches, but Lee had said that the design that Swales' board had agreed to was inadequate.

Planning permission had already been granted and legally-binding demolition and construction contracts signed however, so Lee was forced into the first of many compromises during his reign. Various administrative changes were made, but things tended to carry on as most people employed by the club were on long-term contracts that the already cash-strapped Blues would have been sued out of sight for if they had terminated the contracts. With the new season's capacity reduced to around 24,000 every last penny had to be spent properly and there was no margin for error.

City started the new season well, retaining Horton as manager and adding Nicky Summerbee, the son of Lee's City and England colleague Mike, on the right wing. The return of Niall Quinn from a cruciate knee injury meant the Blues had options up front and were as high as fourth in the table before losing Beagrie to a hairline shin fracture two weeks before Christmas.

Despite reaching the fifth round of the FA Cup and the quarter-finals of the League Cup, City fell away badly in the League and faced yet another relegation scrap. Once more, they saved themselves with two Easter wins, beating Liverpool 2-1 on Good Friday and twice coming from behind to win at eventual champions Blackburn at a rain-soaked Ewood Park on Easter Monday evening. City had the chance of finishing ninth in the League but a 3-2 home defeat by QPR left them two places above the drop zone in the final table. Two days later, Horton was unceremoniously sacked.

The 1995 close season was almost completely taken up by a frantic search for a new manager and proved to be the first real test of Lee's chairmanship: could he attract a big-name manager to drag City up the table and bring the much longed-for success the fans still dreamed of? Name after name was suggested, from Franz Beckenbauer to Spanish coach Arsenio Iglesias (some wag even suggested that one-time Real Madrid reserve goalkeeper and singer Julio Iglesias might be on his way to Moss Side!) and the summer months dragged by.

Then, with less than a month until the new season started, Alan Ball was unveiled as City's new manager, to the dismay of the supporters far and wide, because they perceived that one relegation specialist had simply been replaced by another on the cheap, with the desperate Blues facing the start of the season with no leadership. Ball failed to ingratiate himself with his players and moved most of the senior players on or fell out with the others. City produced their worst-ever start in the top flight, taking a solitary point from their first nine games.

Georgian midfielder Georgiou Kinkladze had arrived on the day that Ball's inaugural press conference was held and at first struggled to make an impact. At one point City lost a League Cup tie 4-0 at Liverpool, only to be humiliated 6-0 at the same venue just four days later. Ball tactlessly admitted to enjoying the game, meaning he'd admired Liverpool's ruthless performance, but the long-suffering fans who had sarcastically sung 'Alan Ball Is A Football Genius' during the game weren't fooled; unless a dramatic change took place the Blues were already doomed.

Typically, City confounded the critics and their own supporters by winning four of their next five games in November and drawing the other. Amazingly, Ball had collected the Manager of the Month award, but of course it couldn't last as only five more wins were achieved throughout the rest of the season.

On the last day of the season, City faced a weakened Liverpool side preoccupied with the following week's FA Cup final, knowing that subject to results elsewhere a draw might be enough to stay up and a win might not be sufficient to save themselves. A poignant minute's silence was held prior to kick-off in memory of Peter Swales, who had passed away in the week leading up to the game. As part of Lee's takeover deal Swales was granted free entry to all of City's home games for the rest of his life, but declined to return to

Maine Road. City missed a couple of chances early in the game and by half-time were 2-0 down and all but buried. A rousing all-or-nothing second half performance ensued as Liverpool slackened off and Rösler's penalty offered hope.

A Kit Symons equaliser raised optimism even higher as news filtered through that at least one of the other strugglers was losing, so a point would be enough. Northern Ireland midfielder Steve Lomas tried to keep the ball at the corner flag to use up time, but substituted forward Niall Quinn rushed down the touchline to tell him that a win was still needed. The game finished as a 2-2 draw and the other results confirmed what most of us had known since the early weeks of the season; City were relegated and Ball had struck again.

It was a personal disaster for Lee, since his first managerial appointment had already resulted in a desperate failure. Vital income from maintaining Premiership status had been surrendered and high wage-earners were sold off to balance the books. Ball kept his job, but Lee gave the club's official magazine an exclusive interview in which he stated that the time for talking was over, the manager had to get results quickly and bring the Blues up at the first attempt or face the consequences.

City played the first game of the new season on a Friday night at home to Ipswich for the Sky TV cameras. Kinkladze's magic created the only goal of the game for Lomas but the East Anglians were unlucky to at least get a point. City followed this up with dismal defeats at eventual runaway champions Bolton and Ball's old club Stoke.

During the second half of the Victoria Ground capitulation both home and away supporters joined in with sustained anti-Ball taunting and in his post-match press conference

Ball had the audacity to publicly blame the *Evening News* City writer Paul Hince for the problems at the club, claiming the columnist's negative coverage had stirred the fans up against the manager. Well, that and the fact that we were absolute garbage, eh Alan?

News filtered through on the following Tuesday morning that Ball had left City by mutual consent. The Blues were already showing signs that they would struggle in this division as well so Lee and his board had no option but to try a new man at the helm. Four embarrassing months followed in which George Graham and Dave Bassett were publicly approached but turned the job down, Bassett even agreeing to come to Manchester but backing out at the last minute when he saw his Crystal Palace side murder City 3-1 and the Blues then lost 4-1 in the League Cup at third division Lincoln. Steve Coppell took over but sensationally quit for personal reasons just 33 days later, leaving his assistant Phil Neal in charge.

The odd win here and there was offset by some dreadful defeats and, by Christmas, City were once more trying to stave off relegation. Tranmere Rovers' 2-1 November win at Maine Road had seen a post-match demonstration outside the main entrance in scenes reminiscent of two seasons before. These were repeated after a Boxing Day home defeat at the hands of Port Vale, and by the time Barnsley had embarrassed us 2-0 at Oakwell the final straw had been placed as the City fans sang 'I'd rather be in Barnsley than Barbados', a reference to Lee's annual holiday taken at a time when the Blues were at their lowest ebb for over thirty years.

Neal pleaded with the board to do something and what happened next was momentous. The ex-Liverpool skipper was replaced as manager by former Nottingham Forest captain and manager Frank Clark.

As with Brian Horton, Clark was lucky in that his first game, a tricky New Year's Day visit to Birmingham, was postponed thus allowing him a full week to install his backroom team, get to know his new squad and bring in a few new faces. Majority shareholders John Wardle and David Makin, owners of the JD Sports high street chain, underwrote a £10 million share issue to keep the club going and enable Clark to deal in the transfer market. Players came and went and Clark enjoyed success, dragging the Blues up the table and into the fifth round of the FA Cup, where they unluckily lost by the odd goal to eventual finalists Middlesbrough. City's rise up the table gave fresh hope of a late push into the play-off positions, but late-season defeats by Bolton, Birmingham and Ipswich put paid to a quick return to the Premiership as City finished in the bottom half of the table. Nevertheless, optimism rose for a renewed promotion effort in the new season.

Reshaped by Clark and wearing a new laser blue strip, City started the 1997/98 season as favourites for promotion, but what followed was arguably a watershed in the club's history.

They failed to win during the first month and were dumped out of the League Cup at the first attempt by Blackpool. Despite thrashing Swindon 6-0, another slide down the table occurred and City were once more in dire danger of relegation.

A late November visit to newly-promoted neighbours Stockport County offered a chance to turn things round, but with the Blues 3-0 down early the fans finally lost patience with Clark and skipper Symons, who was substituted long before the interval.

Lee also suffered the supporters' wrath at a fiery AGM, and by now the knives were out, just as they had been for Swales four years earlier, Dante Friend being instrumental in forming a 'Free the 30,000' protest group. Still in the relegation zone at the end of January and out of the FA Cup, another local derby at home to promoted opposition in Bury brought matters to a head. The Shakers easily outclassed a dreadful City side who were far worse than the 1-0 scoreline suggested.

Demonstrations against Clark, Lee, Barlow and anyone else within firing range continued beyond the final whistle, with season tickets and club mementoes being tossed onto the pitch. Some form of dignity was maintained when the Bury side were sportingly applauded as they took the acclaim from their own fans, but after the game yet another fierce demonstration ensued on the Maine Road forecourt.

Amongst the mayhem David Makin rang BBC GMR's post-match radio phone-in and promised that change was imminent within the next few days. He was as good as his word for, on the following Tuesday, Clark was sacked without ceremony and immediately replaced on the morning of a midweek home game with Ipswich by Joe Royle, who had famously reneged on an agreement to manage City in December 1989.

Royle was left with just 11 games to save City from dropping into the third tier of English football for the only time in their history. Lee had been under siege within the boardroom for months: first his business partner John Dunkerley stepped down from the board due to ill health, then Colin Barlow was dismissed as Chief Executive. Finally, Lee himself was persuaded to step down in favour of David Bernstein, chairman of the French Connection high street clothing chain and a lifelong City fan to boot.

A mixed bag of results left the Blues in the bottom three on the morning of the last game, at Stoke City. As with the situation two years previously, City could win and still go down, but paradoxically a draw might just be enough to save their skins. The Blues destroyed Stoke 5-2, but once again results elsewhere sent them down long before the end of the game.

The fans' by now famous gallows humour surfaced once more as, realising that the drop was now inevitable, they sang 'Are you watching, Macclesfield?' while the Blues ran up their best away win of the season. At the final whistle Royle stood opposite the corner of the away end and applauded the travelling support. They acknowledged his efforts, recognising that if anything he'd been brought in far too late to stave off the inevitable.

But what of Lee? During his resignation speech he revealed that his health had deteriorated during the second half of his time as chairman, and he didn't want his family to see him suffer any longer. His tone was almost apologetic as he then thanked the fans for their support, somewhat ironically since he had been subjected to the same level of vilification that his predecessor had endured, and wished his successor Bernstein the best for the future, reminding everyone that as a City fan himself he wished nothing but success for the club dearest to his heart. He returned to his Stanneylands home near Wilmslow and continues his interests in racehorses to this day.

Time has proven to be a great healer both for Lee and the City faithful, as his difficulties during his spell as chairman have done nothing to diminish the esteem he earned as one of the club's greatest-ever players.

Lee was warmly greeted when taking part in the Parade of

Legends immediately prior to the final Maine Road game in May 2003 and when taking part in a pre-match memorial to former City skipper Roy Paul at a recent FA Cup tie at the City of Manchester Stadium. He was also one of the very first players to be voted into the club's Hall of Fame in 2004.

At first glance Lee's legacy was poor, failing to deliver on his promise to improve the team with better players and to avoid relegation, culminating in the drop into the third tier of English football in 1998. However, look a little deeper and much of what can be recognised as successful at Manchester City today was created on the insistence of Francis Lee. Having seen Manchester United pick the cream of Greater Manchester's youth talent for half a decade, Lee campaigned for the FA to grant City official Youth Academy status, allowing them the facilities to attract and groom the stars of the future. It took a few years, but the likes of Shaun Wright-Phillips, Joey Barton, Stephen Jordan, Nedum Onouha, Willo Flood, Lee Croft, Bradley Wright-Phillips and Stephen Ireland have all come through the Academy, and most of these names have gone on to establish themselves as first-team regulars.

Shaun Wright-Phillips was eventually sold to Chelsea in 2005 for a club record fee of £21 million, easily eclipsing the previous record fee received of £6 million for Nicolas Anelka six months earlier. Micah Richards was recruited from Oldham Athletic but was also brought up through the club's youth system. City's Academy sides have challenged for their league titles regularly over the last five years or so and this year narrowly lost out in the FA Youth Cup final over two legs. Many players have graduated to the first team, saving the club who knows how much revenue in transfer fees, money that would be lost to Manchester City.

In addition, Lee was unlucky in that his takeover coincided with an expensive and urgent project to replace the Kippax Stand terrace and bring Maine Road into compliance with the recommendations of the Taylor Report. Initially, he opposed the plans for the stand which was originally planned, but when it became clear that the existing plans had to go ahead he commissioned a greater plan to completely redesign Maine Road as a 48,000-capacity stadium with unrestricted views and the very best facilities.

Realising that the funds for such a scheme were unobtainable, he proposed that City should apply to Manchester City Council and Sport England with a plan to move into the stadium that would be built after Manchester was awarded the 2002 Commonwealth Games. As a result, City now play their home games at a state-of-the-art 21st century stadium with a 48,000 capacity and containing the very best facilities for the players, staff, spectators, media and corporate visitors.

In effect, the plan for Maine Road has been achieved at a site earmarked for urban regeneration in Manchester, leaving a legacy for the city that will last for centuries. At some time in the distant future, ownership of the stadium will pass to the club, which already pays Manchester City Council a premium on all League match attendances above the 34,000 gate City averaged during their last season at Maine Road.

For all the short-term failings of his chairmanship and the risk of the club going out of business, Francis Lee's short tenure has at least provided the basis for a better long-term future for the club, something which his predecessor sadly could not claim.

MANCHESTER CITY FC – THE ONE THAT WENT WRONG

Eamonn Monks saw his first Manchester City game on a rainy Grand National Day in 1972. It was the visit of Bobby Moore and West Ham United, who have become his favourite 'other' team in the process. City won 3-1 in a game dominated by Rodney Marsh during his early days at the club, and if memory serves him right it was the day the Kippax adopted Chicory Tip's Son Of My Father *as a terrace anthem to commemorate a typically brilliant Marsh performance.*

Derby days, European nights and many relegation or promotion battles followed. £10 (!!) for his first junior Season Ticket in the Platt Lane Stand for 1977–78, how times have changed – the same amount wouldn't get you a junior seat for most single games today...

Nowadays – for reasons of cost – he has to carefully pick and choose his games but still gets along to see the Blues whenever possible. Players, managers, chairmen – and even the ground! – may come and go but the love is still (amazingly) strong.

CHAPTER 11

MANCHESTER UNITED FC – NO TO GLAZER!

BY PAUL EDMUNDSON

IN THE LAZY July heat of 2003, Russian billionaire Roman Abramovich finalised a deal that would see him take over as the owner of Chelsea in a money-spinning deal that would change the face of top-flight English football. Up until then, the Stamford Bridge club had struggled to compete with the cream of English football. In fact, they could barely keep up with London rivals West Ham and Tottenham and, though they had brought home four major trophies in the previous decade, they hadn't landed the championship since 1955.

That lack of success went some way towards explaining exactly why there was absolutely no protest against the concept of a 'unit buyer' (that is, an entrepreneur with a purely financial, rather than emotional, interest in his investment) clutching control of their club. Sure, such a huge takeover deal raised eyebrows at the Football Association and among financial onlookers, but the supporters sat by without any exploration of just what this stranger had planned for their club. In any case, if that question had been asked, it would have been answered within days as the Damien Duffs and the Petr Cechs began rolling into the Chelsea squad, transforming a once average outfit into one of English football's genuine big boys.

With that in mind, let us rewind the clock 105 years to a time when, 185 miles north, 13-year-old Newton Heath battled bankruptcy and faced a real threat of going out of business, like so many other clubs did in their fledging years at the turn of the century.

Step forward John Henry Davies, a wealth brewery owner who bought out Newton Heath. He gave the club a massive cash injection, which turned around the team's fortunes and allowed new manager J. Ernest Magnall to bring in Welsh striker Billy Meredith – one of football's first ever 'celebrity' stars.

As club president, Mr Davies made two other legendary changes, scrapping the green-and-yellow club colours in favour of a red-and-white kit. He also got rid of the club's title, and replaced it with a name now familiar all around the world – Manchester United.

Far from a unit buyer, Mr Davies was something of a philanthropist, keen on promoting the good things football could do for the masses. He paid for the construction of the 70,000-capacity Old Trafford in 1910, for example, without which, Manchester would be a little less united. James Gibson, his son Alan, and Martin Edwards went on to own the club through most of the 20th century, until 1991, when Edwards floated it on the stock exchange and it became a public limited company (PLC). In the two decades leading up to this floatation, the whole mood around Old Trafford slowly changed, both on and off the field.

United fans – and players – lived in the shadow of rivals Liverpool and Arsenal for some two decades, but under a resilient Alex Ferguson's reign, the tide turned. After finishing Division One runners-up in 1989, success opened the floodgates and brought with it trophies in droves.

Not only that, the hooligan element that began in the 1970s forced football to evolve from a mere weekend leisure pursuit to a fierce territorial battleground and, as terrace fighting evolved during the Thatcher years, United's firm, the Red Army, gained prominence and got in regular scraps with arch rivals Liverpool and Manchester City. This success and tribal pride made reds much more confident as the 1990s approached and they began to fend off banter from their long trophy-less neighbours from Maine Road, while taking pride in what the club stood for – what it meant to be a Stretford Ender. As the famous song goes 'we'll beat 'em at home and we'll beat 'em away, we'll kill any bastards who get in our way'.

The formation of fanzines such as *Red News* in 1987, *United We Stand* in 1989 and *Red Issue* not long before, gave fans a forum to voice their thoughts, concerns and protest plans, should the need arise. This new-found passion and feeling of power snowballed even more in 1989 when Michael Knighton came on the Old Trafford scene. Before Edwards transformed the club into a PLC (retaining a 14 per cent stake), Knighton offered £20million for Manchester United and Edwards accepted.

But the deal collapsed when Knighton's backers pulled out – much to the relief of loyal reds, who grimaced at the site of Knighton doing kick ups on their precious Old Trafford surface in a symbolic act of power – an iconic gesture similar to that repeated 16 years later by the Glazer family, although that was met with a much more animated reaction, as we will later see.

The Knighton takeover attempt came in the same year as the Hillsborough disaster, in which 96 people tragically died after a deadly crush of spectators cramming into Sheffield Wednesday's ground to watch an FA Cup semi-final between Liverpool and Nottingham Forest. This, in turn, lead to the Taylor Report, which ruled amongst other things that all clubs in the top two English divisions must have all-seater stadia. A directive that provided as clear an indication as any to the fans that their game was changing forever.

Loyal reds who had been watching football at low cost for decades soon found themselves having to buy tickets for games in advance. A development which made it increasingly difficult for groups of mates to congregate but which also forbade them from standing at matches at all.

Not surprisingly, this more 'civilised' environment, with no troublemakers on the terrace, comfortable seats under shelter and the luxury of being able to arrive as near as you like to kick-off, soon began to attract more families on match-days. By the time Rupert Murdoch – never one to miss a business opportunity – threw BSkyB's hat into the ring in 1992, a move which ultimately led to the creation of the all-singing all-dancing Premier League, Old Trafford provided a readymade advertisement to be piped into millions of middle-class homes showing just what top-level football was really all about.

But by now, United's traditional fanbase had started to notice a dramatic change in their match-day experience. As more families came to games, ticket prices increased, as did the cost of merchandise. More insulting for most was the presence of extra security guards to stop fans standing up during games, even though they had done so for years. While all of this was a slap in the face to veterans who had enjoyed the under-regulated 1970s era, they were quick to realise that these hideous changes would be the very things that would pull in the moneymakers keen to exploit this wonderful new market. You may ask whether that would be a bad thing? Why would it be so terrible if Johnny Moneybags rolled into the Old Trafford boardroom and took charge, pumping in money to improve the squad? In many people's eyes the PLC setup wasn't ideal, but it was the fairest system around at the time.

After all, in theory anyone could be a shareholder and a large group of shareholders could hold paid employees accountable at Annual General Meetings (AGMs). While a large percentage of shareholders would be supporters, even unit investors would be keen to protect their cash by stocking up the manager's coffers so there was more success on the field and future shareholder dividends. In short, the relatively communal approach meant that no one would lose out and no one person could take control.

A private owner, meanwhile, could come in, raise ticket prices, scrap all lines of supporter/club communication and even sell Old Trafford, while millions of reds worldwide stood powerless on the sidelines. That was the worst-case scenario and it was one the loyal 'old guard' supporters were determined to prevent. From that point on they kept one eye on what was happening on the pitch, and the other on all the match-day changes going on behind the scenes as savvy entrepreneurs, like Knighton and Murdoch, tried, and failed, to seize their club from right under their noses.

Knighton wasn't the first to attempt this coup. Media mogul Robert Maxwell had also failed to prise the club from

Edwards in 1984 and, unsurprisingly, Murdoch wanted to outdo his greatest rival by getting his hands on the biggest club in England.

At this point, it's worth explaining the timescale in which Manchester United supporters played out their part in what turned out to be a 17-year long war to halt their beloved team's fall from community grace to mass commercialism and, ultimately, private ownership by a unit buyer. It was almost a full decade after Knighton's attempt before Murdoch put his takeover battle plan into action. And it was another seven years before another unit buyer, American business tycoon Malcolm Glazer, succeeded where Murdoch, Knighton and Maxwell failed.

But in all that time in between, the Stretford End guard never dropped. United fans were always aware something could happen and were never naive enough to believe for a second the PLC system would be in place forever. The suspicion among the hardcore fans never stopped, even though it would have been easy for fans to down arms and be blinded by the on-the-pitch success Fergie's new breed was enjoying. Home-grown players like David Beckham, Paul Scholes, Nicky Butt and brothers Gary and Phil Neville, were combining with the cream of world football, including Eric Cantona and Peter Schmeichel to help United dominate competitions in England and Europe. The reds were crowned domestic champions eight times between 1993 and 2003, FA Cup winners four times in the same period and, infamously, they achieved one of the club's highest honours in 1999, when Schmeichel and Ferguson lifted the European Champions Cup in Barcelona, achieving the treble.

However, rather than be sidetracked by this now legendary triumph, the troops mobilised to stop another unit buyer coming along or at least, to be prepared when it did. One of the most significant points of this mobilisation came in April 1995 when, during a match against Arsenal, the Old Trafford public address system ordered those in the K-Stand to sit down or be thrown out. The move appalled fans who used notorious fanzines like *Red Issue* and *United We Stand* as a forum to appeal to fellow reds to find a better way for the club to address these issues.

The calls for action led to an infamous meeting in the Gorse Hill Hotel, Manchester, attended by what become known as 'The Dirty Dozen' (well-known fans, fanzine editors, fans' author Richard Kurt, local football figures like Manchester FSA chairman Johnny Flacks and others). It was at that point the Independent Manchester United Supporters Association (IMUSA) was born.

This fledgling gathering led to a public meeting at Manchester's Free Trade Hall on 22 April 1995, where more than 200 fans turned up to suggest campaign ideas and get the ball rolling.

Soon after, IMUSA elected a committee, with Andy Walsh as chairman, and adopted a constitution, which promoted ideas like getting as many United fans as possible to become IMUSA members, establishing a dialogue with those in charge of the PLC and to promote and maintain the history and independence of Manchester United.

Traditionally, such supporters clubs' armed with no more influence than being able to get the odd bundle of match tickets have been 'in-house' and, therefore, controlled by the club. In these cases, clubs rarely sought supporters' opinions, and when they do, it comes across as little more than an empty PR stunt.

Indeed, the English football authorities have also followed

this pattern in the latest decade. The only real effort they –
and the government – have made to let fans speak was in
bringing in the Football Task Force, which staged a series of
public meetings around the country in 1998. Little of what
supporters requested was implemented.

The idea behind IMUSA was simple: Manchester United
gets rich off the fans, so if enough fans become IMUSA
members, the PLC must listen to its views. To a certain
extent, it succeeded during the PLC years at Old Trafford.
During its first full season, IMUSA was heavily involved
with the Busby Memorial fund, which culminated in the
unveiling of a statue above the stadium's players' entrance in
tribute to the great man, who survived the Munich Air
Crash, led United to glory as manager in the 1968 European
Cup and sadly passed away in January 1994, aged 85.

IMUSA also gained the club's support for the staging of
'flag day' on which match-going fans would bring banners to
create a special festival atmosphere at certain matches during
the season.

On a more practical note, the group campaigned to
politicians and UEFA for reds to get more tickets for a
European away game against Porto in Portugal, and
persuaded the powers that be to let 5,000 more Manchester
United supporters travel to the game.

IMUSA also got behind those supporters who, after that
initial baptism of fire announcement at the 1995 Arsenal
game, were ejected from the ground simply for standing up
and supporting their team. The group earned a reprieve
for some 40 or so supporters who had been handed
banning orders.

It rallied for the creation of a West Stand Tier 2 at Old
Trafford, which, once in place, became a popular end for

old-guard supporters without season tickets who may have been lodged out of the Stretford over the years.

So how did IMUSA achieve all this?

Back in 1995, it could have gone two ways: the democratic way it did, with fans getting more of a voice than they had previously been given, or it could have become a much more confrontational situation with stand offs between stewards and supporters refusing to sit down at games. In order to restore calm and normality at home games, the PLC were willing to show they were listening to fans, and so things got done.

With the fanzines on their side, IMUSA had a perfect media setup, through which the leaders could gain feedback from supporters, pitch ideas or voice public concern over dealings at the club. Given the stature of the club, the press were always keen to listen to IMUSA's views and approach its leaders, like former chairman Jules Spencer, for quotes on burning issues surrounding Manchester United. In its first three years, those involved with IMUSA gained strength, confidence and a will to fight using effective democratic means; qualities the group would need in September 1998.

As the team fought to win what would be their fifth championship in seven seasons, the PLC and BSkyB (owned by Murdoch) issued a statement through the stock exchange confirming takeover talks were ongoing.

IMUSA, the fanzines and the supporters were immediately on their guard. They had faced this prospect twice before and fought it off both times. The first being when the resistance was far less organised. Meanwhile, the club's value soared by £123 million overnight as boardroom talks went on. It was just a day after that initial statement when Murdoch tabled a £623 million offer for Manchester United

PLC, which was quickly accepted – threatening the club's plurality of ownership for the first time in almost a decade.

With IMUSA leading the way alongside the newly created Shareholders United Against Murdoch (SUAM), there was an outcry from the fans who decided the best course of action was to lobby the government into referring any takeover to the Office of Fair Trading (OFT) – a request which was granted. The view was that the deal would not be in the public interest, because as BSkyB owner and Manchester United owner, Murdoch could make an offer to televise games and accept it on Manchester United's behalf. Then IMUSA secretary, Gillian Howarth, spoke out against the takeover, arguing that, by accepting the offer, the shareholders would prove they didn't listen to the backbone of the club – the match-going supporters. She joined fellow fans in pledging never to sell her shares as a symbolic protest against unit owners.

Within days of the deal, IMUSA and SUAM had created a protest strategy against Rupert Murdoch to, as Andy Walsh said at the time, 'secure the future of Manchester United'. On its launch day, more than 700 protesters gathered for an anti-takeover rally at Bridgewater Hall in Manchester – an event which gained the support of former United players Brain McClair and Sammy McIlroy. The latter veteran urged the fans to 'band together and try and ensure the club remains the property of genuine fans of Manchester United and not just a commodity to be treated at investor wills'. An appeal raised more than £40,000 for IMUSA's war chest, with even Queen guitarist Roger Taylor chipping in £10,000 towards the cause.

IMUSA and SUAM set about trying to delay the OFT review in order to lobby as many groups as possible on the matter and ask then to write to the Government speaking out against Murdoch's proposition. In fact, so many people wrote to the OFT, its fax machine broke twice and it had to extend its consultation period.

It is interesting at this point to compare the lines of attack used by IMUSA, SUAMA and other pro-supporter campaigners with the more primitive methods employed in the past. Gone are the post-match car park 'out!' songs calling for the head of Supporters Enemy Number One. They have been replaced with a need for fans' representatives to have an in-depth knowledge of legal and financial procedures, like competition law and the stock market and also an ability to utilise modern technology.

Speaking after the Murdoch takeover saga, ex-IMUSA chairman Andy Walsh stressed the influence of protesters' communication via the Internet, describing it as 'vital in pulling together distant resources and researching Murdoch's activities. Thanks to Murdoch's past, plenty of people were willing to assist, especially in the field of sport and the media'.

But IMUSA was also keen to use good old-fashioned publicity stunts to raise the profile of the anti-Murdoch bandwagon. So in the week Peter Mandelson was due to consider the OFT's report on whether the takeover deal should be referred to the Monopolies and Mergers Commission (MMC) people from about 20 clubs visited the House of Commons to lobby MPs – and have a 'jumpers-for-goalposts' kick about outside.

Campaigning went on as men in suits wrote reports and debated the legal pros and cons of allowing a takeover until, eventually, in April 1999, IMUSA discovered they had won their biggest victory to date, as the Department of Trade and

Industry announced they would block Murdoch's takeover.

United supporters had defeated one of the world's most powerful men, even after some observers had earlier described the takeover as inevitable, though others said Murdoch would have almost certainly got his way had it not been for the tireless campaigning of IMUSA and SUAM.

The success was rubber stamped when the OFT announced they would ban any media company from owning more than 9.9 per cent of any football club, thus ensuring the reds – and other clubs – would be permanently safe from media organisations.

But just four years later United realised there was a far greater threat on the horizon in the form of a more potentially dangerous breed of moneymen with their eyes on Old Trafford. Abramovich's takeover of Chelsea proved that English football had entered an age where its clubs appealed to some the world's richest men. So could it happen at United? Ironically, even before moneybags Abramovich had made his grand entrance into Stamford Bridge, things were happening on the Old Trafford stock sheets that would have a massive influence on the club's very existence. In March 2003, American business tycoon Malcolm Glazer bought 2.9 per cent of Manchester United PLC. This may at first seem an odd percentage to purchase, but the American would have been only too aware that, once an investor passes the 3 per cent threshold, they must inform the club of their involvement.

Glazer passed this threshold in September that year, but the move remained beneath the radar of the press until the following March when they cottoned on to the potential importance of Glazer's interest in the club. After all, his past sports business interests included buying out American football team the Tampa Bay Buccaneers. At this point, Glazer's people put out a statement saying they had no interest in buying the club. But a year after buying those first shares, Glazer's stake in the club rose to 20 per cent, raising eyebrows considerably.

By October 2004, a three-way confrontation was looming as Glazer gained control of 30 per cent of the club – the maximum any single investor could have without launching a formal takeover bid. Very much aware of this, the PLC paid close attention to proceedings, while the fans stepped up their action and, in somewhat revolutionary fashion, a new group sprung to fruition – the Manchester Education Committee (MEC). Shrouded in mystery and the source of fascination for loyal reds and football fans everywhere, little is known about the size and resources of the MEC, but on more than one occasion they have shown they are willing to protest.

Like all parties monitoring the Glazer approach, the MEC were only too aware that stock market rules prevented Glazer from slowly increasing his share ownership of Manchester United. In order to progress, he had to persuade remaining shareholders to sell their shares to him. He only had to get his hands on 75 per cent of the club before it would lose its PLC status and oblige the remaining shareholders to cave in and make him the sole owner.

With his new takeover-vehicle company Red Football Ltd, Glazer set his sights on charming Irish racehorse enthusiasts J.P. McManus and John Magnier, who between them owned 28.7 per cent of the club. If they sold up, the rest would follow. So as the season progressed, all eyes were on the Irishmen – and the MEC. Aware of the status quo, the MEC struck tactically, hitting at a target that would make Magnier and McManus sit up and listen – their beloved racehorses.

In January 2004, about 30 activists disrupted a race meeting at Hereford, overpowering the shocked authorities on duty and putting up 'Not For Sale' banners. Afterwards, those in command of the MEC warned of further protests codenamed 'Operation Emily Davison' after the suffragette who grabbed the reins of the king's horse during the Derby in 1911, was trampled and died as a result. MEC had made their mark, but didn't strike again until October of that year. This time, Manchester United itself was the target.

MEC members attended a Manchester United reserve game at Altrincham's Moss Lane ground and staged a direct-action protest against the possibility of a takeover. Released the day after, an MEC statement claimed the protest, in which dozens of people invaded the pitch waving another large 'Not For Sale' banner, was an operation to redress a propaganda imbalance in Manchester United's official television channel, MUTV. The stunt raised the MEC's profile skyward overnight and upped public awareness of fans' opposition to any attempt by a unit owner to buy the club.

But, more alarmingly, the MEC statement released after the event hinted at a far more stark form of protest to come. It read: 'This operation should also serve as a warning to any party interested in taking over Manchester United. The MEC would like to stress that in the event of the wishes of Manchester United supporters being ignored in any takeover situation, that we intend to initiate a civil war effectively setting the football club – the supporters – against the company.

'In such a situation it is our intention to render the club ungovernable and actively disrupt all manner of commercial activity associated with Manchester United. The club's sponsors and commercial partners should note that the MEC will view them as legitimate targets.'

Perhaps this new approach was a reflection of just how desperate the situation could get: Edwards wasn't in control to reject the bid like with Maxwell, Glazer's resources were too vast for his funding to fail, like with Knighton, there was no chance of Government intervention like with Murdoch. This time it was the fans against the would-be owner and, as far as the MEC was concerned, the gloves were off. Meanwhile, Glazer hadn't so much as set foot in the UK, let alone Manchester, so the activities of the MEC were just a tiny distraction to him.

In October 2004, he set about doing what he could to buy up the remaining shares, tabling an offer that was, effectively, a bid for the club. But none of the remaining shareholders took the bait. Glazer hit back with vitriol.

Like Murdoch before him, Glazer and his advisors showed tremendous intelligence in what was essentially a game of high-stakes chess. Murdoch got his takeover campaign under way in September, when Parliament was in recess and fans were enjoying the 1998/99 season honeymoon, so there was little chance of immediate opposition.

Apparently inspired by these clever tactics, Glazer carefully picked the time he took his shareholding about the significant 3 per cent mark and, once at 30 per cent, used his PLC voting powers to oust three board members at the club's annual general meeting, further demonstrating his power and how ruthless he was prepared to be. As Christmas 2004 approached, Glazer revised his bid, but it was again rejected, sparking a third offer two months later, which valued the club at £800million. By April 2005, there was still no movement, until the UK Takeover Panel set Glazer a deadline of 17 May to announce whether he intended to buy the club.

At this point, the stakes were higher than they had ever been since Glazer had arrived on the United scene two years earlier, and the club's 14-year tenure as a PLC looked under more threat than ever. Completely aware of this, more than 5,000 reds marched peacefully on Old Trafford before February's Champions League clash with AC Milan in a well publicised event lead by the fanzines, IMUSA and Shareholders United (SU), which had earlier dropped the 'Against Murdoch' part of its name, and launched a campaign to buy as many Manchester United shares as possible.

A smaller protest had taken place at a league game against Arsenal the previous October and, with SU leading the way, supporters were doing what they could to stop Glazer gaining control. In their determination to do everything possible for the cause, fans wanted to vary their protests as much as possible, moving away from match-day rallies to more devious antics. The first of these took place in the weeks leading up to the huge AC Milan rally, when dozens of reds drove into the Old Trafford car park with their horns blaring and full headlight beams shining, getting their message across loud and clear.

Just three days after that vehicle convoy outing, protesting supporters were again to break new ground for football protests by latching on to a craze sweeping the nation – flash mobbing. This is when organisers arrange for a large crowd to appear out of nowhere in a concentrated area to carry out an act in unison, before it disperses just as quickly.

The beauty of this activity is that it is a lot less likely to draw the attention of police than other direct forms of action, pretty much because there is no illegal activity taking place. You're just simply walking into a shop before walking out and if your activities happen to distract other customers, who is to say you are to blame? Campaigners from a wide range of United groups realised they could easily use flash mobbing to target not Glazer or Manchester United, but the companies they did business with.

Corporate giants like Nike and Vodafone were all seen as fair targets, though on the first United flash mob outing on 12 February 2005, those taking part instead targeted the Manchester city centre branches of bookmakers Ladbrokes and sportswear retailers Allsports.

Amid dramatic scenes, hundreds of participators entered the shops, stood there and then opened up an umbrella before making an exit minutes later. Not only did this send confused customers running out of the door, it also sent out a message to these companies that they had were involved in this battle too.

That flash mob was the only one of its kind before Glazer took over, though a new group, Fight For United (FFU) organised two similar protests in 2006, targeting the Manchester City Centre branch of United's club shirt provider Nike, plastering the interior displays with scores of 'Love United, Hate Glazer' stickers, and again against Ladbrokes – this times at multiple branches – to deprive the firm of as much trade as possible on Grand National Day.

Back in April 2005, Chelsea were fast wrapping up their first title in 50 years, their fans delighted with Abramovich's approach to the club, in sharp contrast to the apparent civil war at Old Trafford. But Chelsea's domination on the domestic front meant the press were ready to thrust full focus on the Glazer issue. And on 12th May 2005, they got their story.

Whether it was down to Glazer's generous offer, the effects of the protest or a desire to be out of the limelight, Magnier and McManus sold their share to the American, effectively making him the owner of Manchester United Football Club. Maxwell, Knighton and Murdoch had all failed. Glazer had not.

Any United fan will tell you that this was one of the saddest days of their footballing past – if not their lives – in direct contrast to memories of the 1999 treble season and achieving five championships under Sir Alex Ferguson.

But perhaps because the reds had never been beaten before and could not, therefore, accept defeat, or contemplate the idea of a unit owner controlling the club whose soul belonged to them, the protests went on. On that sombre day, things began to get ugly and the heat was turned up yet another notch. As news of the buyout filtered through, almost 2,000 United fans descended on Old Trafford, almost like someone – or something – had died.

Fans' representatives gave media interviews, while in the background angry supporters screamed anti-Glazer songs, some of them just on the wrong side of suitable for the pre-watershed news. Other protesters burned effigies of their sworn enemy. Five people were arrested for public order offences that night, with three men charged with the offences. Days later, a hardcore of about 100 of those reds who travelled to Cardiff for the FA Cup final against Arsenal marked the occasion by wearing black clothing. And banners began to emerge carrying heart-wrenching messages like 'Manchester United R.I.P 2005' and, more aggressively, 'Glazer, rot in hell'.

The MEC released another statement in June, warning the 'payback would be immense' against all senior figures in the club for their role in the takeover. It would be fair to say those involved, like Magnier and McManus, at times had to look over their shoulders during this tense period but, ultimately, action failed to materialise. That is, with the notable exception of the events on 30 June 2005.

What started as just a normal working day in the summer, fast turned into one of the most violent days in United's long history. One thing reds' protest groups are not short of is good communication links and they came into play more than ever around midday when whispers began to come out about a possible Glazer visit to Old Trafford. As the afternoon went on, the rumours turned to more solid convictions, and names and times were given as the word spread far and wide via the Internet across Manchester and beyond, translating into a physical presence of 300 supporters on Sir Matt Busby Way, in the afternoon.

Their intelligence report had been right. Joel, Avi and Bryan Glazer were in town to size up daddy's new toy and my, what a welcome they received. As the brothers toured the stadium, those that had gathered pelted police with missiles while others built makeshift barriers and roadblocks in a bid to pen in the Glazer brothers. The group was so well organised, it took more than a hundred Greater Manchester Police officers to gain control using dogs and batons. In the end, the only way the Glazers could get out safely was via a police riot van flanked by a massive escort and a show of force from scores of officers.

For some entrepreneurs, such an experience would be enough to put them off their investment, but the Glazers dug in and stood their ground with the sons visiting more often and given a less frosty reception as the 2005/06 season progressed.

Meanwhile, the troops that had lost their battle in the summer were regrouping in another part of Manchester, ready for the next phase. In the previous 12 months, various groups and individuals representing the club's supporters had tried every form of protest they knew: share-buying, pre-match protests, flash-mobbing, pitch invasions, horseracing sabotage and much more besides.

But there was one route they hadn't gone down – a 'Plan B' route that had been first suggested six years earlier – a plan that most probably would have been implemented if Rupert Murdoch had become Manchester United's new owner.

Only a chosen few were aware of this plan until mid-June 2005, when the *News of the World* broke a story on its back page revealing the blueprint, and getting it scarily accurate. It reported how respected United fans were planning to create their own football team and break away from Manchester United, in a bid to start afresh, creating the utopia they craved and seeing what would happen.

The idea stunned fans who had been campaigning hard for months only to lose their club to an American – they had lost, but here was a chance of a silver lining.

Despite this new wave of enthusiasm, nothing happened. There was no word from any fans' groups or anyone else on whether these rumours were true. By July, there was still no news.

Then, a website – fc-utd.co.uk – appeared out of nowhere and gained massive exposure just days after its creation. It was subtle, filled with little content, but the message to readers was there in red, black and white: the people of

Manchester were to get another football club – FC United of Manchester.

Behind the plan were veteran United campaigners. People like Andy Walsh, a spokesperson for IMUSA since its formation and a former chairman of the group, and Jules Spencer, who joined Walsh on the 16-man FC United steering committee, as did other loyal reds like Luke Zentar and John Paul O'Neill.

By mid-July, things had progressed at an astounding rate, with interested parties being invited to donate cash to the club in return for founder membership, the announcement that the team had been accepted to play in the Moore and Construction Solicitors' North West Counties League Division Two (ten divisions below Manchester United), the appointment of a manager, Karl Marginson and the staging of player trials, as well as the organisation of the club's first ever game.

It is worth mentioning at this point that, one of the reasons the club's formation was possible was due to the way those 16 'in-the-know' campaigners handled it. They showed that the way to achieve such a massive goal was to keep everything under wraps. Diligence, which kept them out of the media spotlight and freed them to concentrate on the nuts and bolts of their operation.

The campaign to fight for United had gone from a direct action process back to the style that was victorious over Murdoch – paperwork crunching and red tape busting. Many of that steering committee would tell you they worked long hard hours round the clock during the summer of 2005 liaising with the powers that be to turn FC United from a dream into a reality. In fact, Andy Walsh, who at the time of writing is the general manager at FC, admitted in a Radio 4 interview he was on the verge of renewing his Old Trafford season ticket when he had an 11th-hour change of heart and decided it would be possible to set up a breakaway club.

The hard work behind the scenes was a sign that Manchester United supporters had entered the most important – and exciting – struggle in their history, but unlike the previous months of shareholder wranglings, this time it was in their own hands.

A new sense of liberation swept through Manchester's football community on 5 July 2005, hundreds of FC United well-wishers packed out the Manchester Central Methodist Hall to hear about the club's structure, long-term ambitions and short-term plans. The meeting sparked a flurry of enthusiasm and excitement vented on the messageboard of the new FC United fans website, www.fcunitedofmanchester.co.uk, which was gaining dozens of new members by the day.

Supporters dreamed of years of back-to-back promotions that would eventually land FC United in the Premiership to become the true people's club of Manchester, with exciting cup runs and trips to smaller grounds along the way, all the while knowing that such success in itself would be an act of protest against Glazer.

But caught up in the excitement of this brand new team, devoted Manchester United fans disillusioned at the Glazer takeover soon came to realise they would have to make a choice between two strands of protest – staying at Old Trafford to coordinate the anti-Glazer Fight From Within (FFW) or to leave 'Big United' completely to follow 'Little United' at non-league grounds throughout the northwest.

While this was a massive dilemma for some fans, others had already decided not to give Glazer's Manchester United (or any of the club's business associates) any of their hard-earned money, whether they could give it to an alternative club or not. And others were determined to take a more conservative 'wait and see' approach – that was, to keep going to Old Trafford to see whether an anti-Glazer protest would materialize, or to try out FC United of Manchester to see if the idea actually took off.

As both Uniteds pre-league campaigns got underway, two defining moments set the scene for the 2005/06 season. The first, on 16 July 2005, took place at the home of Nationwide Conference North outfit Leigh RMI, who invited FC United to play their first ever match against them.

On a bright summer's day, eager fans gathered up to three hours before kick off – completely unable to predict the size of the crowd. And by 3 pm, they had their answer. About 2,000 supporters stood on the terraces, cheering the new United out onto the pitch before a match that ended 0-0.

Despite the scoreline, the vast majority of the FC players who turned out that day have described emerging from the tunnel to the sight of those supporters as the highlight of their season – if not their careers. Some of those players had dropped five divisions to play for the club, others were devout reds who had impressed at trials – but all were committed to the cause.

After the match, a friendly pitch invasion ensued, with hundreds of fans lifting up players like Joz Mitten – great nephew of former United legend Charlie Mitten – and singing defiant anti-Glazer anthems.

It was almost like a day of victory. Since Knighton came on the scene 15 years ago, fans had faced the threat of having their team taken from them and now it had happened, things couldn't possibly get worse. But now they had their own team, with failsafe mechanisms in place to stop it ever happening again.

The second of these defining events took place on 9 August, when Big United lined up in a European Champions League qualifier against Romanian opponents Debreceni. A crowd of 51,701 turned up for the midweek tie – among them the three Glazer brothers who sat quite happily unopposed in the South Stand – a far cry from the burning barricades seen two months earlier.

The contrast of these two events made up the minds of many United fans: if that was how the FFW would be in its early days, Lord knows how it would evolve, whereas the passion on show among 49,000 fewer supporters in the FC United trip to Leigh RMI was much more intense – and could even get stronger.

When forming FC United of Manchester, the steering committee took advice from officials from AFC Wimbledon, who themselves launched a breakaway team in 2002 after their beloved Wimbledon moved to Milton Keynes under the 'rebranded' name of MK Dons.

FC was defined as an Industrial Provident Society, run using a simple system of one member, one vote. Each year, the club holds two meetings (an AGM and mid-season meeting) where members would be able to hold a majority vote to elect board members responsible for the day-to-day running of the club. Fans could also get updates on the club's management from the board and vote on important issues. At the first AGM, members chose the club's badge, for example.

All profits are reinvested into FC United's funds (no lining owners' or shareholders' pockets here) and the club's constitution prevented any person or group owning more than one membership, so there was no way an entrepreneur could get his hands on the club or its assets.

After months (years, if the outline plan had been in place since Murdoch's takeover attempt in 1998) of planning, United had their utopia. Previously, the PLC model was seen as the fairest way a football club could practically be run, and this was breaking new ground. While AFC Wimbledon were regularly drawing 3,000-plus crowds in their earlier years, many Wombles would accept their potential maximum draw was far beneath that of FC United of Manchester.

The flawless model, however, didn't stop the critics coming out to question its merits. When promoting the new club to their friends, colleagues and family, FC supporters would routinely get bamboozled with potential pitfalls in the club's system, though none of them have so far have become a reality and affected FC.

Among the doubters were Manchester United chief executive David Gill, who predicted in a newspaper FC United fans would return to Old Trafford when they got bored with life in the lower reaches of the English league when the weather got too bad in winter.

Meanwhile, Old Trafford legends like Bobby Charlton were defending the new Glazer empire, and even Sir Alex Ferguson appeared to have been won over. As the league season began, there was absolutely no sign of any FFW campaign materialising in the Stretford End.

FC United had secured a season-long contract to play at Gigg Lane, the 11,000 capacity stadium belonging to Greater Manchester neighbours Bury. The team was about to embark on a journey into the unknown. Teams in the North West Counties League Division Two usually attracted crowds of about 50 or so people to each game and the standard is basically seen as the first level of competitive football, as opposed to the just-for-fun Sunday league kick-abouts.

As the league season began, attendance records were smashed left, right and centre, as FC United notched up an attendance of 2,590 at Leek CSOB in their first ever league game. A week later, 2,498 turned out at Gigg Lane to witness Little United's first home league game, showing the club's potential to draw equal numbers of supporters for home fixtures and away trips. Match-day operations were more or less completely organised by a handful of volunteers committed to the cause.

In those early days, many supporters would admit to have been pleasantly surprised by the standard of football. For years, they had been accustomed to watching the likes of Cantona, Giggs, Beckham and Keane, and now the fans were witnessing a whole different ball game. But, under Marginson's guidance, FC United were a cut above the rest, losing just one league game in their first 27 of the season, including a 10-2 drubbing of struggling Castleton Gabriels and an 8-1 hammering of Leek CSOB.

This dramatic superiority on the pitch left the fans able to concentrate on their protest in the stands and, as the season went on, they had developed an impressive repertoire of terrace anthems. There were, of course, the more obvious anti-Glazer efforts and chants of 'Are you watching David Gill?' as yet another record attendance was announced (in reference to Gill's earlier predictions).

But other songs would ring out around Gigg Lane and the other grounds Little United would visit – a strong indication about how the club had become not just an anti-Glazer 'reclaim Manchester United' vehicle, but more a wide-ranging campaigning club.

'I don't care about Rio, he don't care about me, all I care about is watching FC' was sang in reference to Manchester United defender Rio Ferdinand's reluctance to sign a new contract with the club until they upped his wages, despite the club having stood by him during a lengthy FA ban.

'And Fergie said: "Go and watch Chelsea." Are you having a laugh? We'll be watching FC?' was first sung after Sir Alex Ferguson was reported to have uttered that phrase to a group of fans who had confronted him about the Glazer takeover in an airport.

And another (self-explanatory) favourite, 'When FC United come out to play, it's three o'clock on Saturday. We don't work for Sky Sports anymore'.

All these songs were indications of how priorities were starting to change among the FC United faithful. Perhaps being physically detached from the new Glazer empire, while being given this new platform to speak from sparked the progression from anti-unit ownership to anti-everything.

It may also be a fact that, for too long, reds had been used to paying four times as much a month in advance, to go to a lifeless stadium where you would sit beside a day tripping part-time fan from London at a game at noon on a Sunday to suit the television cameras, only for the players, whose wages you were paying, to have lifestyles totally detached from your own.

Now, for the first time since the 1970s, supporters were able to pay £7 on the gate to get into a ground where you could stand – alongside your friends nonetheless – sing for 90 minutes at 3 pm on a Saturday and drink with the players in the pub afterwards. United fans had not only turned their backs on all that negativity at Old Trafford in exchange for a near-perfect alternative, they were also fortunate enough to be experiencing it with supporters who shared more than just United blood, but also the urge to protest that gave them the courage to leave Old Trafford in the first place.

But it wasn't just loyal reds getting in on the act. Supporters of neighbouring teams like Bury, Rochdale, Macclesfield and Stockport, also disillusioned with modern-day football, came to matches and waxed lyrical on Internet sites about how refreshing the atmosphere was.

By February 2006, FC United of Manchester had again smashed their attendance record – and that of the North West Counties League Division Two – when 4,500 spectators travelled to the Fylde Coast for the match against Blackpool Mechanics. Despite these large numbers, fans' accessibility to the club continued. General manager Andy Walsh would always make himself available to address any issues, as would the committed team of (voluntary) board members who were basically fans themselves. The players continued to drink after matches in the pub with fans, joining in with songs, signing autographs and generally engaging in the spirit of things. This togetherness helped the club's next stage of progression – its community involvement.

Throughout FC United's debut season, scores of supporters' groups sprang up, representing various parts of Manchester, the North-West and even further afield in the UK and abroad. All of these organisations used the FC United Supporters Group as the central communication point and the overall set up gave supporters a decent springboard from which to organise community activities, like club and charity fundraisers, collections and events. The supporters held collections throughout the season for the Bhopal Medical Appeal, which campaigns to bring medical relief to some of the 100,000 victims of the Union Carbide gas disaster in Bhopal, India in 1984.

Fans also donated blood on match-days and raised cash for eight-year-old FC United supporter Alex Croft, who suffers from cerebral palsy, to get an electric wheelchair. (Alex's family have since reached their target of more than £15,000.)

A friendly match was held at the home of another supporters-run club, AFC Telford, to raise cash for Jamie Turner – a Manchester United fan who was making his way to a match at Southampton when he suffered a completely unprovoked attack by a gang wielding weapons believed to be baseball bats, metal bars and chair legs. Jamie's skull was broken in two and he was in a coma for three weeks and has been trying to lead as much of a normal life as possible since.

In their final game of the season, the FC United team played a match against a celebrity team at Salford De La Salle Rugby Union Club in aid of 21-year-old Chris McGuirk who was paralysed from the neck down in a freak rugby accident.

All of these fundraisers gathered much-needed cash for various causes and underlined the fact that a football club isn't just about the 90 minutes, it's about uniting the community together to achieve great things individuals couldn't do alone. This community element was a pleasant bonus most fans probably wouldn't have expected the club to have been able to do in just its first season. But the supporters still had time to right the wrongs they saw from Saturday to Saturday.

Quite a strong feature of the FC match-day experience was its accessibility to anyone and everyone, including families, who, instead of facing the prospect of paying a three-figure sum for a top-flight match, could pay less than £20 for a family of four for a day out.

With this in mind, the club were keen to offer value-for-money concessionary prices – £2 for home games, and even three games in which children were let in for free (three of the highest attendances Little United enjoyed all season).

The board also strived to encourage other clubs in their division to do the same when FC came to visit. Revenue from matches against FC would usually take care of that club's finances for the next two or three seasons because of the 3,000 per cent increase in gate money, let alone other match-day takings. Most clubs were happy to fix child and senior citizen discounts at £4 or £5, but one club, Darwen, refused to offer any discount. In response, FC fans utilised the supporters groups and the messageboard on www.fcunitedofmanchester.co.uk to organise a boycott of the game and a boycott of merchandising on the day. The campaign ran for just a few days, but just 1,715 turned up compared to 2,762 who attended a match at nearby Colne six days earlier.

Of those who did turn up, few were children and very few people spent money inside the ground. Even Karl Marginson's team joined in with the protest. They shunned Darwen's post-match hospitality and instead went straight home. It was reported afterwards that Darwen had barely made a penny from the fixture. And it sent a message out loud and clear that clubs would have to compromise to FC's way, or face the consequences.

The FC United board also released a statement critical of

a league match postponement at Great Harwood Town with just two hours' notice on a Sunday, by which time about 2,000 reds had made the journey to the ground. The board argued the league should allow referees to call off games the night before because, unlike in top-level football, word doesn't spread via the media, so the fans will still travel. All this mobility would have been arguably unachievable without the vast campaigning experience of he FC United supporters and board members.

When FC held its mid-season meeting, members were invited to vote on whether there should be a sponsor on the shirt, whether the club should change its kit for the 2006/07 season and weather ticket prices should go up. The majority voted 'no' to all.

But even if the majority had voted 'yes', it would be hard to complain about things like ticket price hikes that were decided upon in the fairest way possible, as opposed to the 12 per cent ticket price rises at Manchester United, decided on by one man, who had never even been to see his 'franchise'.

Contrast the goings on at Gigg Lane with the failed FFW in Stretford. In the first year since Glazer took over, just one protest took place inside Old Trafford, and even that was quelled by sharp-eyed stewards within minutes.

It came in a Carling Cup against Barnet in October, when about a dozen protestors unveiled an anti-Glazer flag in the South Stand. Symbolic, maybe, but the feat barely registered among the media or other members of the crowd and has not been repeated since.

Meanwhile, the media was gradually increasing its interest in FC United of Manchester. In that first game against Leigh RMI, reporters from all the major national newspapers attended to cover the political element of the club, though interest was limited during the early league matches.

But once the 'rebel reds' had established a dominant league position and the large crowds began to turn out regularly (so much so that United averaged more than housemates Bury, despite playing six divisions beneath them), the press and the broadcast media began to attend regularly.

Eventually, dedicated Manchester television Channel M began to attend each FC United game for a monthly goals programme, the *Manchester Evening News* started to run regular reports and influencial national newspaper columnists like Oliver Holt in the *Mirror* and Tony Howard in the *Guardian* would write regular features about the rise and rise of the club.

In their first year, FC United came on leaps and bounds. They won not only promotion, but the championship by eight points, achieved a record crowd of 6,023, set up a reserve and junior sides for the 2006/07 season, organised dozens of supporter groups, produced a Premiership-quality programme and launched a witty fanzine called *Under the Boardwalk*, campaigned for community issues and, in summary, established a framework for the future – all this with just three full-time members of staff and hundreds if not thousands of volunteers who had all played their part.

So in one year of Glazer taking over Manchester United, the protest had shifted dramatically, both physically and psychologically.

Right after the takeover, the then vice-chairman of SU (which is now the Manchester United Supporters Trust, MUST) Sean Bones said it might take three or so years for the supporters to regain control of their club. He was undoubtedly right about the long-term approach needed against such an intelligent and influential opponent, but it would take more than three years for FC United to trouble his empire.

That said, a survey carried out in summer 2006 by the Fooball Fans Census showed 19 per cent of Manchester United season ticket holders said they would not renew in the 2006/07 season. If those figures represent all of the club's season ticket holders, we can expect about 10,000 people to ditch Old Trafford.

Some may give up football altogether, but even if 6,000 try out FC United, that would still be a major boost to the club's aims and could ignite a mass exodus to Gigg Lane (where FC United have agreed a deal to play for three more seasons). If such an exodus occurred, we might see a bizarre landscape in which an empty Old Trafford is compared with a buzzing packed-out Gigg Lane and Malcolm Glazer's investment turns out to be a lame duck.

Could the powers that be at Manchester United be running scared? Possibly, but David Gill et al know there will always be an element among the supporters who don't care for the political side and are happy to do what it takes to watch some of the best players in the world week in week out. And there will always be, understandably, people who just cannot bring themselves to leave the club they love.

Whatever happens, the Manchester United fans' movement that has gone on since Murdoch's takeover attempt and beyond looks set to continue way on into the future in the shape of FC United at Gigg Lane and, possibly with the FFW at Old Trafford.

It has hard to see how groups like IMUSA and MUST can achieve much with the vast majority of their most battle-hardened supporters engrossed in FC United, but the more mysterious MEC could make a return in future years, if suitably provoked, though FFU will most likely continue its tactical flash mobbing campaign against Big United's business partners. So it seems that this story of struggle is far from over and a very intriguing future lays in wait.

We have seen Manchester United go from a rather innocent leisure pursuit funded by a philanthropist, to a weekend religion for supporters, who entrepreneurs have then sought to cash in on. A protest movement sprung up to protect this religion and, for a long time, succeeded in using a wide range of protest methods, but ultimately they were too weak to beat one of the richest men in the world. Despite this, they refused to give up and have potentially revolutionised the structure of football.

For the time being, as the FC terraces song goes: 'There's two United's but the soul is one, as the Busby Babe's carry on'.

Paul Edmundson has been a match-going football fan since the age of nine or ten, and though an irregular visitor to Old Trafford, last year he became involved with the protest movement when FC United of Manchester was founded.

With a BA (Hons) Degree in Journalism and extensive reporting experience, he was able to write for various club websites and the match-day programme and keep up good links with members of the team, management, the board and supporters, including many of the leading figures who were involved with various campaigns for Manchester United in the previous decade or more.

After spending a season following the fortunes of FC

United of Manchester, Paul is firmly of the belief that it is not only more enjoyable, but a better form of protest than joining the fight from within at Old Trafford.

From now on, they are his club.

WHAT HAPPENS NEXT? – THE POLITICS OF FANDOM

BY DOUGIE BRIMSON

SUPPORTING A FOOTBALL team is very much a personal thing. For some, it means no more than looking out for the results on a Sunday morning, for others, it's everything. Home, away, pre-season the lot. There are even those who fight for it and others, thankfully, who will do whatever it takes to protect it. But if you've read this far, you will already know that.

I have to say that whilst researching this book, I have been both astonished and humbled at the effort and commitment shown by individuals and groups toward clubs who, in many instances, deserve little or nothing of the kind. I'm not just talking about those who I have been able to include within these pages but to the many hundreds who wrote to me with their own tales of protesting and campaigning.

Yet the more I've read, the more it's struck me that with the exception of specific days such as Fans United, most football protests are by their very nature, localised affairs. Understandable since in the main, most of those involved have work and family to consider and let's face it, few of us give two shits about what goes on at any club other than our own. This is in many ways, short-sighted. Particularly when it comes to football, which, let's not forget, is both our national sport and a multi-billion pound industry. For by keeping it small, we football fans are simply doing ourselves a major disservice. But before we get into all that, let's think about it from a different perspective for a while.

The idea that politics and sport should be kept well apart is one which receives a great deal of support – not least from amongst those already in government, as evidenced by their reluctance to get involved in the furore surrounding the England cricket team's proposed tour of Zimbabwe in 2005 – the stark reality is that they can't for one very specific reason; publicity. Like it or not, in these BSkyB post-Hillsborough days, sport, and especially football, has become an established part of the media circus surrounding mainstream politics.

Our Prime Minister for example, not only basked shamelessly in the afterglow surrounding the successful bid to bring the 2012 Olympics to London but spouts forth about his love of Newcastle United at every opportunity. Even the tradition of baby kissing to canvass votes has long been replaced by the arse kissing of Beckham & Co. Proof that votes and public opinion have become far more important than the concept of embarrassment.

This fawning over the great game is nothing new of course although to be fair, the powers that be have spent equal amounts of time hating the game and those who both play and follow it. Certainly back in the '60s, '70s and '80s, the idea of a major politician admitting to being a lover of a particular team would have been greeted with as much if not more horror than an admission of homosexuality. Back in the very early days of the game, things were even more fractious. Edward III tried to ban it because he thought it was stopping men practising archery and was, therefore, weakening his army. Similarly, the Puritans tried to ban football on the basis that it was fun although a season watching Luton Town would have resolved that!

Yet despite the fact that the game was widely derided as a working class pastime, the authorities were quick to realise the potential influence it had over the masses and the outbreak of World War I saw the game used as a major recruitment tool. Almost half a million men took the King's Shilling as a direct result of football related campaigns. It was, however, the build up to World War II which saw the game take on a real and significant political importance.

Although both Hitler and Mussolini had recognised the value of sport very early on in their careers, in Britain, governments still refused to acknowledge or even understand the potential power of the game. That changed when news broke that the German national side had been invited to play at White Hart Lane on 4 December 1935. With Germany already firmly in the grip of the Nazi party, the media and trade unions were apoplectic and, together with various Jewish organisations, launched a series of protests. However, despite this, the game went ahead with over 1,000 visiting German supporters witnessing their team lose 3-0.

Just three years later, with war already on the horizon, the England team travelled to Berlin Olympic Stadium and during the traditional pre-match introductions, Captain Eddy Hopgood and his side were photographed giving the

Nazi salute. At a time when the Germans had already reoccupied the Rhineland, were fighting alongside Franco in Spain, had just annexed Austria and were poised to invade Czechoslovakia, it was a shameful episode. One made worse by the fact that permission to make the gesture was given by both the FA and the Foreign Office despite the fact that Hitler was not even present but as a result of clear and obvious pressure from Nazi party officials who were well aware of the propaganda value of such a picture.

Incredibly, possibly because they were still smarting from being out-smarted by Hitler in Berlin, the post-war British government still refused to embrace the potential football held for them. Even when England won the World Cup in 1966, politicians were rarely to be seen anywhere, even at the final!

Indeed, with so little regard did the then Prime Minister, Harold Wilson, hold football, that he foolishly called a snap general election right in the middle of the 1970 World Cup! Not surprisingly, with polling just days after England were knocked out at the quarter final stage, he lost.

By then of course, the game had begun to sink into the dark days of hooliganism and as the fans waged war on the terraces of England and Europe, football became a political nightmare. One that few people, let alone politicians, wanted to be associated with. In 1985 that changed with the tragedy of Heysel and the televised riot at Luton because it finally forced the government into action. And that meant Margaret Thatcher.

There is little doubt that Thatcher hated football and the fact that the FA abdicated its responsibility for the hooligan issue allowed her to treat it as a simple law and order problem. In effect, all she did was simply hand a wide range of powers to the police but she also demanded an identity card scheme for fans. Something which was bitterly opposed by all sides, including, oddly, the police who regarded it as unworkable, although elements of it were implemented at Luton thanks to its chairman, David Evans, who just happened to be one of Thatcher's back-bench MPs.

However, although included in the 1989 Football Spectators Act, any idea of ID cards bit the dust on 15 April that same year when 96 football fans died at Hillsborough. The tragedy in Sheffield changed football forever with the subsequent Taylor Report all but demanding an end to the demonisation of football fans.

However, an equally significant consequence of the report was that certain forward thinking chairmen realised that football had been handed the opportunity to rebrand and relaunch itself. By 1992 that process was complete with the formation of the Premiership and a £340 million pound television deal with BSkyB. It was boom time!

Suddenly, football became a popular peg on which politicians could hang their coats. The then Prime Minister John Major, together with MPs David Mellor and Tony Banks, positively exploited their support of Chelsea whilst other lesser names were quick to come clean about their own supporting heritage or, in some cases, simply jump on the bandwagon.

The huge success of Euro '96 further enhanced the game's appeal to the political parties but things really took off in 1997 and the election of New Labour.

With Tony Blair – who famously claimed to have watched Jackie Milburn at St James's Park even though the Newcastle legend had retired when Blair was 4! – at the helm, government was suddenly all about popularity with the masses. The launch of 'Cool Britannia', epitomised by the iconic figure of Spice Girl Geri Halliwell in a Union Jack dress, had New Labour politicians almost tripping over themselves to be photographed with famous and influential musicians, artists, writers and of course, footballers.

But of more relevance was the fact that in the wake of Euro '96, New Labour realised that if the national team were doing well, so would the nation, and so in an effort to garner even more support from the general public, New Labour actively chased the football vote. First it launched a bid to host the 2006 World Cup and then followed this up with the 'Football Task Force'. A much-heralded and brilliant idea in principle but one which ultimately delivered little.

Initially, it all looked positive. The bid was going well with support coming from all sides and even Mellor was receiving glowing plaudits. Then, in 1998, it all started to go horribly wrong. Not for the first time, the catalyst was England's most notorious export and their exploits at France '98.

The footage of English hooligans rioting in Marseille was beamed around the world and although sports minister Tony Banks MP claimed that the trouble had not harmed the bid, it was clear looking back that from this point in, the die was well and truly cast. Inevitably, as this realisation dawned the fear of being associated with a sinking ship soon had the politicians running for cover.

Evidence of this soon surfaced in the *Financial Times*, which reported that Blair had actually withdrawn his support for the £10 million bid after rumours surfaced that FIFA were keen to see the tournament staged in Africa. From that point on, the bid was over, and when England fans were involved in more trouble during Euro 2000, just weeks ahead of the final decision, even the most optimistic supporter must have realised the game was up.

Since then, politicians and particularly government have tended to steer clear of the game, with calls from supporters groups asking for some kind of regulation falling on deaf ears. Even bodies set up by the government such as Supporters Direct and the Independent Football Commission appear to have little real sway. Indeed, New Labour's only real involvement with football these days seems to be the provision of ever more draconian anti-hooligan measures. However, so powerful and influential has the game become that these days no politician worth their salt would disassociate themselves from it totally.

They know full well that football players have become the new royalty and popularity on that scale equals votes. At a time when an increasing percentage of the electorate have become so disillusioned with mainstream politics that they don't even bother to put their cross in a box on polling day, grovelling at the feet of our national sport is a sure-fire way for the local MP to get his or her name in the local papers and into the voters psyche. Should England ever win a major tournament the exploitation of the game for political gain will no doubt border on the obscene.

But power is power and at the end of the day it doesn't matter how many – or how few – votes it takes to get it or what has to be done or said to get them. And as we have seen all too often in recent years, many politicians will do and say just about anything because ultimately, all that matters is that you had more crosses in the box than the other fella.

Whilst in the bigger scheme of things this might appear to have little to do with football, if you think laterally, it actually invites a very interesting debate. Politicians might be widely derided as sleazy leeches feeding off the great British taxpayer but the simple truth is that they are supposed to hold office to represent the people who put them in that office. So why is it that in many instances, they don't?

I am not talking about major domestic or global issues such as the war in Iraq, crime or the immigration debacle, but local and regional ones including those which relate to local football clubs. These are the things which impact more directly on people and upon which much campaigning is done – certainly at local council level.

Yet how many instances have we seen over the years of elected politicians, ranging from local councillors to the Prime Minister disregarding or even ignoring the wishes of local football fans and instead making decisions which have clearly been contrary to their needs? More often than not without good reason. Barnet, Brighton, Luton, Wimbledon… the list goes on and on.

Which begs the question, since nothing scares a politician more than losing votes and therefore power, why do we allow them to get away with it?

After all, ultimately, we, both as citizens and fans, have the capability to take that power not just from individuals, but from governments. We may only have one vote each but there are millions and millions of us and we all have one thing in common, a love of football. So why not use our votes to further our own ends and obtain something which has a special significance to us?

Such thinking has of course, been used at a local level many times. Supporters groups at a variety of clubs, most notably Charlton and the 'Valley Party', have fielded candidates at local council level and direct pressure has certainly been brought to bear on numerous MPs over the years as we have seen in this very book. Hartlepool even found itself electing the local club's mascot H'Angus the Monkey as their mayor!

Here is where we return to the opening of this chapter and the problems associated with thinking small. Why do we do that? Why not go further and take supporter power to its ultimate conclusion? What price a political party with the sole aim of furthering the ideals of the nation's football fans? The Football Party.

Anyone who has read any of my previous books will know that I have talked about this before and on every occasion the response has been huge and universally positive. But more importantly, since I first mentioned it back in 1998 we have seen even more significant problems come to light. More to the point, increasing numbers of football fans have simply had enough of being screwed over and there is growing clamour for some form of significant representation and change.

It might be single issue politics, but it is still nevertheless, politics. And it is certainly nothing new. George Galloway pulled it off in spectacular fashion at the last General Election when he became MP for Bethnal Green and Bow after forming the anti-Iraq War 'Respect' party, whilst former newsreader Martin Bell entered Parliament after standing on an anti-sleaze platform against discredited Tory MP Neil Hamilton.

But this would be much bigger than that, encompassing as it would have to both local football related issues and those which impacted on the wider domestic game. It would also mean more than one candidate and can you imagine the impact the appearance of a single Football Party MP would have in the House of Commons.

That might appear a comical, even trivial notion but think about it seriously for a moment and then ask yourself why not? If Sir Andrew Lloyd-Webber or Dame Judy Dench decided to stand as a prospective MP for the luvvie brigade, not only would no one would turn a hair, but you know and I know that they would attract huge amounts of both publicity and support for whatever cause they were standing for.

So what's the difference between the theatre and football? Well there are only two key differences actually. The first is that one is generally thought of as being highbrow and the other has always been regarded as the domain of the working classes. The second is that football is the only industry, entertainment or otherwise, not driven by its consumers.

If you put a play on in the West End and no one goes to watch it, it closes. Yet a club can turn out any old crap and we'll still go week in and week out in the hope it gets better. We do it because for us it's an obsession and the clubs know that full well. As a consequence, they treat fans as little more than fixed assets the exploitation of which helps them remain at the trough of TV moneylust.

Yet as if that isn't bad enough, it continues to sell itself on the back of the atmosphere and match-day sense of occasion that we create for it and has the nerve to charge us often extortionate amounts for the privilege of doing so! If it wasn't so sad, it would be funny.

This begs the same question, why on earth do we let them get away with it? Well the truth is we don't have to. No one forces us to walk through that turnstile. We all have the choice.

But why shouldn't we go? It is our game after all and ultimately, they are our clubs so why should we let those who run them on our behalf keep taking the piss out of us? Again, we don't have to. Not if we really wanted to stop them. All it would take is the will, the organisation and a lot of hard work. All things which, as we have seen within the pages of this book – and this has been merely the tip of a very big iceberg – football supporters have always had in spades. Change could therefore come relatively easily, all we'd have to do is get everyone thinking a bit bigger.

So how would it work? Well the first thing would be to unite all the various supporting factions up and down the country to bring them on board and once everyone was happy, appoint a steering committee. This could and should be drawn from the upper echelons of either the existing fans organisations such as the FSF as well as from the numerous ISAs dotted around the country, or be highly motivated supporters already heavily involved with different aspects of the game.

Many of these fine individuals already commit huge amounts of time to their footballing responsibilities and most are by nature reasonably militant so this would surely appeal to enough of them.

With a committee in place, the next step would be the development of a party manifesto. Or rather, a battle plan.

This also shouldn't prove too difficult since many of the things it would have to include are problems and issues that many groups are already campaigning for. For example:

1. The appointment of an ombudsman or regulator to oversee the activities of the Football Association, the Football Trust, The Premier League and its members, The Football League and its members and all agents and agents organisations.

2. The appointment of supporters representatives on to the committees of both the Football Association and the Football Trust.

3. The establishment of an independent body to arbitrate in disputes between professional football clubs and local authorities.

4. The appointment of an independent, credible and properly elected supporters representative on to the board of every professional football club.

5. A clampdown on the exploitation of football fans by both clubs and the Football Association.

6. The removal of intimidation in all its forms, be it racial, verbal or physical, from the game.

7. The return of safe terracing.

Once everyone had agreed on these points, then the next decision would be where to start. As someone who always starts at the top and works down, I would forget the idea of fielding candidates for local elections and go for the jugular. That means either a General or European election.

The leadership would then need to decide how many candidates it wanted to field and who those candidates might be. The latter would, in effect, be a done deal with the majority of the leadership aiming for office near their local club with a second string drawn from the more active ISAs. Ideally, that would mean one person standing in at least one ward of each of the major towns and cities with a professional club. More if it were somewhere like Manchester, Liverpool or London for obvious reasons.

A benefit of this is that it would allow potential candidates to draw on help from their fellow supporters, ISA members, mates and family for help with campaigning. Funding could come from all kinds of places ranging from subscriptions to donations – indeed, one would imagine that given the nature of the party, support would certainly be forthcoming from those who have much to gain: the players.

Then, with everything in place, the campaign could be taken out to the masses. First by exploiting local media connections and then through more direct contact with local football fans in the time-honoured fashion of getting out there and meeting Joe Public. Well, almost.

You see the one ace The Football Party would have up its sleeve is that, potentially, it already has millions of supporters the vast majority of whom would actively agree with every word it had to say. All it would really have to do is to let them know what was going on, convince them that the idea is a sound one and make sure they were galvanised into voting come polling day.

Here's where it would get clever because the mechanism to do that is already in place. Both websites and fanzines have proven to be hugely effective tools through which to disseminate information and news in recent years and they would prove invaluable here.

But once word was out about what was going on, it would spread like wildfire anyway. Not just via the web but through word of mouth at games, at work, in pubs, everywhere. Take London as an example. Within the M25 boundary there are now seven Premiership sides with a further six in the Football League. If you throw in all the supporters of other clubs now resident in the Capital city not only do you have a massive fanbase but potentially, a massive powerbase. Obviously not all of those would support the idea but a large percentage would almost certainly be interested enough to think about, if not support it.

Equally, our prospective candidate wouldn't even have to go knocking on any doors to try and canvass votes because they would know exactly where a good percentage of their potential supporters were going to be at least once every fortnight. Thousands and thousands of them. In pre-match and post-match pubs, outside the grounds, even inside. Let's face it, what club would dare stand in the way of something like this? Not only would it risk the wrath of its own fans but it would also stand the very real prospect of alienating someone who might suddenly be in a position of great power both locally and nationally.

Could it work? Could we potentially see one, maybe even more members of Parliament (British or European) elected solely on the objective of campaigning for the rights of the football fan?

Damn right it could. And it would. The comedian, Billy Connolly, once famously said, 'Anybody who aspires to become a politician should automatically be banned from ever becoming one!' but to paraphrase that, 'anybody who needs to become a politician should automatically be allowed to be one.'

Well, football needs something like this, we all need it. You know it, I know it, everyone knows it. At a time when Abramovich's chequebook superiority has all but rendered the concept of a fully competitive Premiership redundant, even some Chelsea fans know it.

So why not? Forget talk of European Super Leagues, Rangers and Celtic in the Premiership and even Premiership 2, should we not be looking at supporter power as being the real future for the greatest of all games?